STUDY SKILLS
THE TOOLS FOR ACTIVE LEARNING

DELMAR GENERAL STUDIES SERIES

STUDY
SKILLS

The Tools for Active Learning

Abby
Marks-Beale

The Reading Edge

Delmar
Publishers Inc.™

I(T)P™

NOTICE TO THE READER

Cover design by Spiral Design

Delmar staff:
Acquisitions Editor: Mary McGarry
Project Editor: Theresa M. Bobear
Production Coordinator: James Zayicek
Art and Design Coordinator: Karen Kunz Kemp

For information, address Delmar Publishers Inc.
3 Columbia Circle, Box 15–015
Albany, NY 12212-9985

Delmar Publishers' Online Services
To access Delmar on the World Wide Web, point your browser to:
http://www.delmar.com/delmar.html
To access through Gopher: gopher://gopher.delmar.com
(Delmar Online is part of "thomson.com", an Internet site with information on more than 30 publishers of the International Thomson Publishing organization.)
For information on our products and services:
email: info@delmar.com
or call 800-347-7707

Printed in the United States of America
Published simultaneously in Canada
by Nelson Canada,
a division of The Thomson Corporation

    4 5 6 7 8 9 10 XXX 00 99 98 97 96

ISBN #0-8273-5437-1

CONTENTS

Part 5 ◆ RESEARCHING AND WRITING PAPERS　*325*

ABOUT THE AUTHOR

Abby Marks-Beale, president and owner of The Reading Edge, develops and facilitates reading and learning efficiency programs for students, educators, and professionals. She provides public and in-house training programs for various universities, community colleges, adult education centers, and corporations. The Reading Edge courses have been approved by the State of Connecticut to provide continuing education credits for Connecticut educators. Before starting her own company, Abby worked for several years with Readak Educational Services as an itinerant reading and learning skills instructor for students in private schools. She gained experience teaching diverse populations including military and international students.

Ms. Marks-Beale is an active board member of The Hartford Critical and Creative Thinking Center and an active local member of The American Society for Training and Development (ASTD). Abby holds a B.A. in Hispanic and French Language and Literature from Boston University and currently is using the information contained in this book to complete a master's degree in Adult Education.

ABOUT THE CONTRIBUTORS

Charlotte J. Foster and **Dr. Thomas G. McCain** were valuable contributors to Chapter 3 on Learning Styles. Charlotte is the founder of Multivariant Learning Systems Corporation of Bernardsville, New Jersey. She specializes in accelerated learning and provides public and in-house seminars to corporations and educational institutions. She is also skilled in the design and development of accelerated learning programs. She is one of four people in the nation certified to deliver the Davis Disorientation Counseling Program for learning disabilities.

Dr. McCain is president of Learning Builders and an educator with more than thirty years of experience at the elementary, college, and university levels. He has presented seminars on the topics of learning and thinking styles, study skills, cooperative learning, career planning, and self-esteem. He has been awarded honors for his service as principal and superintendent of schools.

Louise Loomis was a valuable contributor to Chapter 13 on Critical Thinking. Lou is a former high school science teacher who is now working full time in the field of critical thinking. She is founder of the nonprofit Hartford Critical and Creative Thinking Center, which serves as a resource for information about thinking in New England. The center offers consulting services and workshops on all aspects of thinking and maintains a reference library of books, journals and tapes. Lou believes that critical and creative thinking is an integral part of all learning and would like to see it taught universally at all levels of education.

Nora Bird was a valuable contributor to Chapter 14 on Using the Library. Nora has been an academic librarian for almost a decade. After several positions at Boston area colleges, including Harvard and MIT, she now works at Teikyo Post University in Waterbury, Connecticut. Her career has been dedicated to teaching students how using the library can benefit them not only academically but throughout their entire lives.

TO THE INSTRUCTOR

About This Text

Writing this text-workbook has indeed been a learning experience. I have spent more hours than I can count creating more text than I ever imagined. You might think that I would be concerned about its success. I am not. What I am most concerned about is the future of our educational system. Students are expected to succeed in school but are not taught how. If only they knew how to effectively document the information they hear. If only they were able to read and learn effectively from informational material. If only they could master the testing game. If only they could use critical and creative thinking to become more self-directed. If only they could manage their most precious resource—time. *If only. . .*

In my mind, one fact remains: *No matter how many books are written in the area of study skills, there is still an overwhelming need to teach our students how to learn.*

Study Skills: The Tools for Active Learning was developed to teach students how to take part in any learning process. The information in this book, accompanied by your positive, supportive, and encouraging instruction, will not only improve your students' academic ability, but also boost their learning self-confidence and self-esteem. As a long-term result, students who learn from this text will feel more positive about learning. They will also be better equipped to carry the tools of learning with them into their careers. *Learning how to learn is a lifelong skill.* I hope that use of and success with this text will encourage your students to discover the rewards of active learning—for school, for work, and for themselves.

Features of This Text-Workbook

Both you and your students will find the text is easy to read and easy to follow. It is interactive and conversational in a way that demands student participation. You will be presented with many opportunities to work with your students on improving their verbal and written self-expression skills both in and out of the classroom.

Each chapter of the text builds on the skills and concepts learned in the previous chapter, though they do not have to be studied in order. Every chapter begins with an *introduction* and a series of *learning objectives*, and ends with a *summary* and *subjective review* of material presented. In addition, there are *motivational quotes* sprinkled throughout the text as well as *illustrations and photos* appropriate to each chapter's discussion.

The *five sections* of this text focus on areas that are most important to your students' success. You will find a more detailed description on page xix.

Part 1—The Basics of Active Learning
Part 2—Becoming an Active Reader
Part 3—Taking Notes
Part 4—Studying, Test Taking, and Critical Thinking
Part 5—Researching and Writing Papers

At the end of the text, you will find appendices with answers to exercises in the chapters, a glossary, and a bibliography suitable for reference and research in the area of study skills.

An educational and motivational *audiotape* accompanies the student text-workbook.

About the Instructor's Guide

This text-workbook was written under the premise that in the area of study skills, students should reach for their personal best. This means that many times there is no right or wrong answer—rather there are some that are better than others. You will spend a minimal amount of time preparing for the class because the book is student-centered, not instructor-centered. The course was developed with adult learning theories in mind; therefore, the instructor's role is that of a facilitator of learning, not a director. As a result, the *Instructor's Guide* is a valuable resource for planning your course syllabus and facilitating your students' learning.

The *Instructor's Guide* contains information on how to best evaluate a student's learning given the resources in the text. A student's individual improvement will be the basic criteria for evaluating their progress. There are specific suggestions about using adult learning theories in your course design. For some chapters, transparency masters are included. In addition, the *Instructor's Guide* contains thought-provoking classroom discussion topics as well as optional exercises that will relate what is being learned to "real-life" situations. You will also find several suggested educational games that will make learning fun for you and your students.

Feedback

I ask for your feedback. Every class I teach, I learn something new. Since I am not with you while you are teaching from this text, I am most interested in your comments, questions, and suggestions. I want to know what worked for you and why. I want to know what didn't work for you and why. Most importantly, I'd like to know how you make learning successful. Please send your letters to the address listed on page xxv.

ACKNOWLEDGMENTS

In the past, I had always thought that this section of a book was superfluous, but now I understand why it is one of the most important. If it were not for the support, friendship, and talent of numerous individuals, this text-workbook would have never been written.

To all of the contributors, I am extremely appreciative for their skillful sharing of their expertise and experience. More specifically, to Charlotte Foster of Multivariant Learning Systems and Dr. Thomas McCain of Learning Builders, I am extremely thankful for their collaborative effort and convincing perspective in the area of learning styles. They have been incredibly supportive and thoroughly helpful. To Louise Loomis of The Hartford Critical and Creative Thinking Center, who is dedicating her life to creatively sharing her teachings and perspective in the area of critical thinking, I am truly honored to include her words. And to Nora Bird, an experienced research librarian who truly enjoys teaching others about the ins and outs of a library, I am grateful for her time, energy, and creative contribution to this text.

To my photographer, Ron Jaworski, who patiently worked on this project from beginning to end, I thank him for his time and the quality photos he has produced. I also want him to know how much I appreciated his crouching on the floor of several college classrooms, and wandering the halls and strolling the campus to find the exact photos that this book required. An additional thanks to the Public Relations Department of Manchester Community College (CT) for allowing us to photo-shoot on campus. Thanks also to Joy Bush of Southern Connecticut State University for her photo contributions.

To my pinch-hitter illustrator, Storm Robinson, who was crazy enough to enter this project at the bottom of the ninth with all bases loaded, I thank him for sharing his incredible talent and creativity for this project, on deadline. It is with extreme pleasure that his work is included in this project.

I'd also like to thank Vanda North of The Buzan Centre for her comments and information about Mind Mapping®.

To all of the authors of the books I researched (listed in the bibliography) as well as those I haven't yet found, thank you for your significant contributions to this important field.

To my editor Bob Nirkind for his uncensored editorial feedback, guidance, and support, and to Mary McGarry who believed in me, I thank them both for putting their time, energy, and faith in me. I would have never done this without them!

To all of the reviewers on this project, I am especially thankful. The comments, suggestions, and constructive feedback of the following individuals contributed greatly to both the quality and readability of this text:

- ❑ Carolyn Moffitt, Superior Career Institute, New York, NY
- ❑ Richard Thome, Southern Ohio College, Akron, OH
- ❑ Mark Newton, Gwinett Technical Institute, Snellville, GA
- ❑ James Strate, O.T. Autry Vocational Technical Center, Enid, OK
- ❑ Randy Johnson, Centralia College, Centralia, WA
- ❑ Marie Holmberg, Pima Community Center, Tucson, AZ
- ❑ Paulette Jacques, North Western Community College, Simsbury, CT
- ❑ Victoria Trotter-Washington, Houston Community College, Houston, TX

To Jim Conklin and Al "The Gator" Poneleit of Digital Effigy Music Company of Meriden, Conneticut, I am thankful to them and their creative recording talents for putting together such a dynamic and quality audiotape for the students. Thanks also to Glenn Heavens, Zoë Lynch, Chris "Max" Beale, Mary Conklin, Steven Kennedy and Heidi Elsinger for lending their voices for this project and thanks to JoAn Paganetti for helping me focus on a script format.

And last, but certainly not least, I am most thankful to my husband Christopher, who has been a pillar of support from the start. His genuine love, friendship, encouragement, and patience have allowed me to spread my wings and fly as I have never done before.

Abby Marks-Beale

TO THE STUDENT

Success has always been easy to measure. It is the distance between one's origins and one's final achievements.

- Michael Korda, contemporary author

CONGRATULATIONS! By picking up this book, you have just taken a very important step. You have expressed a powerful desire to learn more about making your learning easier and becoming a successful student. The road to more effective learning begins here.

The Recipe for Learning

The recipe for learning, as written on the recipe card in the following figure, contains the necessary ingredients for becoming a successful student. These necessary ingredients include having *desire*, being *aware* of what you do, having the *knowledge* to do something about it, and then developing the *tools and skills* to be effective. The purpose of this book is to provide you with the opportunity to learn about them all.

Recipe for:
LEARNING SKILLS

Ingredients
  Desire
  Awareness
  Knowledge
  Tools

Procedure
  In your head, locate your learning desire.
Then add awareness and knowledge and
mix together. Combine mixture with your tools
and practice, practice, practice. In a short time
skills will result.

The Recipe for Learning

1. **Desire.** *Study Skills: The Tools for Active Learning* was written for you to succeed. Every success you experience will hopefully encourage you to maintain or increase your desire to know more about learning how to learn.

2. **Awareness.** *Study Skills: The Tools for Active Learning* will make you think about the habits you have created as a student. This will be accomplished through the self-evaluations at the beginning of each chapter, the review materials at the end of each chapter, and the other questions asked of you throughout the text. You will probably find some of your learning habits to be very effective, while recognizing that others could use some improvement. In some areas, you may not have been aware of doing anything at all. Once you become aware of what you have or have not been doing, then you will be encouraged to begin experimenting with the effective habits and tools discussed in this book.

3. **Knowledge.** *Study Skills: The Tools for Active Learning* will also provide you with the knowledge you need to improve your ability to learn. Each chapter contains valuable information that can be easily applied to your daily learning demands. The more active a learner you choose to be, the more knowledge you will learn from this book.

4. **Tools and Skills.** *Study Skills: The Tools for Active Learning* will provide you with the tools you need to build the skills for learning. For a carpenter to build a home, he or she has to know how to use the tools to do the job: hammer, nails, wood, and so forth. Just having them does not make a good carpenter. For a student to learn effectively in school, he or she has to know how to use their learning tools: pen, paper, textbook, etc. This book will not only introduce you to the tools for active learning, but also provide you with the opportunity to begin using them. Continuing to use these tools over a period of time will build your skills.

Who Was This Book Written For?

This book was written for you. You already possess some form(s) of study skills, both effective and ineffective, efficient and inefficient. The book's objective is for you to distinguish effective and efficient abilities from ineffective and inefficient ones. You will also be able to add new abilities to your previously learned ones.

Definitions of Effective and Efficient

Throughout this text-workbook, the terms *effective* and *efficient* are frequently used. They describe the type of student you will hopefully become. It is important to learn and understand these terms to improve your understanding of the material in this text.

Being **effective** means you are capable of producing a desired result. The result of effective notetaking is having good notes to study from. The result of effective reading is reading with good comprehension. Anything that is ineffective does not produce the desired result.

Being **efficient** means accomplishing a job with a minimum amount of time and effort. Efficient study habits are those that take the least amount of time and energy. Efficient reading habits are those that allow you to get what you need quickly without wasting time and energy. Anything that is inefficient wastes time and effort.

Unlearning to Relearn

Unlearning happens every time you learn to do something new. In the case of learning skills, in order to create effective and efficient abilities, you may have to unlearn some of the study habits you have been using for many years. *Unlearning feels uncomfortable and you may not be very effective—at first.* However, feeling uncomfortable is the best way to recognize that you are beginning to break old learning habits or create new ones. This uncomfortable feeling will not last long provided you continuously put your new learning habits into practice.

The Features of This Text-Workbook

This text-workbook is conversational and interactive. It is easy to read and easy to follow. You can learn from it either individually or in a group. Every chapter contains interactive questions and exercises that contribute to the recipe for learning.

Each chapter builds on the skills and concepts learned in the previous chapter. Every chapter begins with an *introduction* and a series of *learning objectives* and ends with a *summary* and subjective *review* of material presented. In addition, there are motivational quotes sprinkled throughout the text as well as *illustrations and photos* appropriate to each chapter's discussion.

The *five sections* of the text each focus on areas that are most important to your success. Part 1, "The Basics of Active Learning," focuses on the basic awareness that all students need in order to begin learning how to learn. These four chapters include valuable information about active learning, your favored learning style(s), your effective study environment, and time management.

Part 2, "Becoming an Active Reader," centers on becoming an active reader. By improving your vocabulary, previewing, reading faster to improve your concentration, and skimming and scanning, you will be able to read more in less time with good understanding and retention.

Part 3, "Taking Notes," focuses on notetaking. Taking effective notes in class from your instructor as well as from your textbooks is vital to doing well on tests and for long-term learning.

Part 4, "Studying, Test Taking, and Critical Thinking," centers on your studying, testing, and thinking skills. Learning and applying the five success factors for studying smart will reduce your study time while increasing your learning. Since learning how to prepare for tests is as valuable as your ability to take a test, you will learn how to create a winning combination. Learning more about critical thinking, or thinking about thinking, will help you do well in school and also in your career and personal life.

Part 5, "Researching and Writing Papers," focuses on the most challenging work a student will ever have to do. Learning how to use a library will help you in school with your papers and also help you find answers to any questions you might have throughout your whole life. In school, writing good papers and essays require planning and organization of ideas. For your career, writing will be a necessary part of any job, and for certain jobs more effective writing will be required.

At the end of this text, there are *appendices* that will assist you with answers to the exercises in the chapters. You will also find a *glossary of terms* specific to this text that you can easily refer to for definitions of vocabulary words. In addition, there is a *bibliography* that includes book titles for more information about getting motivated, building self-esteem, reaching your goals, and exploring careers.

An educational and enjoyable *audiotape* accompanies this text-workbook. It focuses on getting motivated, creating a positive self-concept, and thinking like a winner. The audiotape combines interesting and usable information that you can listen to and learn from over and over again.

Directions for Using the Self-Evaluation Feature

The Self-Evaluation in each chapter, provided it is used honestly and answered accurately, is one of the most important tools of this text-workbook. You use it to evaluate your learning habits at the beginning of every chapter and then to re-evaluate them at the end of the book in the Final Self-Evaluation located in Appendix A. The objective for this exercise is to see where you are now and then hopefully show improvement based on what you learned.

After each chapter introduction, under the subheading of Self-Evaluation, there are ten statements. You are asked to respond with one of the three choices: "yes/always," "sometimes," or "no/never." Your response should be based on your previous knowledge, experience, and current habits. The following self-evaluation for Chapter One includes one student's sample responses.

One Student's Sample Response to Chapter One Self-Evaluation

1. I regularly attend my classes.	(Y)	S	N
2. I sit in the front of the classroom.	Y	S	(N)
3. I actively participate in class discussions.	Y	(S)	N
4. I listen carefully and take good notes in all my classes.	Y	(S)	N
5. I choose a proper study environment for learning.	Y	(S)	N
6. I take notes or write down questions while reading.	Y	(S)	N
7. I am prepared for class (do my assignments on time).	Y	(S)	N
8. I have and follow a study schedule.	Y	S	(N)
9. I ask for help when needed.	(Y)	S	N
10. I learn from my mistakes as a student.	Y	(S)	N

After responding to all ten statements, count the number of Ys you have circled and place that number in the appropriate blank in the "Rate Yourself" section located at the bottom of the evaluation. Then do the same for the Ss and then the Ns. Now multiply the number of responses times the number listed. The following sample is completed based on the preceding example.

Rate Yourself Sample

RATE YOURSELF

Number of Ys ___2___ x 100 = *200*

Number of Ss ___6___ x 50 = *300*

Number of Ns ___2___ x 10 = *20*

Total = *520*

The highest number you can have is 1,000 (10 x 100) and the lowest is 100 (10x10). *Getting the highest number is NOT the objective here—showing honest improvement from beginning to end is.*

Once you have completed the "Rate Yourself" section, turn to the Self-Evaluation Progress Chart in Appendix A at the end of this text. First, transfer your Ys, Ss, and Ns from your "Rate Yourself" section to the appropriate boxes under "Beginning." Then, using the total number of points, complete the bar graph. The sample continues below.

Beginning Evaluation Sample Student Completion

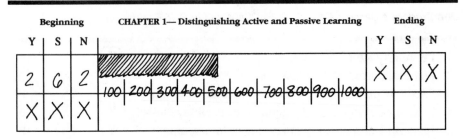

Sometime during your term, depending on your instructor's syllabus, you will be asked to complete all or parts of the "Final Self-Evaluation." The "Final Self-Evaluation" is all of the self-evaluation statements from all 15 chapters, separated by chapter number and name. There are 150 statements in all. If you have completed all of the chapters, then you will eventually be responding to all of the statements. If you have not worked with all of the chapters, then you will only be responding to those chapter statements that you have completed.

After you have finished responding to the statements, you will be following the same procedure for each chapter, except that this time you are going to complete the ending evaluation bar graph and blanks. The sample continues below.

Sample Student Final Self-Evaluation Completion

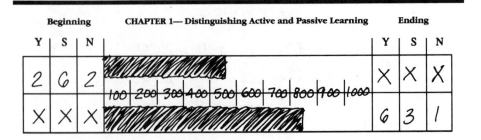

Once all of your Ys, Ss, and Ns have been filled in, total your beginning and ending numbers at the bottom of each page. Then add them together at the end. Compare your beginning and ending numbers. This is one sample of completed totals.

Sample Completed Tally for Both Beginning and Ending Self-Evaluation

Y	S	N		Y	S	N
16	48	16	Beginning Subtotals (Ch 9-15) Ending Subtotals	48	24	8
+				+		
14	40	16	Beginning Subtotals (Ch 1-8) Ending Subtotals	38	25	7
=			(from previous page)	=		
30	88	32	Beginning Total Ending Total	86	49	15

Look at your numbers. What do you see? Hopefully, you will see a shift from a lot of Ns and Ss in the beginning to more Ys and Ss in the end. The more Ys you have, the more efficient and effective learner you have become. The Ss are habits you are working on and put to use as needed. The Ns that still remain are areas you need to pay attention to and continue to work on.

Feedback

I ask for your feedback. Every class I teach, I learn something new. Since I am not with you while you are learning from this text, I am most interested in your comments, questions, and suggestions. I want to know what worked for you and why. I want to know what didn't work for you and why. Most importantly, I want to know everything about what you do to make learning successful. Please send them to:

Abby Marks-Beale
The Reading Edge
PO Box 4212
Yalesville, CT 06492

Enjoy learning!

Abby Marks-Beale

PART 1

THE BASICS OF ACTIVE LEARNING

CHAPTER 1
DISTINGUISHING
ACTIVE AND PASSIVE
LEARNING

CHAPTER 2
DISCOVERING YOUR
LEARNING STYLE

CHAPTER 3
CREATING AN
EFFECTIVE
LEARNING
ENVIRONMENT

CHAPTER 4
LEARNING TIME
MANAGEMENT

CHAPTER 1

DISTINGUISHING ACTIVE AND PASSIVE LEARNING

After studying and working with the information in this chapter, you should be able to:

1. Distinguish between active and passive learning.
2. Outline the advantages of becoming an active learner.
3. Explain how study skills can help you in the future.
4. Explain why and how knowing the purpose and responsibility of every assignment is important to learning.
5. Identify ways to develop a belief in yourself.
6. Summarize the six ways to be active in your learning.
7. Recognize where to look for help.
8. Explain how your health influences your ability to learn.
9. Begin using active learning tools toward your success.

Working harder or longer is not the same as working smarter.

Your first exposure to homework and studying was sometime around the first grade. Your teacher instructed you to go home, do some work, and bring it back the next day. As the years progressed, your homework assignments became more challenging in both size and content. Out of necessity, you probably figured out how to do the work. Some students are more successful with their self-learned study skills than others. Too many students spend more time studying and learning than is really necessary because of ineffective study skills. *Working harder or longer is not the same as working smarter.*

When education is continued beyond high school, many students find that their self-taught study skills are not enough and/or that they are working unusually hard. Just as a car's engine may run for years with little maintenance, so too can some students make it through high school with little attention to study skills. College proves to be a different story! It is only when a car gets a tune-up or a student learns effective study skills that both are able to function more efficiently. Learning IS work, but it can be made a lot easier with the proper skills.

In this chapter, we will help (1) identify the differences between active and passive learning, (2) provide you with simple ideas and strategies toward becoming an active learner, and (3) encourage you to create your own action plan for learning success.

SELF-EVALUATION

The following self-evaluation will give you an idea of how familiar, or unfamiliar, you are with some of the topics and terms discussed in this chapter. After reading each statement, circle the letter (Y, S, or N) most appropriate to your answer. Please answer honestly, rate yourself at the end, and then complete the information for Chapter 1 on page 374 in Appendix A.

When you're learning, you're making use of many tools available to you. What tools do you use for learning?

Y = yes; frequently   **S** = sometimes   **N** = no; never

1. I regularly attend my classes.	Y S N
2. I sit in the front of the classroom.	Y S N
3. I actively participate in class discussions.	Y S N
4. I listen carefully and take good notes in all my classes.	Y S N
5. I choose a proper study environment for learning.	Y S N
6. I take notes or write down questions while reading.	Y S N
7. I am prepared for class and do my assignments on time.	Y S N
8. I have and follow a study schedule.	Y S N
9. I ask for help when needed.	Y S N
10. I learn from my mistakes as a student.	Y S N

<u>Rate Yourself</u>

Number of Ys _____ x 100=

Number of Ss _____ x 50=

Number of Ns _____ x 10=

Total =

To furnish the means of acquiring knowledge is . . the greatest benefit that can be conferred upon mankind.

- John Quincy Adams, Sixth President of the United States

IDENTIFYING ACTIVE AND PASSIVE LEARNING

The terms *active* and *passive* are complete opposites of each other. Being **active** simply means *doing something* while being **passive** means *doing nothing*. Though you can sometimes learn by doing nothing, those who do something are far more effective and successful in their learning.

The following example using the term *osmosis* is helpful in demonstrating the difference between active and passive learning. **Osmosis** is a passive process by which you learn information or ideas *without conscious effort*. As an example, you might have learned how bees make honey just by watching the Discovery Channel on television.

If, however, you place a textbook under your bed pillow before going to sleep, the information contained in the book will not absorb into the pillow nor into your head. In this case, the passive process of osmosis doesn't work, so then you need to become more active in the learning process to absorb the material in the textbook.

Below is a comparison of some passive study habits versus active ones. On the active side (where there is no entry), try to come up with an appropriate study habit and fill in the blank. (Remember that *active* and *passive* are opposites.)

These are just some of the habits that you should be aware of. Throughout this book there will be more detailed explanations of each of these active habits, as well as others. Each explanation will help you to better understand how and why you need to be more active in the learning process rather than passive. As you attend classes, read assignments, take notes, and perform other student functions, it is important to be aware of how active you are in the learning process. The more active, the better!

Active versus Passive Study Habits

Passive Habits	Active Habits
Frequently daydreaming	Listening carefully in class
Taking no notes in class	Taking notes in class
Not doing assignments	_____
Not making notes from texts	_____
Not asking for help (or know when to)	_____
Not participating in class	_____
Skipping classes frequently	_____
Sitting in the back of the room	_____
Having no study schedule	
Studying for a test the night before	Studying for a test ahead of time
Repeating the same mistakes	Learning from mistakes

THE ADVANTAGES OF BEING AN ACTIVE LEARNER

As mentioned earlier, many students are able to make it through their schooling with their own self-learned study skills. Most of these students can best be described as observers, rather than participants, in the learning process. **Observers** learn by paying careful attention to what they see, while **participants** learn by getting involved in the learning process. Beginning electricians can learn a lot by observing someone with more experience install a light switch, but that does not necessarily mean they will be able to perform the same task successfully the first time on their own. If, however, they participate in the installation instead of simply observing it, they will probably be more successful when trying it on their own. Similarly, first-time computer users learn faster and understand more if they are able to work on a computer while learning about it.

Because active learners are involved in the learning process, they understand more when material is introduced. As a result, they learn more with less effort and in less time.

The following old Chinese saying helps to describe the relationship of involvement in one's learning:

Tell me and I will forget;
Show me and I may remember;
Involve me and I will understand.

Think about something you recently learned how to do. It could have been playing a new sport, balancing a checkbook, cooking a meal, or driving a car. Now respond to the following questions.

What did you learn how to do? _____

_____

How did you learn it? _____

_____

Were you told, shown, or involved in the process? _____

_____

In your opinion, what are the differences with each type of learning method?

Telling: _____

_____

Showing: _____

_____

Involving: _____

_____

Which method would you prefer to learn by and why?_____

_____

Becoming an active learner is a simple and rewarding way to get an education without wasting valuable time and money. The information in this chapter will provide you with specific steps you can take to become more involved in your learning process.

Why Study Skills Are So Important

Study skills are the keys to your success as a student. Possessing and using effective study skills means that (1) you will spend less time learning more, (2) you know how to be an active, independent, and self-directed learner, and (3) you can learn anything you will ever want to learn. Not only do these skills help achieve academic success, but also career and family success.

All too frequently students wonder how what they are learning today relates to anything in their future. In Figure 1–1 you will see chapter by chapter how each of the study skills you will read and learn about in this textbook can also be used for your future. You may want to return to this figure later to reinforce what you are learning.

Curiosity is more important than intelligence.
                                        - Anonymous

Figure 1–1 How Study Skills Relate to the Future

Chapter	Chapter Title	Relation to the Future
1	Distinguishing Active and Passive Learning	Active learning is useful for all types of learning activities, including researching careers, learning a new job, and having a family.
2	Discovering Your Learning Style	Understanding that people learn differently will enable you to better understand your own learning abilities. This will help for anything you will ever need or want to learn.
3	Creating an Effective Learning Environment	In order to read or learn anything effectively, you need to know how to set up your working environment to reduce mind-wandering and increase concentration.
4	Learning Time Management	Effective and efficient people use some form of a time manage-

Chapter	Chapter Title	Relation to the Future
		ment system, most commonly a calendar, that schedules time for school, work, and family activities. Without it, many things do not get done.
5	Building Your Vocabulary	Having a good vocabulary helps you to speak, read, and write better, making you a more desirable candidate for many professions.
6	Mastering Reading Assignments	Knowledge is power. Learning to master reading will help you to read professional journals, newspapers, magazines, textbooks, computer manuals, etc., more easily and efficiently.
7	Raising Your Reading Speed	Knowing how to effectively read faster will enable you to read more in less time.
8	Learning to Skim and Scan	Knowing how to skim and scan will help you to read selectively, which promotes concentration and saves time and energy.
9	Taking Effective Notes in Class	Organizing information on paper is a useful skill for school as well as for business activities including meetings, workshops, and writing reports.
10	Taking Effective Notes from Textbooks	Seeking out and noting important information helps you to concentrate, focus, and learn from any reading material.
11	Learning to Study Smart	Knowing how to study smart means you know the factors necessary for success in the real world such as being prepared and learning from your mistakes.
12	Mastering Tests	Tests are not only performed in school. For many professions, there are certificate programs that require passing a series of tests. There are also other types of tests necessary for gaining or keeping employment.
13	Developing Critical Thinking Skills	Critical thinking skills are very important for all of the decisions

Chapter	Chapter Title	Relation to the Future
		you will ever make, including those for your career, in a job, for your family, and for yourself.
14	Using the Library	Knowing how to use a library will enable you to find the answer to any question you may have. It will also help you research schools and career opportunities.
15	Writing Essays and Papers	Writing is a part of most careers. Becoming good at it will help you to perform your job more effectively.

BECOMING AN ACTIVE LEARNER

Active learners can be described as people who are **empowered,** or people who feel capable of learning anything they want, know what they have to do in order to learn (or ask how), and then proceed to learn. Active learners continually seek out ways to make learning easy and rewarding. They want to learn as much as they can in the time they have to spend. Most important, active learners possess a feeling of self-confidence and high self-esteem as a result of their involvement in learning.

Read carefully through the following suggestions for becoming an active learner. After reading each section, you will be asked to choose one of the following statements:

_____ I understand this section and have no questions.
_____ I do not understand this section and will ask my instructor the following question(s):_____

If you have understood what you just read, place a checkmark (✓) next to the statement "I understand this section and have no questions." If, after reading, you are unsure about what you just read and have a question about it, place a checkmark (✓) next to the statement "I do not understand and will ask my instructor. . ." followed by your question(s) filled in the blank.

At the end of this chapter, you will be asked to use the information you have learned to work on an action plan.

Know Your Purpose and Responsibility for Every Assignment

Every assignment has a purpose, and for every assignment you have a responsibility. Your **purpose** is the reason *why* you are doing your assignment and your **responsibility** is *how* you are account-able for it. For example, let's say your computer instructor assigned you to read fifteen pages of your programming textbook and to then answer ten questions about it. To start, open the book to the first page of your assignment, read the title, and think about your pur-pose and responsibility. In this example, your purpose might be "because I want to learn about the topic" or "because I need to learn it for a test later in the course." Your primary responsibility is to answer the 10 assigned questions. However, it is also your responsi-bility to think about how else you might use the information you have learned. You may need it for a class discussion, for a computer program, for a test or quiz, or for some future project.

By taking a few moments to get yourself mentally prepared to do your assignment, you are identifying a reason to begin working (your purpose) as well as a point at which you are finished (your responsibility). Students who keep their purpose and responsibility in mind while doing an assignment find that they not only concen-trate better, but learn and retain more of what they study.

Take an assignment or two that you have to do for a class you are currently taking and consider your purpose and responsibility. Fill in your answers to each of the following questions.

What is your assignment (#1)?_____

What is your purpose?_____

What is your responsibility?_____

_____

What is your assignment (#2)?_____

What is your purpose?_____

What is your responsibility?_____

_____

Writing down this information is not always necessary once you have trained yourself to ask these questions. A mental reminder of your purpose and responsibility can work just as well.

_____ I understand this section and have no questions.

_____ I do not understand this section and will ask my instructor the following question(s):_____

Work in a Good Study Environment

In Chapter 3 we will discuss in detail the ingredients of a good study environment for improving concentration. For now, use the following information to start you thinking about your own study environment and how it compares to the suggested conditions for a good study environment:

❑ A quiet, distraction-free place

❑ A comfortable chair

❑ A clutter-free desk or table

❑ A comfortable room temperature

❑ Good lighting

❑ The materials you need (including pens, paper, highlighter, textbooks, and a dictionary)

Remember, if you need or want to study outside of your home, a school library, an empty office, or conference room can also be suitable locations.

_____ I understand this section and have no questions.
_____ I do not understand this section and will ask my instructor the following question(s):_____

Develop Belief in Yourself

Your confidence in your ability to learn can either make your studying easier or more difficult. If you convince yourself that the work is too hard or too much, or that you can't do it, you will have a hard time. A negative attitude encourages you to give up. If, on the other hand, you are determined to learn as much as you can, no matter how hard or how much there is, you will learn much more easily. A positive attitude encourages you to continue until you succeed.

If you can believe in yourself, in the fact that you *can* do anything you *want*, then you will possess the confidence necessary to succeed in school. You will then also have the ability to succeed in anything you choose to do in the future. You can begin to gain this confidence in yourself by learning to replace failure words with success words.

In the right column below, complete the blanks with the success word that is opposite to the failure word.

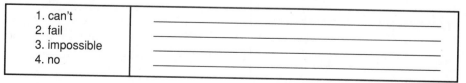

Failure Words	**Success Words**
1. can't	_____
2. fail	_____
3. impossible	_____
4. no	_____

Now create a typical statement including first the failure word, then replacing it with the success word. For example, "I can't read that much in a night" becomes "I can read that much in a night."

1. _____

_____

2. _____

_____

3. _____

_____

4. _____

_____

Think about the difference between the two statements. Which is a more typical statement for you? Are success words part of your vocabulary? If so, good for you! If not, what are you waiting for?

Another way to develop the belief in yourself is to use a coping attitude. A **coping attitude** is neither positive nor negative, but one that helps you cope with the work or situation. Let's see if you can come up with positive or coping attitudes from the following negative ones. Think about or discuss with your classmates the differences you feel there are in your ability to learn with each attitude. In the blanks on the negative side, fill in some of your negative attitudes. Then turn them into positive ones.

Negative Attitudes	Positive or Coping Attitudes
Example: I can't do it.	I can do it or I can deal with it.
I have too much homework.	I need to set aside more time today to do my work.
I dislike my instructor.	_____
The course is too hard.	_____
I don't have time to study.	_____
School is boring.	_____
_____	_____
_____	_____
_____	_____
_____	_____

With any attitude, know that *you* make the choice to think either positively or negatively about your abilities and work load.

If you find out that you didn't do as well on a test as you wanted, which of the following statements is closest to your attitude?

Positive: What a great opportunity to learn from my mistakes!

Coping: What do I need to do better next time?

Negative: I'm either a failure or the test was too hard.

In reaction to each of the following situations, try to create a positive, coping, and negative statement response.

If you found out a week in advance that you have two or more tests in one day:

Positive: _____

Coping: _____

Negative: _____

If your instructor gives a lot of homework or projects:

Positive: _____

Coping: _____

Negative: _____

If you are having trouble learning a subject:

Positive: _____

Coping: _____

Negative: _____

If you have to write a paper and you are not sure how to do it:

Positive: _____

Coping: _____

Negative: _____

Developing a more positive attitude overnight may not be realistic. But by the time you complete this textbook, you will have new approaches to all kinds of learning tasks that will make it easier to think positively about your abilities as a student.

The late Earl Nightingale, a popular speaker on personal development, said that "You go in the direction of your most dominant thoughts." This means that if you think negatively, you will end up with negative results. If you think positively, you will end up with positive results. Remember, the choice is yours.

_____ I understand this section and have no questions.
_____ I do not understand this section and will ask my instructor the following question(s):_____

Take Part in Your Learning Process

More often than not, you probably sit in a classroom staring at your instructor while trying to look interested. Unfortunately, if you are just sitting there, you are probably daydreaming more than listening or learning. It could be that your instructor is not very interesting or that you are just tired or unmotivated that day. *No matter the situation, it is your responsibility to learn the material!*

You can learn under any condition *if* you get involved and actively participate in the class. Active class participation (1) increases concentration, (2) improves listening, (3) seems to make the time go by quicker, and (4) positively affects overall learning. How can you do this? Here are six key ways to take part in your learning process:

Go to Class and "Soak It All In."   One obvious way to increase your potential for learning is to *attend classes regularly*. Classes are a very important part of the learning process. Since learning is an individual activity, there is no substitute for being there.

In every class, you have the choice of acting like a "sponge" or like a "rock." Students who act like a "sponge" soak up all the information through active participation, have a positive attitude, and possess an eagerness to learn as much as possible. On the other hand, students who act like a "rock" generally have a negative attitude and are in effect just sitting there. It should be no surprise that sponges learn more than rocks.

What are you? Are you an active learner, like the sponge who soaks up knowledge, or a passive learner, like the rock who expects knowledge to come to it?

Which are you? _____

_____ I understand this section and have no questions.
_____ I do not understand this section and will ask my instructor the following
question(s):_____

Sit in the Front of the Room.   This is an easy way to ensure your participation in the learning process. Sitting up front limits distractions from other students and gives you a clear view of the instructor and the instructor a clear view of you. Students who sit in front usually sit up taller than those in the back and thus appear more eager and ready to learn. Try sitting in front in all your classes. You will find yourself concentrating better and learning more. It may feel a little uncomfortable at first, but you can get used to it.

_____ I understand this section and have no questions.
_____ I do not understand this section and will ask my instructor the following
question(s):_____

Ask or Answer a Question.   To ask an intelligent question or to respond intelligently, you have to be listening and concentrating. Too many students feel that asking questions makes them look stupid. Actually, students who don't ask questions don't learn nearly as much or as easily as those who do. Remember that you aren't expected to know it all; that's why you are studying—to learn. Your job is to ask questions so that you can learn more.

Questions can be asked during class, after class, or during your instructor's office hours. As long as the question gets answered, it doesn't matter where it is asked. Remember to write your questions down, though; otherwise you may forget them.

By asking questions and participating in class discussions, you take an active role in your learning process. Are you an active participator or just a quiet observer?

Not all questions need to be asked aloud. Just being curious about a topic can help you to learn more. You can gain curiosity by first creating your own list of questions about the topic, then actively seeking the answers to them as you study.

Questions are easy to think of when you use the **5Ws** and **H**: *who, what, when, where, why, and how.* For example, if you were taking a computer course and the day's topic is "Font Styles and When to Use Them," you could think about any or all of the following questions:

1. *What* are font styles?

2. *How* many are there?

3. *What* are they used for?

4. *Why* should they be used?

5. *When* is the right time to change them and *why?*

If you were taking an electronics course and the day's topic is "Measuring with an Oscilloscope," what questions could you ask? (Remember to use the 5Ws and H listed above to help you come up with your questions.)

1. _____

2. _____

3. _____

4. _____

5. _____

Or, if you were taking a Travel/Tourism course and the day's topic is "Handling Cancellations," what questions might you ask?

1. _____

2. _____

3. _____

4. _____

5. _____

Or if you were taking a study skills course and the day's topic is "Active Participation for More Learning," what questions might you ask?

1. _____

2. _____

3. _____

4. _____

5. _____

Think of yourself as a young child, a curious student of the world. By learning to ask questions, you will understand the world better while learning more in less time.

_____ I understand this section and have no questions.
_____ I do not understand this section and will ask my instructor the following question(s):_____

Take Notes in Class. Taking notes is like taking a picture of what happens in your class. Students who take notes listen more carefully, have information to study from, and—most importantly—daydream less. Even if your instructor doesn't require you to take notes, creating your own notes will help you to learn more. Chapter 9 will discuss how to take effective notes in class. In the meantime, take notes as best you can to promote your active participation in learning.

_____ I understand this section and have no questions.
_____ I do not understand this section and will ask my instructor the following question(s):_____

Take Notes while Reading. Taking notes will transform the act of reading, which for many individuals is a passive activity, into an active process. Note taking while reading forces you to concentrate because you are actively seeking out important information to write down. *More concentration means less mind wandering. Less mind wandering means more learning in less time.*

Figure 1–2 shows an effective example of student notes from part of a chapter of the text *Civil Litigation for the Paralegal.* Notice that the notes are written in an easy-to-read format and in the student's own words. When it comes time to study, the student will not have to reread the chapter, but only refer back to his or her notes. In Chapter 10 we will discuss how to take notes from a text in more detail. In the meantime, take notes as best you can to promote active participation in learning.

Figure1–2 Sample notes from Civil Litigation for the Paralegal. Source: Kerley, Peggy, et al. Civil Litigation for the Paralegal. © 1992 Delmar Publishers Inc. Reprinted with permission.

9/24/94
pp 3-22 1-1 What Civil Litigation Is
Civil Litigation = resolving private disputes thru courtesy
Trial or hearing = parties present evidence to judge or jury
Litigation attys¿ assts. = gather ¿ analyze facts/ research law
  - legal doc's prep'd ¿ filed
  - witnesses interviewed
  - other evidence identified ¿ located

_____ I understand this section and have no questions.
_____ I do not understand this section and will ask my instructor the following
question(s):_____

Know When to Ask for Help and Then Ask for It.   Sometimes even the most active participants in a class find that they may still need some help. Help can come from your instructor or from fellow class-mates. Sometimes a library can be useful as well. The time to ask for help is NOT the day of, or the day before, an exam. Studying at least a week before a test will ensure that the help you need will be available when you want it. Instructors generally do not have a lot of sympathy for students who wait until the last minute to ask for help. Chapter 4 will help you learn how to organize your time.

_____ I understand this section and have no questions.
_____ I do not understand this section and will ask my instructor the following
question(s):_____

Where to Look for Help

Though it may seem like you are all alone in your quest for academic success, know that you are not. There are many people you can talk to, places you can go, and material you can read that can help you reach your academic goals.

People You Can Talk To.   There are plenty of people you can talk to who can provide you with almost any information you may need, both about school-related issues and/or personal ones. In the following chart you will see a list of these people on the left and explanations as to how they can help you on the right. Most of these people are specialists and are there to give you help and advice.

People You Can Talk To	How They Can Help You
Course Instructor	❏ Answers questions about the course. ❏ Helps you manage course requirements.
Other students in class	❏ Provide an academic support system. ❏ Provide a network of friends.
Academic Advisor OR Guidance Counselor	❏ Helps you select courses you need to graduate. ❏ Assists in helping you decide on a major. ❏ Lends support for personal problems.
Career Counselor	❏ Evaluates where your interests lie. ❏ Chooses a career. ❏ Assesses employment opportunities. ❏ Provides information on available jobs.
Tutor	❏ Provides academic assistance—e.g., extra help

People You Can Talk To	How They Can Help You
Librarian	❏ Helps you find answers to any question.
Head of a Department	❏ Assists with any problems related to a course—e.g., full enrollment on a course you need.
Department Secretary	❏ Answers questions about department requirements and course offerings.
Resident Assistant (if living on campus)	❏ Advises on campus services and student activities.
Athletic Coach (if on an athletic team)	❏ Lends support for academic problems. ❏ Lends support for personal issues.

Places You Can Go. There will probably be times when you have a question or problem and you don't know whom to go to. If this is the case, then be assured that there are many places you can go. Each location has a staff of knowledgeable people who are there to assist you. To find the specific addresses or phone numbers of their locations, look in your school catalog, campus directory, or telephone directory.

Place You Can Go	How They Can Help You
Learning Skills Center	❏ Assists in the development of reading, writing, math, or study skills that help you meet course requirements.
Tutoring Center	❏ Provides assistance for your coursework.
Library	❏ Provides you with resources to answer any question.
Student Activities Office	❏ Provides information about what is happening on campus.
Student Gov't Office	❏ Provides information about campus events, clubs, and organizations.
Career Development Ctr	❏ Provides information on careers; also evaluates your interests and skills.
Computer Lab	❏ Assistance with computer coursework. Also helps you learn how to use a word processor.
Academic Advising OR Guidance Counselor	❏ Helps you choose your courses and manage your academic life.
Registrar's Office	❏ Handles applications, registrations, grades, and transcripts of the courses you have taken.
Financial Aid Office	❏ Assists you with money matters.
Health Office/Infirmary	❏ Medical advice and/or help.

Material You Can Read.   In addition to people you can talk to and places you can go, you also have material you can read to find the information you seek. A school catalog, usually found in a school bookstore, counseling department, or administration office, will contain a wealth of information about your school's policies, programs, services, and requirements. The catalog usually contains a school calendar which lets you know when classes begin and end, when your holidays occur, when drop and add period deadlines are, and when final exams are scheduled.

A course catalog, usually found in the admissions or registrar's office, will list all of the information you need to register for your courses including dates and times and who the instructor will be. Your school newspaper is where you can get information about upcoming campus events and campus news. It is geared specifically for students because it is written and published by students. Bulletin boards located all over the school are probably your most current source of school information.

_____ I understand this section and have no questions.
_____ I do not understand this section and will ask my instructor the following
        question(s):_____

Learn from Your Mistakes

If you ask successful people how they got to where they are now, they will most likely tell you that while they did a lot of things right, they also made some mistakes along the way. *Mistakes are a vital part in becoming successful, as long as they are learned from.* For students, two common mistakes include:

❑ Forgetting to do an assignment

❑ Not studying for a test, thinking it was another day

Being unprepared either for a class or for a test is a position most students dislike. To prevent these mistakes from happening again, you can use a homework planner to keep on top of your responsibilities (see Chapter 4 for more information) and/or find a study partner who can be relied upon. There are many more mistakes that students can and do make, but the key is to recognize that the mistake has been made and then to act accordingly to prevent it from happening again.

Can you list at least five common mistakes that students make? By first being aware of them, you can prevent them!

1. _____

2. _____

3. _____

4. _____

5. _____

_____

_____ I understand this section and have no questions.

_____ I do not understand this section and will ask my instructor the following
question(s):_____

Take Good Care of Yourself

Your health, or lack thereof, greatly influences your ability to learn. The more mentally and physically prepared you are, the easier it will be to learn. The more tired and stressed out you are, the harder it will be to learn. You have the ability to control how well and how easily you learn by ensuring that you get enough sleep, eat well, and exercise. Health problems increase with behaviors like smoking and drinking alcohol, so it is advisable to avoid them. If _you_ don't take good care of yourself, no one else will.

_____ I understand this section and have no questions.

_____ I do not understand this section and will ask my instructor the following
question(s):_____

YOUR PLAN FOR SUCCESS

You have now read a chapter's worth of information about active learning. Though reading about active learning is interesting, doing something with it is more rewarding.

On the following pages you will find an easy-to-use Awareness and Action Plan for building awareness toward active learning. To use the plan, tear it out of this book and fill one plan out for each class you attend. Photocopy as many as you need. This plan is meant to help you become aware of what you do, or do not do, in your own learning process. The idea is to encourage changes in your habits so that you can move from passive to active learning. Be honest when completing the plan and make sure to complete all the questions.

SUMMARY

1. The terms active and passive are opposite. Being an active learner means you do something to make learning happen, while being a passive learner means doing nothing to make learning happen. Though you can sometimes learn from doing nothing, doing something makes learning more effective and successful.

2. Some of the advantages of becoming an active learner include learning more in less time and learning how to learn anything you want. Active learners also possess a feeling of learning self-confidence and high self-esteem as a result of their involvement in learning.

3. Study skills can help you in school as well as in your future. In addition to your academic success, you will need active learning skills for career and family success.

4. Every assignment has a purpose and for every assignment you have a responsibility. By giving yourself a reason to begin working (your purpose) as well as a point at which you are finished (your responsibility), you will concentrate better, and learn and remember more of what you are working on.

5. If you believe in your ability to learn, then you will possess the confidence necessary to succeed in school. You can begin to gain this confidence in yourself by learning to replace failure words with success words and positive and coping attitudes with negative ones.

6. This chapter describes six of the many ways to be active in your learning. They include going to class and soaking it all in, sitting in the front of the room, asking or answering a question, taking notes in class, taking notes while reading, and knowing when to ask for help and then asking for it.

7. Every school has resources you can turn to to help you answer any question or help you with any problem. These resources include people, places, and reading material.

8. Your health, or lack thereof, greatly influences your ability to learn. The more mentally and physically prepared you are, the easier it will be to learn. The more tired and stressed out you are, the harder it will be to learn.

Figure 1–3 Awareness and Action Plan

Awareness and Action Plan

Your Name_____

Today's Date _____

Name of Class: _____ Instructor Name: _____

Topic(s) of Discussion _____ Class Times: From _____ to _____

Today's Class Format (check those that apply)

___Lecture ___Discussion ___ A/V Presentation ____ Other (please describe) _____

While In Class . . .

1. Did I sit in the front of the room? (circle one)   Yes   No
   If yes, what did I notice about my learning? _____
   If no, what did I notice about my learning? _____

2. Did I actively participate in the class discussion? (circle one)   Yes   No
   If yes, what did I do? _____
      What did I notice about my learning? _____
   If no, what did I notice about my learning? _____

3. Did I listen to the instructor and take good notes? (circle one)   Yes   No
   If yes, what did I notice about my learning? _____
   If no, what did I notice about my learning? _____

4. Was I prepared for class (e.g., doing the homework as assigned)? (circle one)   Yes   No
   If yes, what did I do to be prepared? _____
      What did I notice about my learning? _____
   If no, what did I notice about my learning? _____

5. Did I have a good, positive attitude about learning? (circle one)   Yes   No
   If yes, why did I have this attitude? _____
      What did I notice about my learning? _____
   If no, why did I have this attitude? _____
      What did I notice about my learning? _____

6. Am I familiar with the instructor's style? (circle one)   Yes   No
   If yes, what do I understand about the instructor? _____
      What could I do to succeed with this instructor? _____
      _____
   If no, what did I notice about my learning? _____

At Home/After Class . . .

7. Did I choose a proper study environment? (circle one)   Yes   No
   If yes, what did I notice about my learning? _____
   If no, what did I notice about my learning? _____

8. While reading, did I take notes or write down questions for the instructor? (circle one)   Yes   No
   If yes, what did I notice about my learning? _____
   If no, what did I notice about my learning? _____

In General . . .

9. As a student today in this class, I was _____
   _____

10. For next class, I plan to _____
    _____

_____   _____

Student Signature   Date

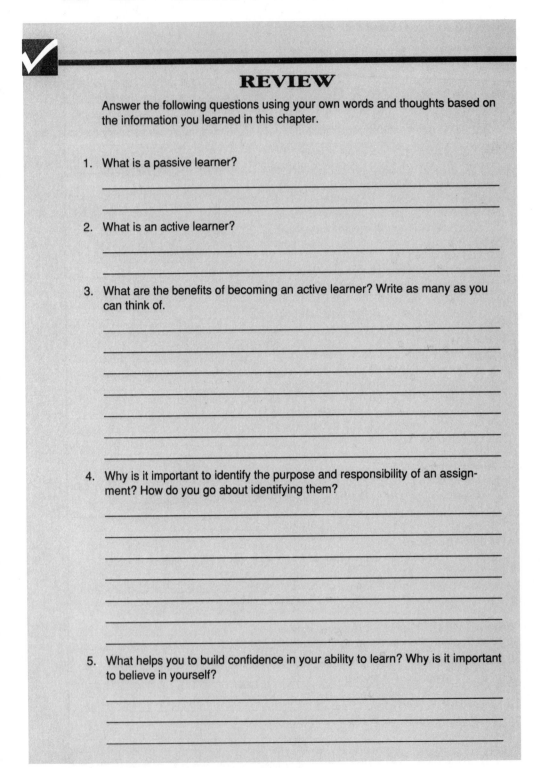

REVIEW

Answer the following questions using your own words and thoughts based on the information you learned in this chapter.

1. What is a passive learner?

    _____

    _____

2. What is an active learner?

    _____

    _____

3. What are the benefits of becoming an active learner? Write as many as you can think of.

    _____

    _____

    _____

    _____

    _____

    _____

    _____

4. Why is it important to identify the purpose and responsibility of an assignment? How do you go about identifying them?

    _____

    _____

    _____

    _____

    _____

    _____

    _____

5. What helps you to build confidence in your ability to learn? Why is it important to believe in yourself?

    _____

    _____

    _____

_____

_____

_____

6. Describe the six ways suggested in this chapter to help you take part in your learning process.

_____

_____

_____

_____

_____

_____

_____

7. What are the 5Ws and H? How can they be used toward active participation and learning?

_____

_____

_____

_____

_____

8. What are you going to do to become more involved in your learning?

_____

_____

_____

_____

_____

_____

_____

_____

CHAPTER 2

DISCOVERING YOUR LEARNING STYLE

After studying and working with the information in this chapter, you should be able to:

1. Define *learning style.*
2. Determine your preferred learning style.
3. Describe the qualities of a sequential learner.
4. Describe the qualities of a random learner.
5. Identify the benefits of learning to adapt to both learning styles.
6. Explain the importance of knowing your instructors' teaching styles.
7. Assess the teaching style of your instructors.
8. Summarize the elements of other learning styles.
9. Begin to apply the information in this chapter to learn more easily.

Your learning style is a reflection of how you absorb information from your world and how you process it.

From the moment you were born you've been learning. Learning is one of the most natural processes of any species—human or otherwise. Before the age of five, you were able to learn more in a given day than you will at any other time in your life. And you performed the act of learning in a very skillful and effortless way. You were so successful that you learned a whole language without any formal instruction. You also learned athletic abilities that you will use for the rest of your life; you learned how to read and react to the expressions on other people's faces; and you learned social skills that you still use today. You learned none of these skills in a classroom, and yet they may be counted among your most significant achievements.

As you continued to learn about the world around you, you began to develop your own style of learning—a style that was comfortable and effective. What you may not have learned is that your developed learning style is entirely personal and entirely right for you. It is different yet similar to the style of others. Most important, it's yours, and the more you know about your style of learning, the more successfully you can adapt it for success in the classroom.

There are many different learning styles. A single chapter is too small to be able to describe them all. However, in this chapter you will learn (1) how to recognize your general learning style, (2) how to identify your instructor's teaching style, and (3) to begin to understand what these learning differences mean. Throughout this book, you will also be given various learning strategies that will enable learners of all styles to learn more easily.

To succeed in the classroom, you need to recognize your own learning style, your instructors' teaching styles, and the difference between the two. Can you recognize your instructors' teaching styles?

SELF-EVALUATION

The following self-evaluation will give you an idea of how familiar, or unfamiliar, you are with some of the topics and terms that are discussed in this chapter. After reading each statement, circle the letter (Y, S, or N) most appropriate to your answer. Please answer honestly, rate yourself at the end, and then complete the information for Chapter 2 on page 374 in Appendix A.

Y = yes; frequently   **S** = sometimes   **N** = no; never

1. I know what learning styles are.   Y S N
2. I know *my* learning styles preference.   Y S N
3. I am familiar with how a sequential learner prefers to learn.   Y S N
4. I am familiar with how a sequential instructor prefers to teach.   Y S N
5. I am familiar with how a random learner prefers to learn.   Y S N
6. I am familiar with how a random instructor prefers to teach.   Y S N
7. I can identify the teaching style of my instructors by the way they are dressed.   Y S N
8. I can identify the teaching style of my instructors by knowing the kinds of questions they ask.   Y S N
9. I can adapt to more than one learning style.   Y S N
10. I know how to adjust my learning style to the teaching style of my instructor.   Y S N

<u>Rate Yourself</u>

Number of Ys _____ x 100=

Number of Ss _____ x 50=

Number of Ns _____ x 10=

Total =

Whatever is received, is received according to the nature of the recipient.

- St. Thomas Aquinas, 13th century
Italian philosopher and theologian

WHAT ARE LEARNING STYLES?

Learning is a natural and constant process of gathering and processing information. Your **learning style** is how you prefer to gather this information and then what you do with it. How you do a lot of things in life—such as where you choose to live, how you dress, what you do for a living, and how you decorate your home—will be a reflection of your learning style—even when you are far from the classroom.

Observers and participants, discussed in Chapter 1, are two kinds of learners with different learning styles. The observer, or more thoughtful learner, prefers to *think* about what is being taught while the participant, or more involved learner, prefers to *experience* learning firsthand. For example, in a drivers' education course, the observer would be content to listen to an instructor lecture or be shown movies while the participant would prefer to get in the car, play with the knobs and buttons and begin driving as soon as possible.

You have probably been aware of differences in people for as long as you can remember. You may have a friend who is neat "as a pin," who keeps a very orderly house or bedroom. On the other hand, your house or bedroom may look like a violent storm has just hit it. For you this may be comfortable, but for others who live with you this may cause some friction—especially if they are neat types. Those of us who are less than neat can never figure out what the concern for neatness is. The interesting thing is that how you approach the matter of neatness is most likely a reflection of your learning style to some extent. Your learning style is a reflection of how you absorb information from your world and how you process it. Your way of dealing with your schoolwork, notebook, and bedroom quite naturally reflects that style.

Another example of how your learning style can influence the way someone does something is in teaching style. An instructor will teach in a style that reflects, or is compatible with, that instructor's learning style. If you can recognize your learning style, while also recognizing your instructor's teaching style, then you will have a greater opportunity to adjust your study skills to meet that instructor's demands and to succeed in that class.

If your learning style is different from your instructor's teaching style, it can make learning a greater challenge. Simply put, if you can't understand what your instructors want and your instructors grade you poorly for not giving it to them, then school and learning can become less than a successful experience.

W *hat we perceive comes as much from inside our heads as from the world outside.*

- William Jones, successful businessman

IDENTIFYING YOUR PREFERRED LEARNING STYLE

I *t is important to understand that your learning style, whatever it is, does not mean that you are better or worse at learning than anyone else. It only means that you have a preference for a certain way of learning.* Your preferred learning style may be considered your comfort zone for learning.

A Learning Styles Assessment

What follows is a learning styles assessment. Circle the *one* letter that completes each statement or answers each question in a manner that is most like you. Go with your first impression—do not think too much about each response. There are no right or wrong answers. When you are finished, tally your responses to discover your preferred style of learning.

1. I consider myself:
   a. Intuitive, relying on hunches and feelings.
   b. Logical, relying on a close study of a situation.
   c. Relying on both a and b the same amount.

2. My bedroom or closet in my room is usually:
   a. A mess—I am not sure what is in it.
   b. Neat and orderly—I can quickly find what I need.
   c. Neat in spots and messy in others.

3. In class:
   a. I have trouble sitting quietly for the whole period.
   b. I have no trouble sitting quietly for the whole period.

4. At a dance, I feel more comfortable:
   a. Dancing a lot.
   b. Talking to friends most of the time.
   c. Dancing and talking about the same amount of time.
   d. I don't like dances.

5. Which phrase describes you best?
   a. I look for and enjoy opportunities to be a leader.
   b. I am perfectly happy being part of the group and letting others lead.
   c. I enjoy both leading and following.
   d. I do not like being a leader or being part of a large group.

6. Which phrase describes you better?
   a. I may exaggerate a bit when telling about an event in which I have been involved.
   b. I always make sure my facts are correct when I tell about an event in which I have been involved.

7. When taking notes in class, I:
   a. Doodle a lot in the margin.
   b. Never doodle because I am too busy writing.
   c. Doodle a little and take notes a little.
   d. Don't take notes or doodle.

8. When it comes to meeting deadlines, I am:
   a. Often late or very rushed at the end.
   b. Usually early or right on time.
   c. Sometimes late, sometimes on time.

9. When learning, I like:
   a. To be active, experimenting and learning by trial and error, field trips, and group exercises.
   b. To listen to teachers, to read a lot, and learn lots of facts and details.
   c. Both a and b equally.
   d. Neither a nor b

10. Which phrase describes you better?
   a. Sometimes I will go into a room and get so distracted I forget why I went in.
   b. When I go into a room, I never forget why I went in.

11. In school:
   a. I tend to daydream a lot.
   b. My mind hardly ever wanders.

12. Which phrase describes you better?
   a. Occasionally I will use my fingers to count.
   b. I do all my math in my head.

13. I study best:
   a. While listening to music.
   b. Without listening to music.
   c. Either with or without music.

14. Which phrase describes you better?
    a. I often have trouble following spoken directions.
    b. I almost never have trouble following spoken directions.

15. Which is more like you?
    a. I get so many new ideas that I don't always carry them through.
    b. I like to plan things carefully.
    c. Both a and b.
    d. Neither a nor b.

16. I am best at:
    a. Art and/or music.
    b. English and/or history.
    c. All of the above.
    d. None of the above.

17. I:
    a. Enjoy sharing my feelings.
    b. Like to keep my feelings to myself.

18. When doing homework:
    a. I have trouble concentrating.
    b. Time flies because I get into most assignments.
    c. Some assignments seem to take forever and in others I lose track of time.
    d. I don't do homework.

19. I consider myself:
    a. Creative.
    b. Not very imaginative.

20. Which phrase describes you better?
    a. I love colors and notice them a lot.
    b. I don't notice colors very much.

Learning Style Assessment Results: Follow the directions below to evaluate the assessment you have just completed.

1. Total the amount of As, Bs, Cs, and Ds and put the numbers in the following blanks:

   As_____   (These responses indicate a random preference.)

   Bs_____   (These responses indicate a sequential preference.)

   Cs_____   (These responses indicate no strong preference.)

   Ds_____   (These responses indicate no preference.)

2. Add together your Bs and Cs, then your As and Cs and put the numbers in the following:

Bs _____ + Cs _____ = Bs and Cs _____

As _____ + Cs _____ = As and Cs _____

3. On Figure 2–1, take the sum of your Bs and Cs and plot it with a large dot on the horizontal line to the left of the vertical line. Then take the sum of your As and Cs and plot it with a large dot on the horizontal line to the right of the vertical line.

4. Now draw a thick dark line connecting the two large dots.

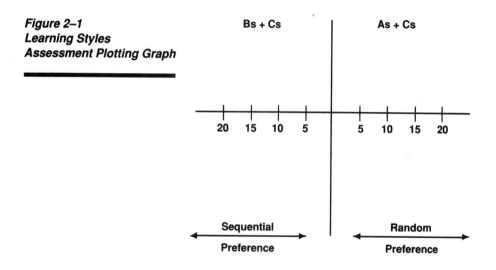

Figure 2–1
Learning Styles
Assessment Plotting Graph

As a result of the learning styles assessment, you can now recognize which learning style you prefer. If your line is more on the left side than the right, then you have a preference toward sequential, or step-by-step, learning. If your line is more on the right side than the left, then you have a preference toward random, or less structured, learning. If most of your line is on one side or the other, then you have a strong preference for that side. And if your line is equally on the left and right, then you have no strong preference.

Having a preference for sequential learning means you tend to learn logically, though you may also possess some qualities of a less structured learner. Having a preference for random learning means that you tend to learn in a less structured manner, though you may also possess some qualities of a logical learner. Having no strong preference means having an equal preference for both styles. This type of learner is the most flexible—able to switch styles depending on the situation.

The following sections will provide you with more information about each of these preferences.

THE SEQUENTIAL LEARNER

A preference toward **sequential learning** means you tend toward a more logical, step-by-step approach to taking in information. You most likely enjoy theory, want order in all things (your room, your study area, your notebook, etc.), require structure in your life (you're a planner), value being on time, desire the details when you gather information, are comfortable with reading and lecture, and need to be in control. For example, if a friend is telling you about a party, you want the details (a complete description of who was there, what they were wearing and doing, what was served, and how it was served), and you want the description to be in your sense of order. (You will be uncomfortable if your friend wanders all over the place, telling you a little of this and a little of that.) Most likely, to keep things on track and in *your* sense of order, you'll start asking questions that guide and control the conversation, and you'll feel impatient when your friend doesn't stay on the topic.

More Sequential Learner Qualities

In addition to the qualities listed above, you will see below a list of other sequential learner qualities. Regardless of your preference, read down this list and place a check mark (✓) next to the qualities that sound like you. If a quality does *not* sound like you, do nothing.

___ I enjoy learning and playing with ideas and theories.

___ I am a critical thinker.

___ I prefer getting data from reading and lectures.

___ I need a sense of personal control.

___ I see play as a waste of time.

___ I am efficiency oriented and keep excellent records.

___ I prefer a single correct answer to a test question rather than several possibilities.

___ I am unable to handle spur-of-the-moment activities.

___ I am a step-by-step problem solver.

___ I work well (and independently) from precise, clear instructions.

___ I want intellectual recognition.

___ I like lab books.

___ I keep my room in very good order.

___ I take pride in neat papers.

Those having a preference toward sequential learning may be able to say that most of these statements are true, while those having a preference toward random learning may say that only a few are true. The more your learning preference is sequential, the more you feel comfortable with many of the descriptive phases above. And more than likely, you are comfortable in school and the structured classroom. Traditional instruction is very sequential!

THE RANDOM LEARNER

A preference toward **random learning** means that you learn in a less structured manner. This means there is a chance that school and math class, in particular, are not some of your more comfortable moments. In fact, you probably live for the discussion of history, literature, and current events, and art class, sports, or band practice. Your papers probably have comments on them such as "lacks organization," "good ideas, but you fail to order them or develop them fully," and "you didn't follow the assignment."

As a random learner, you need examples and comparisons to make the facts stick in your mind, and if the analogy or example is in story form, so much the better. You often have gut sense of the correct answer to questions, but are unable to support them with details or facts. To remember the facts and details of anything, you need to know the "big picture" first—otherwise the details are absolutely meaningless. In your textbooks, you frequently study the graphs, diagrams, and pictures; you might even think that learning would be much easier if textbooks were only illustrations. In any case, you are glad that the pictures and diagrams are there, and you might feel lost without them.

Additionally, as a random learner you are frequently off in many directions at once, and are accused of being disorganized. When you describe the same party to a sequentially preferred friend, you are more interested in giving your impressions of the people at the party and what you thought about them, and may become annoyed when your friend keeps asking you for details.

More Random Learner Qualities

In addition to the qualities described above, you will see below a list of other random-learner qualities. Read down this list and place a check mark (✓) next to the qualities that sound like you. If a quality does *not* sound like you, do nothing.

___ I learn best through discussion, collaboration, and participation.

___ I need a sense of social unity in the classroom.

___ I need personal attention and feedback.

___ I have a vivid imagination.

___ I am sensitive to heated debates that I perceive as conflict.

___ I enjoy looking at things from many viewpoints.

___ I have a broad range of interests.

___ I am creative.

___ I dislike routine and authority.

___ I need to do things my own way.

___ I get uneasy if there is no outlet for action.

___ I enjoy active presentations that use the eyes, ears, and even the body while learning.

___ I have little sense or regard for time.

___ I work on several projects at once.

Those having a preference toward random learning may be able to say that most of these statements are true, while those having a preference toward sequential learning may say that only a few are true. The more your learning preference is random, the more you feel comfortable with many of the descriptive phrases above. As a random learner, it is quite probable that school is not always comfortable for you, and that you need to force yourself to be disciplined and orderly to be successful in a sequential world.

If you are a random learner and you have pushed yourself to

Sequentially preferred learners are often identifiable by their neat, organized desks, while random preferenced learners are most often identifiable by their less organized approach to learning. Which type of learning preference do you have?

be more sequential (organized, orderly, and neat), you may have discovered that after a while, acting sequential becomes easier. Research shows that you can change or adjust your learning style to different tasks, and, more important, that to do so expands your thinking capability tremendously. You may, in fact, be well ahead of the sequential thinker, who didn't have to adjust much in high school. Imagine what it's like for the sequential learners when they enter a very random classroom!

LEARNING TO USE BOTH STYLES OF LEARNING

I*t's important to know that we all use both styles of thinking and learning—sequential and random. The more you use both, the more efficient your thinking and recall capability becomes. In fact, it benefits memory and thinking to use both styles.*

To practice using a style that is not your preference is like learning to use your nondominant hand. On the line below, write your full name using your nondominant hand. (If you are right-handed, use your left; if you are left-handed, use your right.)

How comfortable was it? Probably not very. Eventually, however, with practice you can become ambidextrous and more capable of using whichever hand is best for the situation. You become a "switch-hitter"—the much valued baseball player with the ability to face either a right- or left-handed pitcher. To practice in a style that is not your own is to develop the ability to face either the random or sequential instructor with equal success.

D**o what you can, with what you have, where you are.**
- David Sarnoff, American radio and television pioneer

IDENTIFYING TEACHING STYLES

N*o matter who your instructor is, the fact remains that your job is to learn and succeed in every class.* Every instructor teaches differently. Some will be easy to understand, others very difficult. Some will be likeable, others not. The best strategy you can have is to first observe your instructors, learning as much as possible about their teaching styles and habits, and to then find ways to adjust to each instructor's style.

As much as it is your instructor's job to understand you, so too is it your job to understand your instructor. What is your instructor's expectation of you? Are your instructor's lectures organized or disorganized? Is a lot of information provided on handouts or is it written on the board? Are the homework assignments useful to class discussion or are they just preparatory for a test? What kinds of tests are usually given? Are the "pet-peeves" of your instructor obvious? Answers to these and other questions can help you gather information about each of your instructors.

Now that you have discovered something about your own learning style, let's look at how to identify your instructors' teaching styles. *It is important to realize that instructors' teaching styles are mostly an extension of their learning styles.* Most instructors teach in the mode they are comfortable with for learning.

Before continuing, stop for a moment and think about your past instructors. Recall one or two instructors with whom you really felt in tune. You always knew exactly what they wanted on tests, and you enjoyed their classes. What did they do in class? How did they ask questions? Did they want one correct answer or did they want your thoughts or opinions? Then think of one or two instructors with whom you always felt at odds, never knowing exactly what they wanted or never being able to give them quite what they asked. Jot down your thoughts in the spaces that follow. If you only had one type of instructor, imagine what the other type would have been like.

If you are a sequential thinker, you probably would prefer to skip this part and get right on to the descriptions of the two types of instructors. Please do this exercise anyway. It is good practice for getting into a random mode of thinking—imagining, recalling how a class felt, having a gut sense of information before you actually read it. Go with it—go random for a moment to improve your thinking skills.

The teacher to whom I could relate: _____

Dressed: _____

_____

_____

_____

Lectured or taught: _____

_____

_____

_____

Asked questions like:_____

_____

_____

_____

Did things like: _____

_____

_____

_____

The teacher to whom I could _not_ relate so well:_____

Dressed: _____

_____

_____

_____

Lectured or taught:_____

_____

_____

_____

Asked questions like:_____

_____

_____

_____

Did things like: _____

_____

_____

_____

The Sequential Instructor

The characteristics of the sequential instructor, quite naturally, are similar to those of the sequential learner. You might recognize one of your teachers whom you recalled with these sequential characteristics:

❑ Idealistic, systematic, and organized

❑ Likes facts and details

❑ Values sequential thinking

❑ More interested in data than people

❑ Prefers informational forms of instruction such as reading and lecture

❑ Can sometimes be completely unaware of the emotional climate in the room

❑ Seeks efficiency

❑ Is a decision maker

❑ Usually has well-planned classroom routines

❑ Tends to be a firm disciplinarian

❑ Black and white, right and wrong; no partial credit, stresses correctness and facts

Do any of these traits match some of your observations in the previous exercise?

... **D**ominance is part and parcel of the normal human condition . . . as a result, we are handed, footed, eyed and—in a general sense—brained.
- *Ned Herrmann, contemporary author and educator on brain research*

Sequential instructors tend to be more serious in class and prefer lecturing to leading group discussions. How many of your teachers are sequential instructors? (Photo courtesy Joy Bush, Southern Connecticut State University)

The Random Instructor

The characteristics of the random instructor, as you can surely guess, are similar to the random learner. More specifically they include:

❑ The warmth of a person who enjoys people

❑ Nonjudgmental and supportive (values others' opinions)

❑ Prefers role play, open discussion, and small group work

❑ Will often individualize instruction

❑ Prefers to create own course of study

❑ Gives imaginative assignments

❑ Assumes learning is a function of interest

❑ Prefers self-discovery, experience, and a variety of instructional modes

❑ Tends to follow what he or she feels like doing rather than a lesson plan

❑ Classroom may be viewed as disorderly by instructors of other styles

❑ Stresses concepts and conclusions

Do any of these characteristics match, in some way, one of the instructors you described in your previous exercise? Can you guess with some certainty what type of instructors you described in these exercises—was one random and the other sequential?

Quick Ways to Assess Your Instructor's Teaching Style

Based on the instructor qualities described previously, it may be challenging to easily identify which style your instructor prefers. A simple way to quickly determine your instructor's style is to focus on these four key steps:

1. Look at how your instructor is dressed.

2. Listen for clues in lecture or class.

3. Determine what kinds of questions your instructor asks.

4. Observe your instructor's behavior.

Look at How Your Instructor Is Dressed. Sequentials are more inclined to wear muted colors that blend and match with every part of their outfit. They dress in "sets," or outfits, and one outfit usually doesn't get mixed with another.

Randoms tend to have more relaxed, more colorful, and more casual clothing. Randoms don't like boredom.

Listen for Clues in Lecture or Class. Sequentials deliver a lecture in specific order (that's primary), probably use a lot of outlined notes (never deviating), use a monotone voice with very little humor (remember that they are apt to see play as wasteful), and always stick to the topic. They will make the clear connections to relevant topics that they think you should have and not allow you to wander far off the topic.

Randoms will tell stories, use metaphors, analogies, and humor, and allow for "wanderings" during a lecture. During a history lesson they will tell the "story of history" and describe and develop its characters. Such a lesson may sound more like a conversation than a lecture.

Determine What Kinds of Questions Your Instructor Asks.   Sequentials will ask questions that ask you to recall and recite facts, data, or specific theories. They tend not to ask for your opinion, especially if they are the type of sequential who is comfortable only with one correct answer.

Randoms will ask questions that demand that you interpret, give an opinion, suggest an application, form a connection to some other subject area, or provide for multiple answers.

Observe Your Instructor's Behavior.   Sequentials will stand behind a lectern or table. They will write notes on the board in outline form, but without abbreviations. If they use an overhead projector, they'll use a black pen only—no colors. Their lecture delivery tone will be restrained and, at the worst, will consist of one-word utterances. They will have a low tolerance for students sitting on the floor, preferring that they sit at desks or tables in straight rows—"classroom style."

Randoms will wander around the room, and perhaps gaze out the window, or better yet, sit on the windowsill and play with the venetian blind cord. They will scribble fragments of ideas on the board, use arrows to connect one fragment or idea to another, and use abbreviations or even pictures to illustrate ideas. Randoms will gesture with their hands and their vocal tone will vary from soft to animated. They might even tolerate students sitting on the floor or using two chairs—one for their legs.

Sequential instructors like to point out information on the blackboard or with overhead projectors, while random instructors take a more relaxed approach to classroom instruction. How many of your teachers are random instructors?

Both teaching styles have a place in instructional settings. More than likely, you will not encounter any one instructor who is purely sequential or random. As you read through the previous descriptions, you could probably recall some of your past teachers in each style. Use the preceding descriptions to help you identify individual teaching styles so that you can plan your study strategy in the future now that you know what each type of instructor considers important.

LEARNING FROM STYLE DIFFERENCES

It can often be to your advantage if your instructor teaches in a different style than you prefer. For example, a random instructor can help a sequential learner develop creativity through those imaginative assignments that ask for concept development and conclusion. Recent research shows creativity is close to the truly successful learning experience.

Sequential instructors will help a random learner develop discipline to get the job done before the random learner wanders off on a tangent (or two or three), creating unnecessary work. Experiencing and adapting to both styles will definitely help your learning and thinking, and create a tolerance and appreciation for differences. Remember that there is power in developing your ability and flexibility to be a "switch-hitter." The more you are able to adjust your style to that of your instructor, the more success you will have as a student.

Figure 2–2 is a worksheet designed for you to learn more about your instructor's teaching style. Bring a copy of this worksheet to each of your classes and complete it as best you can. Add any other notes you think are important related to each instructor's style. If you are in the same class as another student who is learning about learning styles, you may find it interesting to compare your worksheets at the end of the class.

Figure 2–2 Learn More About Your Instructor's Style

Class _____ Instructor's Name _____
Office Phone_____ Office Hours _____
Required Text(s) _____
Other Required Materials _____
How long teaching here? _____ Other subjects taught? _____
  1. Primary instructional mode: (circle one)
Lecture/Seminar   Lab   Discussion Groups   Combination of _____

2. Does active class participation figure into the final grade? Yes or No
3. Does the instructor provide: (check those which apply)
    _____ syllabus? _____ study guides? _____ reading list?
    _____ work at chalkboard? _____ handouts? _____ other? _____
4. Does the instructor require: (describe those that apply)
    homework _____
    papers _____
    outside reading _____
    extra-credit projects _____
    other _____
5. What kind of tests are given? _____
6. How would you describe your instructor's style of dress?
    _____
7. Is your instructor's lecture style organized or random? _____
8. What types of questions does your instructor ask? (circle those that apply)
    recalling or reciting of facts   questions with one answer
    specific theories   questions with more than one answer
    your opinion   interpretation
    suggest an application   form a connection
9. How would you describe the behavior of your instructor?
    _____
    _____
10. Other observations and information: _____
    _____

OTHER LEARNING STYLES

In addition to the sequential and random styles for learning, there are several other learning styles worth mentioning. If you would like more information about any of these learning styles theories, consult your local library. You will probably find them listed under psychology, the brain, and/or learning styles.

Left Brain/Right Brain Theory

Left brain/right brain theory, also known as **hemisphericity**, is closely related to the sequential and random learning theories previously discussed. This theory says that the brain has two hemispheres, a left side and a right side. Each side represents certain qualities. In effect, a left-brain person tends to resemble a sequential learner while a right-brain person tends to resemble a random learner. Some people who have done research and written about this theory include Roger Sperry, Kenneth and Rita Dunn, and Ned Herrmann.

Visual, Auditory, and Kinesthetic Learning Theories

We are all influenced by our senses. **Sensory theory** states that we all have a preference for taking in our information either visually (through our eyes), auditorily (through our ears) or kinesthetically (through our body movements). John Grinder and Richard Bandler have done research and written about this theory.

Visual learners prefer using their eyes to learn. They need to see demonstrations, pictures, and visual aids. They love to see writing on the board and want to write down everything—otherwise they may forget. The tend to talk fast and spell well. Visual learners tend to use statements like "I *see* what you mean," "*show* it to me," or "I get the picture."

Auditory learners prefer using their ears to learn. They would rather hear lectures rather than see demonstrations. They do not feel a great need to write things down because they tend to be comfortable relying on what they hear. They also work well in partners and teams. Auditory learners tend to use statements like "I hear you," "that sounds good to me," or "I'm glad you mentioned that."

Kinesthetic learners prefer using their body to learn. They would rather be physically involved in their learning, like the individual who wants to play with the knobs and buttons of the car. Being comfortable is important to kinesthetic learners. As a result, they tend to move around a lot, fidgeting and slouching in their chairs. Kinesthetic learners express themselves through their body language. They tend to use statements like "I grasp what you mean," "you're on the right track," or "that really tickles my fancy."

Many people have a combination of more than one of these preferences. For example, a visual-kinesthetic learner learns best by watching and experiencing while auditory-kinesthetic learner learns best by listening and experiencing.

From these brief descriptions, can you identify which style of learner you might be?

Social and Independent Learning Theories

Social and independent learning theory says that some people prefer to learn independently while others prefer to learn in a group. If you prefer to learn independently, then it is possible that you are also introverted, preferring to rely on your own thoughts and feelings. If you prefer to learn in a group, then it is possible that you are also extroverted, preferring to rely on others' thoughts and feelings.

SUMMARY

1. Your learning style is a reflection of how you absorb and process information.

2. Your preferred learning style is also considered your comfort zone for learning.

3. A preference for sequential learning means that you tend toward a more logical, step-by-step approach for taking in information.

4. A preference for random learning means that you tend toward a less structural means of taking in information.

5. Your preferred learning style does not mean that you are any better or worse at learning than anyone else. It only means that you have a preference for a certain way of learning.

6. Learning to adapt to both styles will make learning easier in any situation.

7. Instructors' teaching styles are generally a reflection of their preferred learning style. Discovering their learning style and adapting to it can make learning easier.

8. To assess the teaching style of your instructors, you can look at how your instructor dresses, listen for clues in their lecture or class, determine what kinds of questions they ask, and observe their behavior.

9. There are many other learning styles in addition to the sequential and random. These include left brain/right brain theory, visual, auditory and kinesthetic learning theory, and social and independent learning theory.

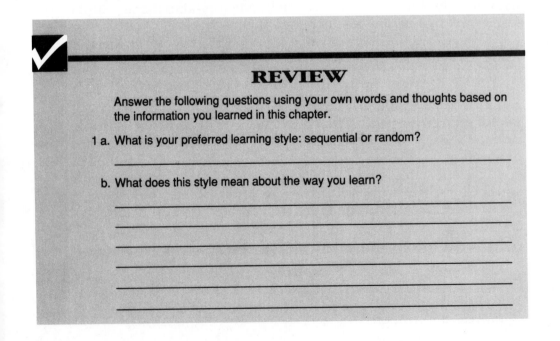

REVIEW

Answer the following questions using your own words and thoughts based on the information you learned in this chapter.

1 a. What is your preferred learning style: sequential or random?

_____

b. What does this style mean about the way you learn?

_____

_____

_____

_____

_____

2. Can you also learn using the "other" style (meaning if you are random, can you learn in sequential style and vice versa)? Explain your answer in your own words.

_____

_____

_____

_____

_____

_____

3. What can you do to figure out your instructor's preferred teaching style?

_____

_____

_____

_____

_____

4. Why do you think it's important to know your instructor's preferred teaching style?

_____

_____

_____

_____

_____

5. After studying this chapter, what have you learned about the way you learn? What do you think you can do in order to make learning more successful for you?

_____

_____

_____

_____

_____

_____

_____

CHAPTER 3

CREATING AN EFFECTIVE LEARNING ENVIRONMENT

LEARNING OBJECTIVES

After studying and working with the information in this chapter, you should be able to:

1. Identify the influences that affect the way you learn.
2. Identify distractions that cause you to mind-wander.
3. Explain the effects of mind-wandering.
4. Discuss when mind-wandering is effective.
5. Specify ways to increase your concentration.
6. List and discuss the ingredients of an effective physical learning environment.
7. Outline the ingredients of an effective mental learning environment.
8. Begin to create an effective learning environment.

T he most important reason for creating an effective learning environment is to increase your concentration while studying.

Learning can be very rewarding. It can also be very challenging, often frustrating, and almost always time consuming. There are many influences that affect the way you learn. These same influences affect the amount of time and energy you spend in the learning process. The most important influences are those in your learning environment.

An effective learning environment is one in which concentration comes easily and more learning results. An ineffective environment can cause you to waste time and makes learning difficult. *The most important reason for creating an effective learning environment is to increase your concentration while studying.* You can learn how to increase your concentration through choosing the appropriate influences in your physical and mental environment.

In this chapter, we focus on helping you to (1) become aware of the influences in your learning environment, (2) understand how these influences affect you, and (3) create an effective learning environment for improving your studying and learning. We will also help you discover the opportunities available to you to make your learning easier and more enjoyable.

Which photo more closely resembles your study area?

SELF-EVALUATION

The following self-evaluation will give you an idea of how familiar, or unfamiliar, you are with some of the topics and terms discussed in this chapter. After reading each statement, circle the letter (Y, S, or N) most appropriate to your answer. Please answer honestly, rate yourself at the end, and then complete the information for Chapter 3 on page 374 in Appendix A.

Y = yes; frequently   **S** = sometimes   **N** = no; never

1. I study in a quiet, distraction-free environment.   Y S N
2. I study without a radio or television.   Y S N
3. I avoid taking phone calls while studying.   Y S N
4. I study at a desk or table with good lighting.   Y S N
5. I am aware of, and can change, the room temperature.   Y S N
6. I am aware of, and try to take care of, mental distractions before I study.   Y S N
7. I am usually relaxed when I have a lot of studying to do.   Y S N
8. I know several ways to increase my concentration while studying.   Y S N
9. I know I CAN learn anything I WANT to.   Y S N
10. I enjoy learning.   Y S N

<u>Rate Yourself</u>

Number of Ys _____ x 100 =

Number of Ss _____ x 50 =

Number of Ns _____ x 10 =

Total =

Surely a man has come to himself only when he has found the best that is in him, and has satisfied his heart with the highest achievement he is fit for.

- Woodrow Wilson, 24th President of the United States

YOUR LEARNING INFLUENCES

A **learning influence** is something that affects the way you learn. Some influences are helpful in keeping your concentration; others are distracting. The helpful influences are considered positive, while those that are distracting are considered negative.

Think about the influences that affect your studying. In the left column below, create a list of as many influences as you can think of that affect the way you read and study. Include specific influences like how you feel, what you think about, where you are, etc. Then, in the right column, determine whether the influence is positive (helpful), negative (unhelpful), or both (sometimes helpful, sometimes not).

List of Influences	Positive, Negative, or Both
Example: Being Tired	Negative
Time of Day	Both*

(* = If you choose to study in the morning and your concentration is good at that time, then the influence is positive. If you choose to study in the late evening and your concentration is poor at that time, then the influence is negative.)

Once you have listed as many influences as you can, compare them with some of your classmates' lists. You may remind someone of an influence they did not think of and you may be reminded of one yourself. Add more influences to your list as you think of them.

Mind-Wandering and Concentration

Concentration is vital to learning. When you are concentrating, you are focused on the learning material and content. **Mind-wandering**, on the other hand, is the enemy of concentration. Also known as **daydreaming**, mind-wandering is a momentary lack of concentration or focus. It can last a second, five seconds, thirty seconds, or longer. Mind-wandering is a natural and very human characteristic. Chances are that you, like most students, are a "master daydreamer," not only in the classroom but also while reading and studying.

When you study, some mind-wandering may be helpful to your learning. If you are building knowledge by thinking about something related to what you are studying, mind-wandering can be productive. For example, if you are learning about the installation of electrical plugs in a house, and your mind wanders to the time you were three years old and got an electrical shock when you stuck your finger in a socket, then that thought is useful to your learning. But if your mind is wandering to thoughts about the coming weekend or the milk that you have to buy on the way home, then it is not productive. These nonproductive thoughts break your concentration, slow down your studying, interrupt your learning process, and affect your ability to understand the information you are reading.

Causes of Mind-Wandering. It is interesting to recognize how many distractions break your concentration, even for a moment. Think about the distractions that get your mind wandering when you are reading or studying. Be as specific as you feel comfortable with and list as many distractions as you can think of below.

1. Example: Being hungry	**11.** _____
2. _____	**12.** _____
3. _____	**13.** _____
4. _____	**14.** _____
5. _____	**15.** _____
6. _____	**16.** _____
7. _____	**17.** _____
8. _____	**18.** _____
9. _____	**19.** _____
10. _____	**20.** _____

Once you have listed as many distractions as possible, compare them with some of your classmates' lists. You may remind someone of a distraction they did not think of and you may be reminded of one yourself. Add more distractions to your list as you think of them.

Now, looking at your list, place a check mark (✓) next to the distractions that are productive or helpful and place an (X) mark next to those that are neither. It is interesting to discover just how many distractions are not helpful to the learning process!

Have you recognized any distractions that you would like to get rid of forever? You may be aware of distractions that you might like to avoid or do something about, but chances are that they will happen again. Using hunger as an example, you may be able to get rid of it by eating something, but that is only temporary. Eventually you will get hungry again.

Under the most ideal circumstances, a human being can only concentrate for about twenty minutes before mind-wandering sets in. Children have concentration periods that last an average of only about 20 seconds! It is amazing that we ever learned anything with such small amounts of concentration.

Effects of Mind-Wandering.   If you mind-wander on your way home from class, you might miss your bus stop, drive past your exit, or, even worse, get into an accident. When you mind-wander while you are reading or studying, it is having an effect on your ability to learn. What do you think are the effects of mind-wandering on your learning?

_____

_____

_____

_____

_____

Remember that mind-wandering is only good when it relates to the material you are studying.

Reducing Mind-Wandering.   Since mind-wandering is a natural and human characteristic, you can never get rid of it forever. Think about it: If you were asked to never daydream again while reading or studying, could you do it? The answer is no! Nonetheless, even if you can't get rid of it, you can at least learn how to reduce it. By reducing mind-wandering, you will be able to learn more in less time with better concentration.

The very first step in reducing mind-wandering is to catch yourself doing it. You can do something about mind-wandering once you are aware that you are doing it.

Throughout this chapter and the rest of this book, we will be providing a lot of suggestions and techniques toward increasing your concentration. We expect that you will find these suggestions helpful and you are encouraged to keep track of them using Figure 3–1.

Figure 3–1
Ways to Improve Concentration While Studying

List as many ways you can think of that help you to develop good concentration while studying. As you continue to work through this book and learn other ways to develop good concentration, refer again to this page and add more. If you run out of room, add another piece of paper and keep adding them!

Ways I Can Improve My Concentration While Studying

1. Catch myself daydreaming! _____
2. _____
3. _____
4. _____
5. _____
6. _____
7. _____
8. _____
9. _____
10. _____
11. _____
12. _____
13. _____
14. _____
15. _____
16. _____
17. _____
18. _____

Increasing Your Concentration

Earlier in this chapter, you created a list of learning influences and decided whether each influence was positive, negative, or both. Using the columns on the next page and the information you just learned about mind-wandering and concentration, rearrange your learning influence list into the two categories: *mind-wandering is a result of* and *concentration is a result of.* Add to either side of your list as you think of things to include. (Hint: The negative ones are usually on the mind-wandering side and the positive ones are usually on the concentration side!)

Mind-Wandering is a result of:	Concentration is a result of:
Examples: Being tired	Being well-rested
Studying late at night	Studying earlier in the day

Review your list. Begin to become aware of these influences and how they affect the way you study and learn. Keep in mind that you have some control over the amount of mind-wandering you do while reading and studying. For example, if you tend to daydream a lot because you are tired, just getting a good night's sleep will allow you to concentrate better, work faster, and learn more. There is no sense in staying up all night if you are not able to concentrate.

Remember to add any influences from your list above to Figure 3–1 "Ways I Can Improve My Concentration While Studying."

In the next section, we will give you more information about increasing your concentration by controlling your learning environment.

L earning is not attained by chance. It must be sought for with ardor and attended to with diligence.

- Abigail Adams, 2nd First Lady of the United States

YOUR LEARNING ENVIRONMENT

As human beings, we react to our environment. When it is warm, we get sleepy. When it is noisy, we get distracted. When we have a lot on our minds, we have a hard time concentrating on our work. A **learning environment** is the combination of learning influences that are present while you are studying.

There are two learning environments: physical and mental. Your physical environment includes where you are and what is around you. Your mental environment includes influences such as your attitude, how you feel, and what you think about.

Both the physical and mental environments in which you study *directly* affect the amount of concentration you have when working. In turn, the amount of concentration you have then directly affects how much you learn and how much time you spend in the learning process.

Your Physical Learning Environment

Your **physical learning environment** is the place where you choose to study. It may be at the library, in your bedroom, in the kitchen, or at work. It could be seated in a reclining chair, on a couch, or at a desk or table. It could be noisy or quiet. It could be filled with clutter or be neat and organized.

A good physical learning environment consists of a combination of positive learning influences that allow you to concentrate easily while studying.

In the left column of the table at the bottom of this page, we have listed a series of negative physical influences on your concen-

Physical Influences

Mind-Wandering is a result of:	Concentration is a result of:
Example: Studying on a bed or couch A cluttered study area Poor lighting Too hot or too cold Eating Listening to music In front of a television Receiving phone calls Other people around	Studying at a desk or table _____ _____ _____ _____ _____ _____ _____ _____

The library is one place where you might choose to study. Is this a good physical learning environment? Why or why not?

tration while studying. In the right column, fill in the blank space with a positive physical influence. Some of these influences may look familiar from your own list of learning influences on page 51.

Once you have filled in the right column, look at both sides and compare one line at a time. Place a check mark (✓) on the left side, the middle, or the right side that is closest to your current physical environment. For example, if you study on a bed or a couch most of the time, place a check mark on the left side of the line next to that statement. If you study about half the time on a bed or couch and the other half at a desk or table, place your check mark directly on the center line. And if you study at a desk or table, place your check mark on the right side of the line.

If all of your check marks are on the right side, you have an effective environment that allows for plenty of concentration for studying. If not, and you would like to learn more about creating this effective environment, read on!

Choosing Where You Study. For years, students have chosen their bed, the floor, a couch, or a comfortable chair on which to study. We associate these locations with relaxing and/or sleeping. A desk or table, on the other hand, are places that we associate with working. If you think about it, that's why classrooms are filled with desks, *not* beds! By trying to study in a place where you usually relax, you will find studying more challenging as well as time consuming.

By moving to a desk or table to do your studying, you can get more work done with better concentration and in less time. A desk or table also has a convenient writing surface and plenty of space to spread out. At the other locations, you are constantly being distracted either because you have to move to a different body position or you are trying to balance the study material. Consider the following equation:

Some places you choose to study are positive learning environments while others are not. Can you tell which of these illustrations shows a positive learning environment? Why?

$$\text{If a Bed} = \text{Sleep,}$$
$$\text{and a Desk} = \text{Work,}$$
$$\text{then a Bed} \neq \text{Work.}$$

Your desk top or table top should be clean except for the study materials you need for that session. There should be enough room for your elbows, a textbook, a notebook, and any other material you are working with. If your desk or table has clutter on it, move it out of the way. You have some learning to do and clutter distracts.

Good lighting is always important. It is difficult to study when there is not enough light (or too much light) in the room.

Room temperature is also important. A room that is too hot makes you sleepy, while one that is too cold makes you think about getting warm. You end up focusing more on how warm or cold you are than concentrating on your studying. By working in a comfortable temperature, your concentration will have a fighting chance and more effective learning can result.

Food and studying don't mix well. Think about it. When you are eating and studying at the same time, which gets more of your concentration? The food, of course! Though you can get some studying done while you eat, you will be more effective if you eat first, then study. We seem to concentrate better on one thing at a time.

Tuning Out What's Around You.   Studying without distractions is another excellent way to learn more in less time.

Listening to anything but your own thoughts interferes with good concentration while studying. Getting rid of distractions like a radio, television, telephone, or other people can greatly increase the amount of learning you can accomplish in a shorter period of time.

Though you may disagree, listening to the radio does interfere with your ability to learn. You may be able to "tune it out" most of the time, but when a song that you like comes on, you may find yourself tapping your feet, humming along, or daydreaming. Think about it: When you study with the radio on, your brain has to focus on two activities instead of one; studying and listening. By cutting out the listening, your brain is better able to concentrate on the studying.

Try the following simple experiment: During your next homework session, study without the radio for ten minutes. Then turn the music on as you usually do and study for another ten minutes. In which ten-minute period did you either get more done and/or learn more? Some say that the silence is more distracting than the radio, but that too can be "tuned-out" with a little practice.

Watching television also interferes with your concentration when studying. Instead of just studying, you are both listening and watching. In a half-hour period, if you only do your work at the commercial breaks, you might get lucky and get five minutes of work accomplished! Even being in the next room, where you can hear your television, can be very distracting. Your concentration should be on your studying, so it is a good idea to stay away from televisions when trying to learn.

Receiving telephone calls during your study time is both distracting and time consuming. Thanks to human beings and answering machines, you have the ability to hold your calls until you have completed your work. If you chose to study between 7:00 and 8:30 in the evening, you can leave a message on your answering machine or tell the person taking messages for you to let your callers know that you will return their calls after 8:30. This will allow you uninterrupted time for studying while not missing any phone calls.

Studying with other people around can make concentrating difficult. If you study in a public place like a library, there will always be people moving around and whispering, though it is usually quiet. If you study at home, your family may interrupt you more often than necessary. In both cases, you have the ability to prevent some distractions. At the library, you may be able to find a quiet corner of the building where not many people go. At home, if you explain to your family your need for uninterrupted time and then go into a room and close the door, you will have a better chance of increasing your concentration during the time you have set aside to study.

Your Mental Learning Environment

Your **mental learning environment** is what your mind thinks about while you are studying. In order to learn anything, concentration is necessary. But as we have already discovered about mind-wandering, we will always have some natural breaks in our concentration. It is during these breaks that we sometimes talk to ourselves. We may say negative or nonproductive things like "I don't know how I'm going to finish all of this tonight" or "I'm going to fail the test tomorrow." Or we may say positive or productive things like "I really learned a lot today" or "I'm glad I've kept up with my assignments." The kind of self-talk you choose is based on your attitude and your physiology.

Developing Self-Confidence.   Your confidence in your ability to learn and to study can either make your studying easier or more difficult. In Chapter 1, we described how important it was to develop belief in yourself. You were also given the opportunity to begin thinking positively. Review this section now to refresh your memory.

Making the commitment of being a student is a positive step toward your future. There is every reason in the world to think that you can achieve anything you want. Developing a positive attitude about your ability to learn makes the amount of time and energy you spend that much more enjoyable. Only you are in charge of your own attitude and learning!

What are the benefits of having a positive attitude?

Becoming Aware of Your Physiology.   Your **physiology**, simply defined as how your body feels, affects your thoughts and concentration while studying. If you are feeling tired or ill, you will daydream a lot and think more about getting some sleep than about the work in front of you. You may try to continue to study, but you will waste a lot of time and find the task of learning difficult.

Or you may decide that getting some sleep will help you learn more easily later so that you don't waste your time or do more than necessary.

Your physiology changes throughout the day, with certain times of day better for studying than others. Your ability to concentrate is easier when you are feeling well and more difficult when you are not. Planning study time around your peak times of the day or in relationship to how well you feel will make the time you spend more effective.

Complete each of the following blanks below with your response:

Example: If I am tired, <u>learning is difficult and I daydream a lot. I</u> <u>also waste a lot of time.</u> _____

If I am rested, _____

_____

If I am hungry, _____

_____

If I am not hungry, _____

_____

If I feel ill, _____

_____

If I feel well, _____

_____

Compare your responses to those of your classmates and discuss the effects of each. Talk about what you might do to improve your concentration in all of the above situations.

SUMMARY

1. There are many influences that affect the way you study and learn. Being rested is a positive influence, while being tired is a negative one.

2. Concentration is vital to learning. Mind-wandering is the enemy of concentration. There are many causes of mind-wandering, most of which are distractions such as being hungry.

3. Mind-wandering causes you to lose concentration and waste time. It can also prevent you from understanding what you are trying to learn.

4. Mind-wandering is effective *only* when it relates to the material you are studying.

5. Reducing mind-wandering is the same as increasing concentration. There are many ways to improve your concentration while studying. The first is to catch yourself doing it.

6. An effective physical learning environment consists of an appropriate place to study without distractions and being able to tune out what's around you.

7. An effective mental learning environment consists of self-confidence and an awareness of how you are are feeling.

REVIEW

Answer the following questions using your own words and thoughts based on the information you learned in this chapter.

1. What are learning influences? Which ones influence your learning the most?

_____

_____

_____

_____

_____

_____

2. What is the relationship between mind-wandering and concentration?

_____

_____

_____

_____

_____

_____

_____

_____

3. How is mind-wandering both a good and bad influence on studying?

_____

_____

_____

_____

_____

_____

_____

4. What can you do to create good concentration for studying?

_____

_____

_____

_____

_____

_____

_____

5. From what you learned in this chapter, which pieces of information are most useful in helping you create an effective learning environment?

_____

_____

_____

_____

_____

_____

_____

CHAPTER 4

LEARNING TIME MANAGEMENT

After studying and working with the information in this chapter, you should be able to:

1. Gain awareness of how you currently spend your time.
2. Identify several short-term and long-term goals.
3. Recognize how much time you really need for studying.
4. Use a term calendar to schedule school-related dates and social events.
5. Use a weekly study schedule to plan daily assignments and responsibilities.
6. Define procrastination and identify several ways to overcome it.
7. Explain the importance of setting study goals and planning rewards.
8. Begin applying the information in this chapter to effectively manage your time and reach your goals.

T**he most important way to gain more time is to plan it.**

The following is not a trick question: How many hours are there in a day? _____ The answer to this question is simply twenty-four hours. No matter what you do, you cannot get any more time out of a day.

So why do students complain that there is not enough time? As you progress either into higher level courses or into more content or career specific ones, the assignments become more challenging, the homework becomes more abundant, and you will find an over-all need to spend more time studying. If you work and go to school, you have to make time for both. If you are involved in ath-letics at your school, then you have to work out a schedule that will include your practice and workout time in addition to your class and study time. If you are a working mother or father, your class and study time will add to your job and family responsibilities.

Many students wish for more time, but don't realize that they are the only ones who can create it. If you took a good look at how you currently spend each twenty-four hours, you might find that there are things you can do to make better use of this time.

"Work smarter, not harder" is one of the important ideas expressed throughout this book. In the area of time management, being smart about how you use your time is an important step toward making your learning easier.

In this chapter, we will (1) help you to understand where your time is spent, (2) help you to recognize how much time you really need, and (3) offer you helpful tips and suggestions for planning your time wisely.

How do you spend the twenty-four hours you have in a day?

SELF-EVALUATION

The following self-evaluation will give you an idea of how familiar, or unfamiliar, you are with some of the topics and terms discussed in this chapter. After reading each statement, circle the letter (Y, S, or N) most appropriate to your answer. Please answer honestly, rate yourself at the end, and then complete the information for Chapter 4 on page 374 in Appendix A.

Y = yes; frequently   **S** = sometimes   **N** = no; never

1. I know what is important to me.		Y S N
2. I know where my time is spent.		Y S N
3. I make time to study.		Y S N
4. I study as early in the day as possible.		Y S N
5. I keep and follow a homework assignment planner.		Y S N
6. I keep a term calendar.		Y S N
7. I plan ahead for assignments due in the future (e.g., tests, writing papers, etc.).		Y S N
8. I set study goals for myself.		Y S N
9. I reward myself when I reach a study goal.		Y S N
10. I know what procrastination is and recognize how it affects my ability to manage my time.		Y S N

<u>Rate Yourself</u>

Number of Ys _____ x 100=

Number of Ss _____ x 50=

Number of Ns _____ x 10=

Total =

The indispensable first step to getting the things you want out of life is this: decide what you want.

- Ben Stein, contemporary author

WHERE DOES YOUR TIME GO?

Where *does* your time go? Actually, it doesn't go anywhere. Just like money, you spend it. You have twenty-four hours to spend each day and each day you spend it in different ways.

There are basically two ways to spend time: wisely and unwisely. *Spending your time wisely* means you are spending it well or productively, usually toward a goal such as doing well in school. Spending your time wisely toward a goal of doing well in school may include such activities as going to class, doing research in the library, or studying. *Spending your time unwisely* means you are not spending your time well, and are in effect wasting it. Spending your time unwisely toward the goal of doing well in school may include such activities as watching television, talking on the phone, or just "hanging out."

You cannot nor should not spend all your time wisely. But neither should you waste all your time. As a student, you need to learn how to balance the time you spend between wise and unwise activities.

Identifying Short-Term and Long-Term Goals

What is important to you? If you can truly know what is important to you today, tomorrow, or five or ten years from now, then you will be able to recognize whether your time is being spent wisely or whether it is being wasted.

What IS important to you? Do you want good grades? Do you want to be a good mother or father, or daughter or son? Do you want to be active in your community? Do you want to be a first-rate nurse, electrician, landscaper, etc.? What are your goals?

A **goal** is something that you want to have, do, or be. There are short-term goals and long-term goals. A **short-term goal** is usually considered something you want to achieve within the next six months or a year. Examples could include buying a new car, deciding on a major course of study, doing well in school, or planning a surprise party. A **long-term goal** is usually something that takes longer than six months or a year to achieve. Examples could include getting a college degree, becoming a computer programmer, or having a family.

On each of the first five blank lines below, list some of your short-term goals. Then on the next five, list some of your long-term goals. Be as realistic as possible. For example, if you say that one of your short-term goals is to have a million dollars, you may find this goal unrealistic or difficult to achieve. Note that you are being limited to five goals because working toward even one of them takes a lot of time and energy. If you find it difficult to come up with five, make sure to write down at least one.

Identifying Short-Term Goals

Example: <u>I want to do well in school.</u>

1. _____
2. _____
3. _____
4. _____
5. _____

Identifying Long-Term Goals

Example: <u>I want to get a college degree.</u>

1. _____
2. _____
3. _____
4. _____
5. _____

Return to this list several times in the next day or two and add or clarify them as you think about what is important to you.

Identifying your goals is the first step toward managing your time. The next step requires planning and action in order to achieve them because you can't *do* a goal. Take each of your goals previously listed and write what actions you believe you need to do in order to achieve them. Be as specific as you possibly can.

Short-Term Goals Action List

Example: <u>To do well in school</u>, I need to:

❑ Study smarter
❑ Attend my classes
❑ Do my assignments on time
❑ Participate in class discussions
❑ Follow directions
❑ Manage my time well

1. To _____, I need to:

- ❑ _____
- ❑ _____
- ❑ _____
- ❑ _____
- ❑ _____
- ❑ _____

2. To _____, I need to:

- ❑ _____
- ❑ _____
- ❑ _____
- ❑ _____
- ❑ _____
- ❑ _____

3. To _____, I need to:

- ❑ _____
- ❑ _____
- ❑ _____
- ❑ _____
- ❑ _____
- ❑ _____

4. To _____, I need to:

- ❑ _____
- ❑ _____
- ❑ _____
- ❑ _____
- ❑ _____
- ❑ _____

5. To _____, I need to:

- ❑ _____
- ❑ _____
- ❑ _____
- ❑ _____
- ❑ _____
- ❑ _____

Long-Term Goals Action List

Example: <u>To get a college degree</u>, I need to:

❑ Secure loan(s)

❑ Research colleges with programs I am interested in

❑ Choose and apply to several colleges

❑ Find and work with an academic advisor

❑ Do well in my classes

❑ Manage my time well

1. To _____, I need to:

  ❑ _____

  ❑ _____

  ❑ _____

  ❑ _____

  ❑ _____

2. To _____, I need to:

  ❑ _____

  ❑ _____

  ❑ _____

  ❑ _____

  ❑ _____

3. To _____, I need to:

  ❑ _____

  ❑ _____

  ❑ _____

  ❑ _____

  ❑ _____

4. To _____, I need to:

  ❑ _____

  ❑ _____

  ❑ _____

  ❑ _____

  ❑ _____

5. To _____, I need to:

  ❑ _____

  ❑ _____

❑ _____

❑ _____

❑ _____

When learning to manage your time, knowing what is important to you helps you plan your time according to *your* needs, not someone else's. Becoming aware of how you spend your time now is the first step to planning how to spend your time in the future.

The Daily Activity Log

Keeping a **Daily Activity Log,** a listing of activities that you do from the time you get up until you go to sleep, is a simple way for you to see how you spend your time. To help you begin to discover how you spend your time, complete the Daily Activity Log in Figure 4–1 for one typical day. (To make writing easier, you can reproduce it using a copy machine that can enlarge it.) Write down how you spend your time being as specific as you can. Use the sample log in Figure 4–2 as an example.

Once you have completed a Daily Activity Log, take a look at it and answer the following questions:

	# of Hours
How much time do you spend *sleeping?*	____
How much time do you spend *eating and grooming?*	____
How much time do you spend *commuting?*	____
How much time do you spend *attending classes?*	____
How much time do you spend *studying/doing homework?*	____
How much time do you spend *working at a job?*	____
How much time do you spend *in sports or leisure activities?*	____
How much time do you spend *socializing with friends?*	____
How much time do you spend *watching TV?*	____
How much time is *not accounted for?* (no activity listed)	____
What else did you spend your time doing? _____	____

From your answers to these questions and according to what you have listed as what's important to you, do you think you are spending your time wisely? If doing well in school was listed as important to you, and you spend a lot of time watching television, socializing with friends, running errands, or if you have no idea where your time has been spent, then you are probably wasting a lot of your time.

Figure 4–1
A Blank Daily Activity Log

DAILY ACTIVITY LOG

6:00 AM		4:30	
6:30		5:00	
7:00		5:30	
7:30		6:00	
8:00		6:30	
8:30		7:00	
9:00		7:30	
9:30		8:00	
10:00		8:30	
10:30		9:00	
11:00		9:30	
11:30		10:00	
12:00 PM		10:30	
12:30		11:00	
1:00		11:30	
1:30		12:00 AM	
2:00		12:30	
2:30		1:00	
3:00			
3:30			
4:00			

Figure 4–2
A Sample Daily Activity Log

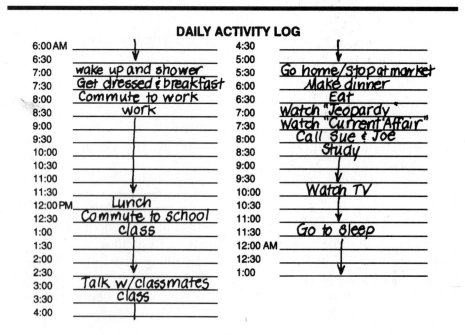

DAILY ACTIVITY LOG

6:00 AM		4:30	
6:30		5:00	
7:00	wake up and shower	5:30	Go home/stop at market
7:30	Get dressed & breakfast	6:00	Make dinner
8:00	Commute to work	6:30	Eat
8:30	work	7:00	Watch "Jeopardy"
9:00		7:30	Watch "Current Affair"
9:30		8:00	Call Sue & Joe
10:00		8:30	Study
10:30		9:00	
11:00		9:30	
11:30		10:00	Watch TV
12:00 PM	Lunch	10:30	
12:30	Commute to school	11:00	
1:00	class	11:30	Go to sleep
1:30		12:00 AM	
2:00		12:30	
2:30		1:00	
3:00	Talk w/classmates		
3:30	class		
4:00			

The Weekly Activity Log

A **Weekly Activity Log** is the same as a Daily Activity Log, but it is completed for a full week, or seven days in a row. To get an accurate account of how you spend your time, complete the Weekly Activity Log in Figure 4–3 this week, recording every activity you did for each of the seven days. If time does not allow you to do this, then complete the log to the best of your ability based on your current weekly activities. Make sure you are specific in the activities on your log and make sure it is complete. Use the sample log in Figure 4–4 as an example.

Once you have completed the log, answer the following questions based on the information you wrote down.

# of Hours

How much time did you spend *sleeping?* _____

How much time did you spend *eating and grooming?* _____

How much time did you spend *commuting?* _____

How much time did you spend *attending classes?* _____

How much time did you spend *studying/doing homework?* _____

How much time did you spend *working at a job?* _____

How much time did you spend *in sports or leisure activities?* _____

How much time did you spend *socializing with friends?* _____

How much time did you spend *watching TV?* _____

How much time is *not accounted for?* (no activity listed) _____

What else did you spend your time doing? _____ _____

_____ _____

From your answers to these questions and according to your goals, do you think you are spending your time wisely?

Your Weekly Activity Log will also give you some information about how much time you are spending in other parts of your life. Hopefully, you can apply the information in this chapter to help you manage them also.

I was taught very early that I would have to depend entirely upon myself; that my future lay in my own hands.

- *Darius Ogden Mills, American educator*

Figure 4–3
A Blank Weekly Activity Log

Weekly Activity Log				For Week of _____			
Time	Monday	Tuesday	Wednesday	Thursday	Friday	Saturday	Sunday
6 AM							
6:30							
7							
7:30							
8							
8:30							
9							
9:30							
10							
10:30							
11							
11:30							
12 PM							
12:30							
1							
1:30							
2							
2:30							
3							
3:30							
4							
4:30							
5							
5:30							
6							
6:30							
7							
7:30							
8							
8:30							
9							
9:30							
10							
10:30							
11							
11:30							
12 AM							

Figure 4–4
A Sample Weekly Activity Log

Weekly Activity Log   For Week of _____

Time	Monday	Tuesday	Wednesday	Thursday	Friday	Saturday	Sunday
6 AM	Get up	Get up	Get up	Get up	Get up		
6:30	shower & bkfst						
7	Go to work						
7:30							
8							
8:30							
9						Get up & read paper	
9:30							
10						Mow lawn	
10:30							Baked cookies
11							
11:30						Food shop	Brunch w/ Chris
12 PM	lunch go to school	lunch	lunch go to school	lunch	lunch go to school		
12:30	Class		Class		Class		
1						Laundry	
1:30							Study
2							
2:30							
3	Class		Class		Class		
3:30							
4						Study	
4:30	Go home watch TV	workout	library research	work-out	Meet John for dinner		
5							
5:30			Go home-watch TV				Watch TV
6	Dinner	watch TV		Volleyball			
6:30			Dinner		Went to movies	met Julia for dinner	
7	Phone calls	Dinner		Go home-Dinner			
7:30	Fix window		Phone calls				Dinner
8		Phone calls	Study	Phone calls		John's Party	Phone calls
8:30	Read newspaper			Watch TV			
9	Study	Read newspaper					Study
9:30		Study					
10	Read in bed	watch TV		Study	out for ice cream		watch TV
10:30			Take Bath				
11	watch News		watch TV		Home/TV		
11:30	Go to sleep	Go to sleep	Go to sleep	Go to sleep	Go to sleep		Go to sleep
12 AM							

HOW MUCH TIME DOES A STUDENT REALLY NEED?

For the purposes of this book, we will concentrate on how much time you spend as a student in class and the time you need for studying and school-related projects. As a general rule, the amount of study time you need is based on the number of hours you attend class each week. For every hour you spend in a classroom, you should have *at least* an equal number of hours set aside for homework and studying. So if you are in class for six hours a week, then you should have at least six hours of study time planned per week. If you require more time to learn, as many students do, you may need at least two hours of study time for each class hour.

How many hours are you in class per week? Use your Weekly Activity Log and the following equation to figure it out. An example has been completed based on an English course that meets one and a half hours a day, three times a week.

Example:

Subject	# class hrs/day	×	#of meetings/week	=	# hours/week
English	1 1/2	×	3	=	4 1/2

Subject	# class hrs/day	×	#of meetings/week	=	# hours/week
_____	_____	×	_____	=	_____
_____	_____	×	_____	=	_____
_____	_____	×	_____	=	_____
_____	_____	×	_____	=	_____
_____	_____	×	_____	=	_____

Total # Hours/Week _____

Taking the total number of hours per week you are in class, look at your Weekly Activity Log and see if you find at least an *equal* number of hours scheduled for study time. If you do, good for you! Read on and you will learn more about how to manage your time.

Using a Term Calendar

Being a student means that you will be spending time going to class and doing homework. But it also means that you have to spend time studying for exams, doing research, creating projects, and writing essays and papers. The best way to make sure that you have time for everything you have to do and want to do is to plan it out using a term calendar.

A **term calendar** is an overview of assignments, papers, projects, etc., that are due on a certain date. A term calendar acts as an engagement book for your personal or work life. Most successful working professionals have a similar form of a time management system. They usually keep a pocket calendar, like the term calendar, or some type of date book. (Office supply stores have a variety of calendars to choose from.) This allows them to make and keep appointments that are important to their work. Mothers and fathers also keep a calendar to keep track of their children's doctor appointments, lessons, and social activities as well as their own. So it makes sense that a student use a calendar to keep track of important school and personal activities.

To complete a term calendar, you need to have a **syllabus**, or schedule of assignments, from each instructor of every class you are taking. These are usually handed out the first week of classes. If the instructor does not have a syllabus, you can still complete a term calendar using what you already know and make changes or additions as time goes on.

Once you have your syllabus (or syllabi—plural), then follow the steps below to complete your term calendar in Figure 4–5. (To make writing easier, you can reproduce it using a copy machine that can enlarge it.) You can use Figure 4–6 as an example. Use a dark pencil or erasable pen so if assignments or dates change, you can easily make any necessary changes.

How to Complete Your Term Calendar

Step 1: Label the "Week" column with *either* the number of the term week OR the dates the week includes (e.g., a semester runs an average of sixteen weeks while a quarter term might last twelve weeks).

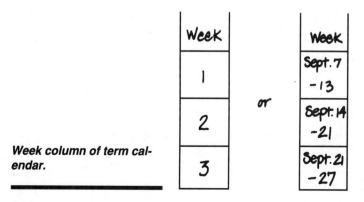

Week column of term calendar.

Step 2: Fill in your school holidays and important school events.

Step 3: From the information provided on your syllabus, mark down important dates such as tests, quizzes, projects, and papers due. (Daily assignments should NOT be written on this form; rather they should be written on the study schedule explained in the next section.)

Step 4: Once all important school-related dates are included on the term calendar, write in any important social events that you already know about, such as family get-togethers, parties, concerts, etc.

What you now have is your calendar of events for the term. The events of dates may change, but you can keep track of them here. Your term calendar will help you to plan your time according to your needs. For example, if today is Wednesday and you know that you have a test next Wednesday, you can plan to study a little each night starting tonight so that you will not have to cram the night before. Also, knowing that you will not be available on a certain day or evening should tell you well in advance to plan your study time around the event. Another great reason to keep a term calendar is to help you to never forget an assignment, paper, or appointment.

Figure 4–5
A Blank Term Calendar

Calendar for _____ Term ____

Week #	Monday	Tuesday	Wednesday	Thursday	Friday	Saturday	Sunday

Figure 4–6
A Sample Completed Term Calendar

Calendar for ___Fall___ Term _95_

Week #	Monday	Tuesday	Wednesday	Thursday	Friday	Saturday	Sunday
1 Sept 7-13	Labor Day	School Begins					
2 Sept 14-20							
3 Sept 21-27			Trigonometry Quiz			Julie & Jack's Wedding	Family Dinner
4 Sept 28-Oct 4					Electronics Quiz		
5 Oct 5-11							
6 Oct 12-18	Columbus Day					Eric Clapton Concert	
7 Oct 19-25			Trigonometry Mid-Term		Electronics Mid-Term		
8 Oct 26-Nov 1	Blue print Reading Quiz						
9 Nov 2-8				Motor Control Project Due			
10 Nov 9-15	Veterans Day		Trigonometry Quiz				
11 Nov 16-22		Nursing Project Due			→ TO PHILADELPHIA →		
12 Nov 23-29			→ THANKSGIVING BREAK →				
13 Nov 30-Dec 6	Electronics Final		Trigonometry Final		School Ends		

Your term calendar will be especially helpful to you in planning time for completing papers and projects. Typically, papers and projects need a lot of time, and should not be done all at once. For example, if today is Tuesday and you have a paper due six weeks from today, you can plan out each of the stages:

Week 1:	By this Friday	Decide on a topic
Week 2:	Tuesday	Start doing research
Week 3:	Tuesday	Continue doing research
Week 4:	Tuesday	Write outline of paper
Week 5:	Tuesday	Write first draft
Week 6:	Sunday	Revise
	Tuesday	Hand in

Take a look at your semester calendar. See if you are able to add any activities that will allow you to plan in advance for your tests, papers, and projects. As the term progresses, you can add or change any of the information you have written down. The key is to learn to rely on your term calendar for all of your planning needs.

Now that you have a term calendar for keeping track of school-related dates and social events, you will still need a way to keep track of your daily assignments and responsibilities.

Using a Weekly Study Schedule

Using a **weekly study schedule** is an effective way to keep track of your assignments and plan your study time according to your term calendar. When you were in grade school, you might have carried a small pocket notepad to write your assignments down. Or you might have written them down inside your notebooks or textbooks. Now that you are older, it is important to have one place to keep track of all your study demands.

Figure 4–7 is a blank weekly study schedule. (To make writing easier, you can reproduce it using a copy machine that can enlarge it.) Since this page represents one week in a term, you will need to make enough copies of this form to equal the number of weeks in your term. For example, if you have twelve weeks of classes in your term, you will need twelve copies. Once you have your copies, follow the simple steps below in how to use your study schedule. See Figure 4–8 as an example.

How to Fill In a Weekly Study Schedule

Step 1: Before you can use your weekly study schedule, you need to set it up with all of the day and week information for the term. This is done once at the beginning of the each term. At the top left of the schedule, where it says "**Study Schedule** for Week # ___", you can fill in the blank in two ways, either by using the week number (one through twelve if twelve is the number of weeks in your term) or writing in the actual dates (Sept. 7–13, Sept. 14–20, etc.).

Step 2: Where it says MON _____/___, TUES. _____/____, etc., fill in the exact weekly dates such as MON <u>Sept. 7</u>, TUES. <u>Sept. 8,</u> and so on. Note that the schedule only goes Monday through Friday. This is because you will be writing down your specific assignments and you usually do not get any new assignments on a weekend.

Step 3: The next step is to write down the subjects you are taking, from the hardest, or most challenging, to the easiest, or least challenging, going across the top line. This is done so that you will pay attention to your hardest subject first. When doing homework, most students put off doing the hardest subject for last, when they are either too tired or just not willing to spend the time with it. *If, however, you do your hardest subject first, you will have a much better chance of succeeding in that class.* If you are only taking one or two classes, you can use a modified version of this by whiting out or eliminating several of the vertical lines that make the boxes bigger.

Figure 4–7
A Blank Weekly Study Schedule

Study Schedule for Week # _____

SUBJECT >>> (hardest to easiest)					
MON. ____ / ____					
TUES. ____ / ____					
WED. ____ / ____					
THURS. ____ / ____					
FRI. ____ / ____					

Study Schedule for Week # ___5___

SUBJECT >>> (hardest to easiest)	Physics	Mechanical Drawing	Computer Programming	English Composition	
MON. Oct / 5	p. 62- Evans problems 1-4 write complete solutions.	work on machine spec	NO CLASS	For Wed. Write a one page essay on my career goals	
TUES. Oct / 6	p. 71- Evans problems 6-12 write complete solutions	Make corrections to spec	Read Chap. 3 "How to read Error Messages" do ques. @ end of Chapter	work on essay due tomorrow	
WED. Oct / 7 Get Joe's Birthday Card	NO CLASS	Finalize spec to hand-in tomorrow	Go to lab and test program -keep journal of error msgs.	P. 36- 40 Read Warriner's P. 41 - 42 do exer. A, B & D	
THURS. Oct 8	Review for Quiz tomorrow	Begin wire drawing for Wed. next week	Go to lab and revise Steps 6-24	NO CLASS	
FRI. Oct / 9 Call Sue re Sunday brunch	p. 76- Evans problems 1-3 write complete solutions	NO CLASS continue wire drawing	Read Chap. 4 "If, when" commands 20 ques. @ end of Chapter	NO HOMEWORK	

Figure 4–8
A Sample Completed Study Schedule

Step 4: Using your semester calendar, fill in on your study schedule any important information such as tests, papers and projects due, and school holidays. As the semester progresses, you again will be making changes to it.

Step 5: Fill in any important information such as tests, papers and projects as they appear on your term calendar. Include school holidays, but do not add your social events—this schedule is for study-related information only. It is recommended that you write your assignments on the day you receive them; however, some students prefer to write their assignments down the day before they are due. Whatever you do, make the schedule work for you!

Step 6: You can carry both the weekly study schedule and the term calendar with you at all times, either in a folder with pockets or, better yet, in a three-ring binder. When you are given a new assignment, or if a date or assignment changes, you can make changes to your planners easily. Add or change any of the information as you need, and most of all, make it work for you!

Plan your work for today and every day, then work your plan.

- Norman Vincent Peale, contemporary author and self-help author

PLANNING YOUR TIME

What you have been doing up to this point in this chapter is first figuring out where your time is actually spent and then discovering several ways to keep track of it, using the term calendar and weekly study schedule. What we haven't worked on yet is how to plan your schedule so that you can do everything you need to do and still have time left over for things you *want* to do.

There are several ways to make sure that you can have more time in a day. *The first and most important way to gain more time is to plan it!* It's like getting in a car and going somewhere. If you know where you are going and have a plan to get there, such as a road map, then you will get there without wasting time. If you do not have a plan, then you will be wasting your time and will take longer to get where you want to go, if you even get there at all!

A second way to gain more time in a day is to do more in less time. You are learning in this book how to study smarter, which includes how to study more in less time. Using active study strategies will help you to gain more time. This can be as simple as doubling up on activities. For example, if you have three errands to do on your way to school, instead of doing one at time, you might be able to combine them and make one round-trip instead of three. If you commute on a bus or train, or carpool, you could study on your way to school or work. While eating lunch, you could review your notes. Use your imagination as to how you can get more done in less time.

Yet a third way to gain more time is to use short periods of otherwise wasted time. Activities like commuting or eating lunch can be time wasters, but they can be put to good use. In your Daily and Weekly Activity Logs, see if you have any wasted time that could be turned into unwasted time. Do you have a free half hour between classes where you can either socialize with friends or study? If doing well in school is important to you, you might choose to study sometimes instead of socialize. Do you watch a lot of television or talk constantly on the phone? This time can easily be put to better use by reducing your television time and limiting your telephone time. Furthermore, it's always a good idea to carry some of your study material or homework with you, because you never know when you will have to wait on a line or in someone's office. If each day you found an extra twenty minutes of study time, in one week you would have an extra two hours and twenty minutes! To secure your academic success, ask yourself, "What can I do to do more in less time or use otherwise wasted time?" Write some of your thoughts below:

_____

_____

_____

_____

_____

Sometimes even the best planned schedules get into trouble because of unplanned events. When this happens, and you need to make a choice regarding what to do, the question you need to ask yourself is "What is the best use of my time *right now*?" Your answer will make sense based on the things that are truly important to you. Take this scenario:

Cousin Sheila comes into town unexpectedly and wants to take you to dinner. You have planned several hours of studying because an assignment is due the next day and you also have a quiz. What do you do?

If being a good student is important to you, then you would kindly thank your cousin, explain your situation, and perhaps offer to go out with her for ice cream after you have completed your work. What would you do in these following situations?

Situation #1: It's 5:00 p.m. on a Monday night. You have a test on Friday that you want to study for tonight between 5:00 and 6:00 p.m. You are scheduled to go to a community meeting at 6:00 p.m. that will not be over until at least 9:00 p.m. Your friend calls you on the phone to chat. Nothing very important, just a conversation. What would you do?

_____

_____

_____

Situation #2: It's 7:00 p.m. on Wednesday night. You have an oral presentation due on Friday and you have already done your research. You still need several hours of preparation time to get ready for the presentation. Because of work and other family commitments, you have no other time before Friday to do this assignment. Your husband/wife/son/daughter needs your immediate help cleaning out the basement. They can't do it without you. What would you do?

_____

_____

_____

_____

Procrastination and Other Time Wasters

Look at Figure 4–9. According to a study done by Lillian Chaney of Memphis State University, this is a list of the top ten time wasters as reported by high school and college students. As you read down the list, place a check mark (✓) next to those time wasters you use most. Are you a big time waster?

Not too surprisingly, procrastination was reported as the biggest time waster of them all. **Procrastination** means to put off doing something unpleasant or burdensome until a future time. Students are, unfortunately, excellent procrastinators. They put work off until the last minute, cramming to get it done, but then hoping to do well with it at the same time. The reality is that only a few students can really cram well. The others just *think* they can. (See Chapter 11 for more about cramming.)

Figure 4–9
The Top Ten Time Wasters

___

1. Procrastination
2. Watching television
3. Visiting friends or socializing
4. Daydreaming
5. Figuring out how to do an assignment
6. Physical problems, such as lack of energy
7. Sleeping too much
8. Lack of planning
9. Waiting for others
10. Talking on the phone

Published in *Business Education Forum*, April 1991, pp.8-9. Results from a study by Lillian H. Chaney, Professor of Management, Memphis State University, Memphis, Tennessee. Reprinted with permission.

What are some of the reasons why you put things off until a future time?

_____

_____

_____

_____

_____

What happens as a result of your putting things off?

_____

_____

_____

_____

For students, some of the top reasons for procrastinating include:

❏ An assignment that is too big or overwhelming, such as a paper, report, or final exam

❏ An unpleasant assignment

❏ Fear of the assignment, such as being afraid you won't know the answer

If you put off an assignment too long, you may not get it done on time. The assignment also may not be a quality job or may not be completed as the instructor wanted. It can sometimes be embarrassing and frustrating when you are caught behind in your work. Remember, difficult subjects do not get any easier when they are put off! So what can you do to reduce procrastination?

Since procrastination means doing nothing, then simply doing something is the way to overcome it. Here are some actions to consider:

1. *Start small.* If your assignment is too big, remember that you cannot eat pizza whole, but you can eat it one bite at a time. So if you take your big assignment and break it down into bite-size pieces, you will be able to break through your procrastination. For example, when studying for an exam, if you study a little each day instead of all at once, the job won't seem to be as large.

2. *Realize how miserable you'll be until it's done.* If you don't want to add unpleasantness into your life, remind yourself how good it will feel to finish the assignment instead of putting it off. Then get started!

3. *Tell yourself you are wasting time.* You ARE wasting time if you are not working on your assignment. If time is valuable to you, then why waste it?

4. *Be accountable to someone else.* If you set a deadline with someone, you will be less likely to break it. For example, if you arrange to meet a friend at 4:00 p.m. once you have finished your math problems, you won't want to disappoint him or her.

5. *Add variety.* If you do not enjoy studying a certain subject, try using other study methods such as flash cards or studying with a friend. Or just mix the unpleasant subject with more pleasant ones.

6. *Promise yourself a reward.* When you finish doing your assignments, give yourself a reward.

In the next section on study goals and rewards, you will better understand this approach.

Study Goals and Rewards

Doing activities according to what is important to you sometimes means that you can't do what you want to do for the moment. Many times, the last thing you want to do is study. You would rather watch television or go out with friends. But if doing well in school is truly important to you, then you have to force yourself to study.

How often do you feel like studying? If you waited until you felt like studying, you might never open a book! So how do you motivate yourself to study when you don't feel like it? Or when you are tired? Or when you are very busy?

By setting a study goal and then rewarding yourself for reaching that goal, you will find studying easier. You will also have a higher level of concentration because you are determined to complete the work on time. A **study goal** means completing your assignment(s) in a reasonable time frame. A **reward** is something you give yourself in return for your effort. For example, suppose you have to read a chapter in your computer textbook and then write your own operations flowchart. You also need to review your wiring diagrams for a quiz the following day. In your estimation, this work should take you no more than an hour and a half. If you begin doing your work at 6:30 p.m., then your study goal should be to complete the work by 8:00 p.m. At 8:00 p.m., when the work is completed, you can reward yourself with something that is not work, such as watching television, eating a favorite snack, or exercising. By deciding ahead of time what your reward is to be for reaching your study goal, you will be motivated to finish your work as quickly as possible and have more time to do whatever you want. This is one of the best ways to study smarter, not harder.

How would you reward yourself for reaching a study goal? Make a list below of everything you can think of.

Rewards

Watch my favorite television show

_____

_____

_____

_____

_____

_____

Tonight, or the next time you sit down to study, think about setting a study goal and then rewarding yourself upon its completion. This way, you will be less tempted to interrupt your study time with phone calls or other things that generally interfere with getting your work done in a time efficient way.

Other Ways to Master Your Time

What follows is a creative list of other ways that you can master your time. See if any of them may be useful to you. Then, at the end of the list, add a few of your own ways to better master your own time.

1. *Prepare for the morning the evening before.* Put out your clothes, make lunches, pack your books.

2. *Get up fifteen minutes earlier in the morning.* Use it to plan your day, study, or get caught up on the news.

3. *Don't rely on your memory.* Write your assignments, appointments, and due dates on a calendar.

4. *Schedule a realistic day.* Avoid planning for every minute. Leave time to get to appointments and allow extra time for studying.

5. *Leave some room in your day for the unexpected.* This will allow you to still get what you need done without losing time. If the unexpected never happens, you will now have more time for yourself.

6. *Do one thing at a time.* If you try to study two subjects at once, you will become confused. Concentrate on the here and now.

7. *Let things slide from time to time.* The world will not come to an end if you do your laundry on Sunday instead of Saturday.

8. *Learn to say "No!"* Say no to social activities or invitations you don't have the time or energy for.

9. *Get enough sleep.* When you are well rested, you are more capable of handling anything that comes your way.

10. *Learn to relax.* Take deep breaths, stretch, and/or exercise to relieve tension and stress.

11. _____

   _____

12. _____

   _____

13. _____

   _____

14. _____

   _____

SUMMARY

1. There are twenty-four hours in a day, no more, no less. To spend it wisely means you are spending it productively toward a goal. To spend it unwisely means you are wasting time.

2. Knowing what is important to you and having short-term and long-term goals will help you make wise choices for how you spend your time.

3. Students need to plan at least one hour of study time per week for every hour in class.

4. A term calendar will help you keep track of school-related dates and social events.

5. A weekly study schedule will help you keep track of your daily assignments and responsibilities.

6. Procrastination is putting off doing something unpleasant or burdensome until a future time. Ways of overcoming procrastination include starting with small actions, adding variety to the task, and promising yourself a reward at the end.

7. Setting a study goal means planning to do a certain amount of work in a given time. When you have achieved your goal, you deserve to give yourself a reward in return for your effort. Setting study goals and planning for rewards can help you save time and make studying rewarding.

REVIEW

Answer the following questions using your own words and thoughts based on the information you learned in this chapter.

1. Why is it important to learn how to manage your time?

_____

_____

_____

_____

2. Why is it important to know your goals?

_____

_____

_____

3. What is a Daily Activity Log used for?

_____

_____

_____

4. What is a Weekly Activity Log used for?

_____

_____

5. What is a Term Calendar? How do you use it? Be specific.

_____

_____

_____

_____

_____

6. What is a Weekly Study Schedule? How do you use it? Be specific.

_____

_____

_____

7. What are you going to do to reduce procrastination?

_____

_____

_____

_____

_____

8. Describe how setting study goals and then rewarding yourself for reaching them can help make studying easier.

_____

_____

_____

_____

_____

_____

9. From the formats explained in this chapter to keep track of your time, which one(s) do you find most useful and why?

_____

_____

_____

_____

_____

_____

10. As a result of working through this chapter, what are you going to do to learn how to manage your time?

_____

_____

_____

_____

_____

_____

_____

PART 2
BECOMING AN ACTIVE READER

CHAPTER 5

BUILDING YOUR VOCABULARY

After studying and working with the information in this chapter, you should be able to:

1. Define background knowledge.
2. Identify how your background knowledge affects your ability to build your vocabulary.
3. Describe two ways to build vocabulary using background knowledge.
4. Explain why skipping unfamiliar words is sometimes effective.
5. Describe the best time to use a dictionary.
6. Identify four types of dictionaries.
7. Use notebook paper and/or an index card to track vocabulary.
8. Explain how to read a dictionary entry.
9. Identify two ways to effectively learn the technical terms of your trade.
10. Begin using the information in this chapter to help you build your vocabulary with minimal effort and time.

. . . **M**ost successful people have a strong vocabulary and use it whenever they speak, read, and write.

Think for a moment:

❑ Do words have meaning?

or

❑ Are words given meaning depending upon the way they are used?

If you believe that both statements are true, you are right. Every word has a specific meaning *and* words change their meaning depending upon how they are used. So how can you ever learn all of the meanings of words? The best you can do is to know what choices you have as well as to realize that there may be more than one meaning to every word you know.

By building a strong vocabulary, you can:

❑ Communicate better, orally and written

❑ Read with good comprehension

❑ Understand more about many areas of interest

❑ Become successful at whatever you choose to do

The last point may surprise you, but it is true that most successful people have a strong vocabulary and use it whenever they speak, read, and write.

In this chapter, we will (1) look at your choices for building your vocabulary, and (2) focus on how you can use your background knowledge to help you to learn new words more easily.

There are many ways to build your vocabulary. In your learning process, do you ever use books such as those shown in this photo?

SELF-EVALUATION

The following self-evaluation will give you an idea of how familiar, or unfamiliar, you are with some of the topics and terms discussed in this chapter. After reading each statement, circle the letter (Y, S, or N) most appropriate to your answer. Please answer honestly, rate yourself at the end, and then complete the information for Chapter 5 on page 374 in Appendix A.

Y = yes; frequently   **S** = sometimes   **N** = no; never

1. When I come across a word I do not know, I use context clues to figure out its meaning.   Y   S   N

2. When I come across a word I do not know, I use prefixes, roots, and suffixes to figure out its meaning.   Y   S   N

3. When I come across a word I do not know, I use a dictionary to find its meaning.   Y   S   N

4. When I come across a word I do not know, I ask someone what it means.   Y   S   N

5. I know that there will be new vocabulary to learn for every class I take.   Y   S   N

6. When I am reading a textbook chapter, I create my own vocabulary list for the chapter.   Y   S   N

7. I keep track of my new vocabulary words either on index cards or in a separate notebook.   Y   S   N

8. I keep a dictionary close to me when I study.   Y   S   N

9. I think I have a good vocabulary.   Y   S   N

10. I am interested in learning new words.   Y   S   N

Rate Yourself

Number of Ys _____ x 100=

Number of Ss _____ x 50=

Number of Ns _____ x 10=

Total =

Almost all men are intelligent. It is the method they lack.

- F.W. Nichol, business educator

USING YOUR BACKGROUND KNOWLEDGE

Your **background knowledge** is what you already know based on your previous experiences and/or learning. It is a very important tool for all learning, including new vocabulary. If, for example, you already know how to change the oil of a car, you then have some background knowledge in the way cars are put together and function. If you were taking a course in automotive repair, this information would be useful to your learning more about a car's workings. Without knowing how to change a car's oil, or knowing anything about this area of the car, your job of learning is not as easy.

Using your background knowledge is also a powerful tool for building your vocabulary. Since you already know and use many words, you can use them to help increase the size of your vocabulary.

The ways for building vocabulary include (1) looking for context clues, (2) using word structures, (3) skipping words (only at certain times), (4) using a dictionary, and/or (5) asking someone.

Though we will discuss each of these ways of building vocabulary, the ones you will be introduced to first are those that encourage you to figure out the meanings of words using the dictionary you already have—your brain! *If you can figure out word meaning on your own, you will build your vocabulary more quickly and easily.*

Looking for Context Clues

Gaining a good understanding of what you are reading without wasting time can be accomplished by using context clues. **Context clues** are the words surrounding the unknown word that provide clues, or hints, to the meaning of the vocabulary word. Many times, by using these clues, you will be able to predict, or take a guess at, the meaning of the word. Since getting an exact dictionary definition is not always necessary and sometimes not possible, you can, nonetheless, get a definition good enough to work with the passage you are reading.

For example, in the following sentence see if you can predict the meaning of the word in italics:

Though the weather was not in their favor, the research team was *optimistic* that their mission would be successful.

Optimistic could mean _____

In this sentence, *optimistic* could mean hopeful or positive. Was your guess close to these? Though they are not the same definitions, both provide you with enough of a clue to understand the sentence and to continue your reading.

Try these sentences:

1. In the concert hall, the enthusiastic fans *congregated* around the band like bees around honey.
Congregated could mean _____

2. The telephone company helped the assistant save space on her desk by *consolidating* the four telephone lines into one.
Consolidating could mean_____

3. After listening to the *interminable* speeches, the graduates were tired and anxious to leave the heat of the auditorium.
Interminable could mean _____

In these examples, guessing the meaning of a word based on the other words surrounding it helps you to understand what you are reading. In addition, it also helps you to save time. Sometimes, however, the context clues are not enough to help you guess the meaning of the unknown word. For example:

Mononucleosis is commonly found among young people who work hard and do not eat well or get enough sleep.

In a case like this, figuring out the definition through context is not possible. The next option for learning vocabulary, using word structures, will be more helpful in finding the meaning of a word in such an instance.

Using Word Structures

Word structures are what words are made out of: prefixes, roots, and suffixes. A **root word** is the basic part of a word that conveys the word's foundation or origin. The other two parts are added to a root and each change the word meaning. A **prefix** is the part of the word that is added to the beginning and a **suffix** is the part of the word added at the end. Each of these parts is a link to a chain of meaning.

If you learn to identify the meaning of one or more parts of a word, you will be able to closely predict the meaning of a word.

In the last example above, the word *mononucleosis* is made up of all of these parts.

With this information, the word structure meaning of mononucleosis is "the condition of one cell." In human beings, there are two kinds of blood cells, red and white. Mononucleosis is the condition where one cell overtakes the other, or, in this case, the white blood cells overtake the red ones. This can be caused by a viral

Type of word structure	Word	Meaning of word structure
prefix	mono	one
root	nucle(us)	cell
suffix	osis	condition of

infection as a result of not eating or sleeping well, and/or working too hard.

A part of one word can be found in many other words. A list of some other words that contain the word "mono" follows. Notice how the meaning of mono—one—is present in all the definitions.

Example	Definition
monorail	**one** rail
monograph	to write about **one** thing
monochrome	**one** color
monomania	thinking of only **one** idea or thought
monopoly	only **one** seller of a product of service
monocular	seeing with **one** eye
monogamy	marriage to **one** person at a time
monologue	a talk by **one** speaker
monomial	(in algebra) consists of **one** term only
monoplane	an airplane with **one** set of wings
monosyllabic	describing a word with **one** syllable
monotony	doing **one** thing over and over again

Now it's your turn. In each of the following lists, you will see across each line a part of a word, then its meaning, and then an example. In the blank spaces, think of other words that use the same part of the word with the same meaning. Use a separate piece of paper if your list gets long.

Prefix	Meaning	Example and its meaning
bi	two	<u>bi</u>nocular = seeing with **two** eyes
		_____
		_____
		_____
		_____
in	not	<u>in</u>separable = **not** able to be pulled apart
		_____
		_____

Prefix	Meaning	Example and its meaning
		_____
		_____
re	again, back	reconstruct = to build **again**
		_____
		_____
		_____
		_____

Root Word	Meaning	Example and its meaning
bio	life	microbiology = study of small **living** things
		_____
		_____
		_____
		_____
dem	people	epidemic = affecting a lot of **people** (e.g., a disease)
		_____
		_____
		_____
		_____
graph	writing	monograph = **writing** about one thing
		_____
		_____
		_____
		_____
nov	new	renovate = to make **new** again
		_____
		_____
		_____
thermo	heat	thermostat = device that measures **heat**
		_____
		_____
		_____
		_____
		_____

Suffix	Meaning	Example and its meaning
able	capable of	portable = **capable of** being carried
		_____

		_____
		_____
		_____
ation	the act of	coll<u>ation</u> = **the act of** putting things together
		_____
		_____
		_____
ous	full of	relig<u>ious</u> = **full of** belief in religion
		_____
		_____
		_____
		_____
		_____

These are just a few of the common prefixes, roots, and suffixes that you can learn. In Appendix B you will find more words to practice with. Try doing a few at a time. Every word part you can recognize is another valuable addition to your background knowledge.

What PREFIX best describes the action for the ROOT word SLIME?
A. PRESLIME
B. DESLIME
C. UNSLIME

What SUFFIX best describes the action for the ROOT word SLIME?
A. SLIMEY
B. SLIMED
C. SLIMER

SKIPPING WORDS

Skipping an unfamiliar word is not the best way to build your vocabulary. However, it is an effective way to avoid wasting your time while still understanding most of what you've read or heard. The trick is to make sure you understand enough.

Read the following two paragraphs. Of the two, which contains an italicized word which you think could be skipped and which do you think needs to be defined?

Paragraph #1:

> A scanned photograph can be cropped using desktop publishing software, which makes cropping electronically a relatively simple procedure. If you must crop a photograph by hand, never draw crop marks directly on the photograph.

Paragraph #2:

> Illness has always been a part of the human condition. Care has been given according to the folkways and beliefs of society. Care also depends on the knowledge and kinds of treatments available.

In the first paragraph, the word "crop" appears several times and describes a concept that would be lost if you did not know what "crop" meant. ("Cropping" means to show which part(s) of the whole are *not* to be reproduced.)

In the second paragraph, the word "folkways" serves as a descriptive word that doesn't seem to carry a lot of important meaning to the sentence. ("Folkways" means the traditional patterns of life common to people.) In this case, you might skip figuring out the word in paragraph two and spending your time figuring out the meaning in paragraph one.

If you decide that skipping a word would not greatly affect your understanding, then it is a good decision. But if you don't understand what is being said because you don't know the word, then you should try to figure out the meaning of the word.

USING A DICTIONARY

Using a dictionary is a common way to find out the meaning of unfamiliar words if they cannot be determined otherwise. By keeping a dictionary nearby during your study sessions, you will be able to use it more easily and will most likely use it more often.

Using a dictionary, however, takes a lot of time. Imagine that you are reading your textbook and you come across an unfamiliar word. If you can figure it out by using your brain as the dictionary (by using context clues or word structures), you will be able to continue your reading within a few moments. If you cannot figure it out using your brain, or if you have chosen not to try on your own, and reach for the dictionary first, the process will take a lot more time. You will have to stop where you are reading, find a dictionary, come back to your reading, and locate the unfamiliar word again. You will also need to see how it is spelled and look it up in the dictionary, flipping a few pages forward and a few pages backward until you find the word. Then you will probably find that the word has more than one meaning, so you will have to look at each meaning and see which best fits with the context of your reading. Once you have found the meaning of your word, you would close the dictionary and try to remember where you were in the reading and what it was about. This process takes *much* longer than using context clues and word structures.

The other problem with using a dictionary is your ability to remember the word a week or month later without looking for it again in the dictionary. You don't always remember new things the first time you come across them. This is why using a dictionary as the only way to find the meaning of unfamiliar words is a less effective way of learning new words.

But you can learn to remember words through the use of repetition or frequent review. Smart dictionary users write down the unfamiliar word on either a piece of paper (Figure 5–1) or an index card (Figure 5–2). The word goes on one side of the card or paper and the meaning goes on the other side. This gives you the ability to review the words repeatedly without wasting time looking them up more than once in the dictionary. In a short time of reviewing the words, they will become part of your background knowledge for use in the future.

Types of Dictionaries

There are several types of dictionaries. An **unabridged dictionary** is the most complete type of a dictionary because it includes all words and definitions. An **abridged dictionary** is a shorter version of an unabridged dictionary. It is smaller in size because it doesn't contain all of the words or definitions. However, an abridged dictionary is useful for most student vocabulary uses. Abridged dictionaries are the most popular as well because they

Figure 5–1
Using Notebook Paper for
Learning New Vocabulary
Terms

Chapter 7 p.91-97	Wind and the Landscape
erosion =	a wearing away of land due to wind or waves. - it happens over time
dunes =	sand deposited by wind in the form of hills or ridges.
Transverse dunes =	long, wavelike ridges - found on beaches
Parabolic dunes =	contain a blowout in the center with high-ridged sides.
barchan dunes =	crescent-shaped dunes
waves =	formed by wind blowing over water
wave period =	time required for a wave to go the distance of one wave length.
tsunamis =	waves created by earthquakes - very large and destructive.

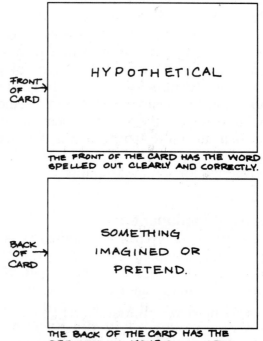

FRONT OF CARD →

HYPOTHETICAL

THE FRONT OF THE CARD HAS THE WORD
SPELLED OUT CLEARLY AND CORRECTLY.

BACK OF CARD →

SOMETHING
IMAGINED OR
PRETEND.

Figure 5–2
Using Index Cards for
Learning New Vocabulary
Terms

THE BACK OF THE CARD HAS THE
DEFINITION IN YOUR OWN WORDS.

are smaller to carry and keep on a shelf. Many dictionary publishers also sell a pocket or vest dictionary that is popular with students. You can carry it with you to school while leaving the larger, more complete one at home.

A **thesaurus** is a type of dictionary that contains only synonyms and antonyms. **Synonyms** are words that are similar in meaning to the vocabulary word and **antonyms** are those words that are opposite in meaning. A thesaurus is useful for expanding your background knowledge and for writing essays and reports. The Merriam-Webster Thesaurus provides information for the following examples:

Word	Meaning	Synonym	Antonym
danger	the state of being exposed to injury, pain, or loss	hazard, jeopardy, peril, risk	security
silence	absence of sound or noise	noiselessness, quiet, quietness, quietude, soundlessness, still, stillness	din, uproar, noise

Another type of dictionary is a **walking dictionary**. This is not a book, but rather a person, such as a relative, instructor, or friend you ask to help you figure out the word you don't understand. *Before asking a walking dictionary the meaning of a word, you should try to figure it out on your own.* This type of person can be very helpful to you *if* he or she knows the answer. He or she can save you time and energy, but cannot help you to remember the word when you come across it again. This is another good reason to write these words down on a separate piece of paper or on index cards. This will increase the chances of your remembering the word when you see it once more.

How to Use a Dictionary

Before reading this section, make sure a dictionary is next to you. Though you may already be familiar with how to use a dictionary, we suggest you use this section as a review. If you are unfamiliar with how to use a dictionary, read this section to build your background knowledge.

Using a dictionary is simple once you know how to read the entries. In the introductory pages of a dictionary, you will find keys to help you understand the symbols and/or abbreviations used. Locate the keys in your dictionary now. Write the names of each of the keys on the following lines:

A dictionary entry consists of a word and its definitions. Every entry contains five parts: syllables, pronunciation, part of speech, the definitions, and the word origin.

Syllables. Each word is broken down into syllables, or parts of a word. For example, the word *circulate* is broken down into three syllables:

Cir • cu • late

Pronunciation. The way each syllable is pronounced, or sounded out, is indicated by special symbols. These symbols are explained in detail in the introductory pages of the dictionary.

Cir • cu • late (sûr′kyə lāt′)

Part of Speech. The part of speech follows each word and is indicated by an abbreviation—for example n. for noun, v. for verb, adj. for adjective. When more than one definition is given, the part of speech is given before the definition.

Cir • cu • late (sûr′kyə lāt′) *v.*

The Definitions. Most words have more than one definition. The definitions are numbered. When looking at a word with more than one definition, make sure to look at all the definitions before deciding on its meaning. The first definition given may not be the correct one for your use.

In the sentence below, which meaning of the word "circulate" is best? _____

The manager opened the doors to *circulate* fresh air into the crowded, smoky ballroom.

> **Cir • cu • late** (sûr′kyə lāt′) *v.* **1.** to move in a circle or circuit; move or pass through a circuit back to the starting point, as the blood to the body. **2.** to pass from place to place, from person to person, etc. **3.** to be distributed or sold, esp. over a wide area. *-v.t.* **4.** to disseminate or distribute. [Lat. *circulare* to encircle].

Some dictionaries may include a sample sentence to show you how a word is used and/or provide a list of synonyms.

Word Origins.   Word origins indicate where the word comes from, or its **etymology.** The word origin can be listed in various places in the word entry. In the previous example, it is found at the end of the entry. Looking at the end of this definition, you will see that the word *circulate* comes from Latin (Lat.). This can help you to learn more about where words come from and their related word structures.

Now that you know how to read a dictionary definition, you can feel more comfortable using the dictionary as a reference tool. Practice using this tool by looking up the following words and writing each of their five parts in the blank spaces provided. Use the keys provided in the introductory pages of your dictionary to understand the symbols and/or abbreviations used.

absorption

Syllables_____

Pronunciation _____

Parts of Speech _____

The Definitions _____

_____

_____

_____

_____

Word Origins _____

gravity

Syllables_____

Pronunciation _____

Parts of Speech _____

The Definitions _____

_____

_____

_____

_____

Word Origins _____

retainer

Syllables_____

Pronunciation _____

Parts of Speech _____

The Definitions _____

_____

_____

_____

_____

_____

Word Origins _____

transcribe

Syllables_____

Pronunciation _____

Parts of Speech _____

The Definitions _____

_____

_____

_____

_____

_____

Word Origins _____

Man's mind, stretched to a new dimension, never goes back to its original dimensions.

> - *Oliver Wendell Holmes, 19th century*
> *poet and novelist*

TECHNICAL TERMS OF YOUR TRADE

For every course you take, there is a vocabulary unique to the subject matter. Your job as a student is to learn as well as use this vocabulary while speaking and writing. You learn these terms from your instructor's lectures, your textbooks, and other related projects or experiences. In your textbooks, the terms are easy to locate because they are often printed in italics or boldface and there may also be a vocabulary list at either the beginning or end of a chapter. In addition, some textbooks also have a **glossary**, or a specialized dictionary, at the back of the book to help you quickly find the specific meaning of a word given in the text. Locate the glossary of this textbook and find three unfamiliar terms. Write the word and its definition below.

1. _____   _____
2. _____   _____
3. _____   _____

Create Your Own Glossary

If you have a vocabulary list for your chapter, you will find learning the words easy if you write the words and their definitions in your notebook or on index cards *before* you read the chapter. This will give you valuable background knowledge that will help you to better understand the information you read. You will also see the word and its meaning several times by the time you have completed the chapter. Remember that this makes learning easier because you see the information several times. And you now have an instant study tool to use when reviewing for a quiz or test.

Use Word Structures

Using what you know about prefixes, roots, and suffixes will be very useful in learning the specialized terms of your course. For example, if you were taking a medical or science course, the following word structures are common. Note how the meaning of the word part relates to the meaning of the word.

anti- = against
> **anti**coagulant = a drug that prevents the formation of blood
> > clots
> **anti**septic = prevents growth of germs
> **anti**body = blood cells that prevent infections

cardio- (a) = heart
> **cardio**logy = the study of the heart
> tachy**cardia** =rapid heart beat
> myo**cardia**l infarction = a heart attack

-ectomy = to take out; remove
> hyster**ectomy** = to remove the uterus of a female
> tonsill**ectomy** = to take out the tonsils
> laryng**ectomy** = to remove the larynx or voice box

-itis = inflammation of; swelling
> tendon**itis** = an inflammation of the tendons
> phleb**itis** = a swelling of the lining of the veins
> bronch**itis** = an inflammation of the windpipe

If you were taking a paralegal studies or government course, the following word structures are common. Note how the meaning of the word part relates to the meaning of the word.

appel- = to appeal to, to ask for help
　　　appellant = a person bringing an appeal
　　　appellee = a person who is against an appeal
　　　appellate jurisdiction = the power of a court to appeal a
　　　　　　　　　　　　　　 trial court's actions
jur- = to judge; having to do with justice; to swear
　　　jurisdiction = the power of a court to judge a particular case
　　　jury = a group of people who judge a court case
　　　juror = a person on a jury
　　　jurisprudence = a body of laws; having to do with law

　　The most important vocabulary activity you can do is to become aware that every course you take will have a unique vocabulary and that your job is to learn it. Learning how to learn the new terms is easy when you apply the information provided in this chapter.

SUMMARY

1. Your background knowledge is what you already know based on your previous experiences and/or learning.

2. The more background knowledge you have, the easier it is to figure out word definitions using the dictionary you were born with—your brain.

3. Looking for context clues and using word structures are two ways to build vocabulary using background knowledge.

4. Skipping unfamiliar words is *not* the best way to build your vocabulary. You can, however, skip an unfamiliar word when you believe your understanding would not be greatly affected.

5. Using a dictionary helps you find the meaning of unfamiliar words. The best time to use it is when you cannot figure out the word meaning by using your background knowledge.

6. There are four types of dictionaries: unabridged, abridged, a thesaurus, and a walking dictionary.

7. An active way to keep track of your vocabulary is to write any new word and its definition on either notebook paper or index cards.

8. Reading a dictionary entry means identifying and understanding its five parts: syllables, pronunciation, part of speech, the definition, and word origin(s).

9. Learning the technical terms of your trade is easier if you create your own glossary and use word structures.

REVIEW

Answer the following questions in your own words based on the information you have learned in this chapter on building your vocabulary.

1 a. What is background knowledge?

_____

_____

b. How does your background knowledge influence your ability to build vocabulary?

_____

_____

_____

_____

_____

c. What do you think background knowledge has to do with learning in general?

_____

_____

_____

_____

_____

2. Why is having a good vocabulary important to being a good student? What can an effective vocabulary do for you in the future?

_____

_____

_____

_____

_____

_____

3. What are some of the ways to figure out the meaning of an unknown word? Describe at least three.

_____

_____

_____

_____

_____

_____

_____

4. When is "skipping a word" a good decision?

_____

_____

_____

5. What would you explain to another student about how to build vocabulary?

_____

_____

_____

_____

_____

6. What is the most important thing(s) you learned from this chapter?

_____

_____

_____

_____

_____

CHAPTER 6

MASTERING READING ASSIGNMENTS

LEARNING OBJECTIVES

After studying and working with the information in this chapter, you should be able to:

1. Identify the difference between nonfiction and fiction reading material.
2. Explain the importance of identifying your reading purpose and responsibility before you read.
3. Describe the procedure for previewing a nonfiction textbook.
4. Describe the procedure for previewing a nonfiction chapter.
5. Begin previewing on your own nonfiction reading assignments.

A little preparation can make the time you spend worthwhile. . . .

Getting through reading assignments may be one of the most challenging tasks for you, especially because they are required and not of your own choosing. Your reading assignments vary in length and content and are generally used for classroom discussions, homework assignments, quizzes, tests, or sometimes just for your own information.

Looking at a roadmap to plan your trip before leaving makes the journey enjoyable, comfortable, and relaxing. Without that map, the same journey could be unpleasant, frustrating, and time consuming. What preparation can you do before reading an assignment that parallels studying a roadmap?

In this chapter, you will begin to climb the Active Learning Staircase toward becoming an active reader. We will focus on a reading skill called *previewing* that you can use with all of your textbooks. Previewing is a powerful tool to help you gain background knowledge. The more background knowledge you have, the easier it is to read and understand any written material.

SELF-EVALUATION

The following self-evaluation will give you an idea of how familiar, or unfamiliar, you are with some of the topics and terms discussed in this chapter. After reading each statement, circle the letter (Y, S, or N) most appropriate to your answer. Please answer honestly, rate yourself at the end, and then complete the information for Chapter 6 on page 374 in Appendix A.

Y = yes; frequently   **S** = sometimes   **N** = no; never

1. I know the difference between nonfiction and fiction material.   Y   S   N

2. I know what previewing is and I can do it effectively.   Y   S   N

3. I know how to preview a nonfiction book or magazine.   Y   S   N

4. I know how to preview a nonfiction chapter or article.   Y   S   N

5. I always know the purpose, or reason why, I am reading.   Y   S   N

6. I know in what way I am responsible for each
reading.   Y   S   N

7. If there are questions at the end of a chapter, I look
at them before I read.   Y   S   N

8. I know where to find the main ideas in nonfiction
reading material.   Y   S   N

9. I always know the organization of my material
before I read.   Y   S   N

10. I am confident when approaching my reading
assignments.   Y   S   N

<u>Rate Yourself</u>

Number of Ys _____ x 100=

Number of Ss _____ x 50=

Number of Ns _____ x 10=

Total =

T here are those who travel and those who are going somewhere. They are
different and yet they are the same. The successful is the one who knows
where he is going.

- Mark Caine, contemporary author

THE ACTIVE LEARNING STAIRCASE

B ecoming an active learner involves becoming an active reader.
Look at the Active Learning Staircase in Figure 6–1. The left
side curves upward showing the level of each activity from
passive on the bottom to active toward the top. Each step indicates
an activity and how low or high it is on the Active Learning Staircase.

Just reading, the activity listed on the bottom step, is the
most passive form of reading. If, for example, your assignment is

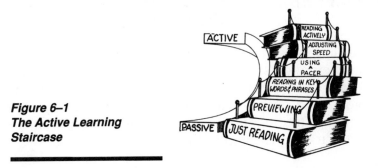

Figure 6–1
The Active Learning
Staircase

to read from pages 50 to 65, you open the book to page 50 and begin reading, almost word-for-word, until page 65. While reading, your mind probably wanders quite a bit. When you finish reading, you are happy to have completed the assignment. However, you have only the slightest idea of what you just read and will have trouble answering any detailed questions about it from either the book or your instructor. When it comes time to review this assignment for a test, you end up having to reread most of the chapter because you don't remember what it was about or, because of time limitations, you don't review it all.

Think about or discuss with your classmates the following questions: Does *just reading* sound familiar? If you read this way, how well do you learn? Do you spend your time wisely or wastefully? How well do you think you will do on a test if you read and study this way? Do you think this is the only way to read? Do you know of any other ways to approach your reading assignments?

The highest reading step on the Active Learning Staircase, **reading actively**, means that you are using some or all of the reading efficiency tools shown on the steps in between just reading and reading actively. You are able to reduce mind-wandering while increasing how much you learn. In the following chapters, you will be learning the tools for active reading one at a time:

❑ Previewing (this chapter)

❑ Reading in key words (Chapter 7)

❑ Reading in phrases (Chapter 7)

❑ Using a pacer (Chapter 7)

❑ Adjusting your reading speed (Chapters 7 and 8)

The first step up the Active Learning Staircase is previewing. To better understand how to preview, you first need to know the difference between nonfiction and fiction reading material.

THE DIFFERENCE BETWEEN NONFICTION AND FICTION

Nonfiction reading material is *factual* in nature. Textbooks, encyclopedias, and certain magazine articles are some examples of nonfiction material. Factual material contains a lot of information on many topics and can be challenging to learn from. Learning from nonfiction can be made easier with the application of the tools presented in this chapter.

What are some examples of nonfiction that you are currently reading?

_____

_____

On the other hand, **fiction** reading material is _imaginative_ in nature. It is composed of invented ideas. Novels, short stories, and certain magazine articles are some examples of fiction material. Imaginative material is easier to read because it generally centers around one topic or story. The challenging part of fiction reading is the ability to follow the story line and then be able to interpret its meaning. Figure 6–2 lists several examples of each type of material.

Figure 6–2
Nonfiction and Fiction Reading Materials

Nonfiction	Fiction
Textbooks	Novels
❏ _Design Guidelines for Desktop Publishing_	❏ _A Portrait of the Artist As A Young Man_ —James Joyce
❏ _Retail Buying: From Staples to Fashions to Fads_	❏ _One Hundred Years of Solitude_ —Gabriel Garcia Marquez
❏ _Civil Litigation for the Paralegal_	❏ _Waiting to Exhale_—Terry McMillan
Magazines	Short Story Collections
❏ _Time_	❏ _Heat_—Joyce Carol Oats
❏ _Utne Reader_	❏ _Descent of Man_—T. Coraghessian Boyce
❏ _Rolling Stone_	❏ _Enormous Changes at the Last Minute_—Grace Paley
Newspapers	Poetry
❏ _The New York Times_	❏ _Earthlight_—Andre Breton
❏ _The Wall Street Journal_	❏ _Howl and Other Poems_—Allen Ginsberg
❏ _The Washington Post_	❏ _Shaker, Why Don't You Sing?_—Maya Angelou

What are some examples of fiction that you are currently reading?

_____

_____

The information in this chapter will concentrate on reading nonfiction material since most of your education centers around factual learning. (For more information about reading fiction see Appendix C, "Previewing Fiction.")

PREVIEWING

Previewing is looking over your material *before* reading it to discover clues to its contents. It is an active approach to reading and an important tool for successfully completing all reading assignments. By previewing, you learn how the material is organized, what and where the main ideas are, and what exactly will be covered in the reading.

Consider the possible answers to the following questions either on your own or with a group:

❑ Why do you suppose football teams look at films of their opponents' previous football games *before* facing them?

❑ Why do people ask for directions or look at a map *before* going anywhere? What else do they do to find directions?

❑ Why do many people look in the newspaper to find out what each film is about *before* going to the movies? What else do they do to find this information?

The first question above responds to the need for *preparing a plan of attack*. Football teams must create a strategy of attack against their opponents, which they can do more easily if they know the typical strategies their opponents have used in previous games. This gives them a competitive edge on the playing field.

The second question speaks to the need for *mapping out a direction*. Without directions, people get lost, frustrated, and may never reach their destinations. On the other hand, with directions people are able to get where they want to go without getting lost, without being frustrated, and can reach their destinations in a reasonable amount of time.

The third question responds to the need for *using time effectively*. If you blindly select a movie, with no idea of what kind of film it is (horror, comedy, action-adventure, etc.) or who is starring in it, you may end up wasting your time, as well as money, watching something you wouldn't have gone to see had you known better. A little preparation can make the time you spend worthwhile and enjoyable.

How does this relate to your reading assignments? When approaching a reading assignment, most students open their book to the assignment and, without thinking about or choosing a plan of attack, begin reading from the first word to the last. This approach to reading is *passive* (remember the difference between the passive vs. active learner discussed in Chapter 1). Active readers, on the other hand, prepare a plan of attack, map out a direction, and create a course of action for using their time wisely.

The most serious drawback commonly mentioned by beginning previewers is that they feel it takes a lot of time. At first, it may take ten minutes to preview a ten-page chapter. However, once you know what to look for and are skilled at finding the information quickly, it should take you no longer than five minutes. The benefits of spending time previewing *before* reading are that (1) it builds background knowledge for easier learning, (2) it helps to transfer new information into long-term memory because you will have seen the material more than once, and (3) it helps you to be active in your reading by having a plan of attack and a mapped out direction. Though it may take some time to save time, the time you spend previewing is well spent toward learning!

FINDING YOUR PURPOSE AND READING RESPONSIBILITY

The first step in previewing any reading material is to learn the purpose of your reading and in what way you are responsible for it. In Chapter 1, knowing your purpose and responsibility was presented as a way to become actively involved with all of your assignments. Here it is specific to each reading assignment.

The **purpose for reading** is best defined as the reason why you are reading. It can be as simple as "because I want to read it for my own information" or as challenging as "my instructor assigned it and I will be responsible for the information."

A **reading responsibility** means in what way you are accountable for the information you are reading. Reading responsibilities may include becoming familiar with the information for a class discussion, possessing the ability to successfully take a quiz or test based on this information, or simply incorporating the information into your knowledge for future use. Each responsibility requires a different amount of reading and study time. For example, if your reading assignment is to prepare for a class discussion, you do not need to spend a lot of time studying the information; you need only be familiar with it.

Without a purpose or knowing your reading responsibility, you are a passive reader who wastes time and is directionless. With a purpose and knowing your reading responsibility, you are an active reader who is efficient with time and proceeds with a clear direction.

Think about an upcoming reading assignment. Write it down next to Assignment #1. What is your purpose and reading responsibility? Write them down as well. Now list more assignments if you have them.

Assignment #1: _____

Purpose: _____

Responsibility: _____

Assignment #2: _____

Purpose: _____

Responsibility: _____

Assignment #3: _____

Purpose: _____

Responsibility: _____

PREVIEWING A TEXTBOOK

Previewing a textbook is easy once you know what to look for. It should be done once at the beginning of a course to familiarize you with exactly what kind of a learning tool it is. (Keep in mind that textbooks are nonfiction, and that other types of nonfiction, such as magazine articles and procedure manuals, can also be read using these same guidelines.)

Previewing a text is accomplished by focusing on each of the following elements.

The Title and Subtitles

The **title** of a textbook tells you what the topic, or main idea, is. For example, a text entitled *Automotive Electronics* tells you that it will contain information about the electronic workings of a car. However, the text may not necessarily provide information about changing a car's oil or tires. A **subtitle** gives you more information. For instance, *Automotive Electronics: An Advanced Course* suggests that the basics will not be discussed and more difficult topics will be emphasized.

To answer the questions in this chapter, you will need one of your course textbooks. If you do not have one with you, use this textbook.

What is the title of your textbook? What does it suggest to you about its topic?

_____

_____

What is the subtitle of your text, if any? What additional information does it tell you about the book's topic?

_____

_____

The Author

Chances are that you will have never heard of your text's author. So why even look at the name? Because the qualifications of the author or authors is important. Is he or she a specialist in this area? Do they have any college degrees or related work experience on the topic? This information can be found on a book's title page (for example: Dr. John Jones, Ph.D, Professor of Auto Mechanics at XYZ College), on a page entitled "About the Author," or sometimes at the end of the book. (See page xiii of this book for information about me.)

What can you tell about the author(s) of your text?

_____

_____

The Copyright Date

A text's copyright date is found on the left-hand page either immediately before or immediately after the title page, and is usually located next to the symbol ©. The **copyright date**, sometimes referred to as the publishing date, tells you how recent or how old the information in the book is. For example, if you are taking a computer course and the book you are assigned is five years old, then developments in the field over the last five years will not be covered. If there is more than one copyright date, this indicates that the book has been either revised, updated, or is popular enough to require another printing. If 33 percent or more of a book has been revised, reworded, or rewritten, the title will indicate this by naming the edition (2nd edition, 3rd edition, and so on).

Look at the sample copyright page for *Design Guidelines for Desktop Publishing* in Figure 6–3. The copyright date is 1992. Because the information in this book centers around computer technology, this information would remain current for approximately three to five years. At that point, you would probably be studying out-of-date information, because new technology will have been created. This is the first edition of this book because there are no other copyright dates or reprinted editions listed. Now look at your own text.

What is the copyright date of your text? What does it tell you about the book?

_____

_____

What is the edition of your text?

_____

The Preface

The **preface** of a textbook is usually found after the table of contents. The preface may also be referred to as the foreword or introduction. It tells you why the author wrote the book and/or what you need to know about how the book is organized.

Read the preface of your text. What information does it give you?

_____

_____

_____

The Table of Contents

Nonfiction books are written in outline form. The **table of contents** is the outline of the text. By reviewing the table of contents, you can better understand the strategy the author used in writing the book, learn what will be covered, and discover what direction he or she intends for communicating the information to the reader. Most textbook outlines are divided into *units* or *parts*, indicating a general topic, as well as *chapters*, indicating more specific areas of discussion.

Review your table of contents. How is the author's outline presented to you? Does it help you to better understand the structure of your book?

_____

_____

_____

Figure 6–3
Copyright Page from Design Guidelines for Desktop Publishing

Cover design by Spiral Design

Delmar Staff

Executive Editor: Lucille Sutton
Senior Acquisitions Editor: Mary McGarry
Project Editor: Carol Micheli
Project Coordinator: Wendy A. Troeger
Design Coordinator: Karen Kemp

For information, address Delmar Publishers Inc.
2 Computer Drive West, Box 15-015
Albany, New York, 12212

Copyright © 1992
by Delmar Publishers Inc.

Printed in the United States of America
published simultaneously in Canada
by Nelson Canada,
a division of The Thomson Company

10 9 8 7 6 5 4 3 2 1

Library of Congress Cataloging-in-Publication Data

Mantus, Roberta.
  Design guidelines for desktop publishing / Roberta Mantus.
    p. cm.
  Includes index.
  ISBN 0-8273-5075-9
  1. Desktop publishing. 2. Printing, Practical—Layout—Data processing. I. Title.
Z286.D47M345   1992
686.2'2544—dc20   91-44244
                                                        CIP

The Appendix, Index, Glossary, and Bibliography

The *appendix, index, glossary,* and *bibliography,* usually found at the back of a book, are some of the resources that an author provides you with for further information. By previewing them, you will always know that these resources are available to you. Too many students do not realize that a valuable learning tool is right in their own hands.

An **appendix** contains supplementary information that further explains a subject in the text. It might also contain an answer key to questions found in the text.

An **index** is an alphabetical listing of names, places, and topics along with the numbers of the pages on which they are mentioned or discussed. The index is helpful when searching for specific information, especially when researching a specific topic.

A **glossary** is a list of terms with accompanying definitions. If your book is called *Computer Basics,* the glossary would have the jargon, or vocabulary terms, relating to computers. Though a regular dictionary may contain the same vocabulary terms, the textbook glossary gives you practical definitions for use in your course.

A **bibliography** tells you what reading resources the author used in writing the book. You can use the bibliography to do further research on a specific related topic.

Does your text have an appendix, index, glossary, or bibliography? If so, check them on the following list and include the starting page number.

_____ Appendix page # _____

_____ Index page # _____

_____ Glossary page # _____

_____ Bibliography page # _____

How will the information in these resources be helpful to your learning?

_____

_____

_____

_____

Figure 6–4 is a quick reference worksheet that you can use for previewing a textbook. It is meant to guide and remind you of what to look for. Copy it and use it for all of your textbooks this term. After locating the information for previewing a text several times, you will probably be able to preview without the worksheet.

If you forget where to find any of the information, review this section as needed.

Figure 6–4
Previewing A Textbook

A Quick Reference Tool

The following is a list of information needed for previewing a textbook or any other nonfiction reading material. Before each item is a blank space for you to put a check mark once you have previewed it. After each item, you can include any related information you feel appropriate or important. As you become used to previewing nonfiction texts, keep this list as a reminder tool.

_____ Title:
_____ Author(s):
_____ Copyright Date:
_____ Preface or Introduction:
_____ Table of Contents:
        _____ Units or sections:
        _____ Chapters:
_____ Appendix:
_____ Index:
_____ Glossary:
_____ Bibliography:
_____ Other Comments:

PREVIEWING A TEXTBOOK CHAPTER

Once you have previewed a textbook as a whole, you are ready to preview a single chapter. Previewing a chapter will provide you with the detailed information needed to prepare your plan of attack, map out your direction, and create a course of action for using your time wisely.

Turn to a chapter in your text. Before reading the chapter, or any nonfiction reading material, it is important to preview the following ten pieces of information:

1. The title
2. Headings and subheadings
3. The length of material
4. Introductory paragraphs
5. Topic sentences
6. Summary paragraphs
7. Boldface and italicized words

8. Margin notes and footnotes
9. Illustrations and captions
10. End of chapter questions

The Title

The **title** of a chapter tells you the topic, or main idea, of the chapter. A title alone may not tell you what specifically will be discussed, but it will give you a general idea of the subject matter involved.

Headings and Subheadings

Headings and **subheadings** provide you with more specific information about the chapter as well as the outline of the information. Publishers usually indicate headings and subheadings by printing them on separate lines or in slightly larger print than the rest of the text. Figure 6–5 illustrates these in more detail.

Figure 6–5
Headings and Subheadings *Source: Clodfelter, Richard.* Retail Buying: From Staples to Fashions to Fads. © *1993 Delmar Publishers Inc. Reprinted with permission.*

This is a heading → **Factors Affecting Merchandise Assortments**

When planning merchandise assortments, you will want to provide a variety of merchandise that is best suited for your customers' needs and consistent with your store's image. As you develop the assortment plan, there are several key factors that must be considered. They include: 1) type of merchandise carried; 2) store policies; and 3) variety of merchandise available.

This is a sub-heading → **Type of Merchandise**

The type of merchandise your store or department carries will affect your assortment planning. There are many methods used to categorize merchandise, and each one requires the development of a different type of assortment plan. Merchandise can be divided as fashion or basic (staple) merchandise or classified as convenience or specialty goods.

This is a subheading to the above. → Fashion or Basic Merchandise

Merchandise can be grouped into two broad classifications—fashion or basic (staple) merchandise. Fashion merchandise has high demand over a relatively short period of time, usually a season. Appeal for fashion merchandise is limited, which causes customer demand to end abruptly. In order to maximize sales, fashion buyers must quickly identify "best sellers" in their merchandise assortments and place reorders immediately. As the selling season progresses, few or no reorders should be placed. Consumer demand could end quickly, leaving you in an overstocked position, and then even substantial markdowns may not move unwanted merchandise.

The Length of Material

The **length of material** is important because it tells you how much time you can expect to spend on the reading. If it is a long assignment, you might want to break your reading time into smaller, more manageable sections. Previewing a chapter's length helps you to plan the time you'll spend reading and allows you to take more control over your study time.

List the title, headings, and subheadings, in order, of your chapter. Then count the number of pages in the chapter and fill in the appropriate blank. Use a separate sheet of paper if necessary.

Title: _____

Headings and Subheadings: _____

_____

_____

_____

_____

_____

_____

_____

_____

_____

_____

_____

_____

_____

Length of material: _____

How much time should you spend on it? _____

Introductory Paragraphs

Introductory paragraphs are the first several paragraphs of each chapter. They are, in effect, the start of your reading journey. These paragraphs give you an overview of what you will be reading. Some texts have an outline of the chapter on their first page. If your text has one, look it over because it will tell you what will be discussed.

Topic Sentences

Topic sentences in nonfiction material are almost always found in the *first sentence of every paragraph*. They provide you with the main idea of a paragraph. Though there may be more than one topic sentence in a paragraph, you need only preview the first sentence. By looking at the topic sentences before actually reading your chapter, you will know specifically what information will be presented and in what order.

When previewing topic sentences, be careful not to read every sentence in the paragraph. Until you become accustomed to previewing, you will tend to passively read from the first word to the last. Here you are asked to actively look only for topic sentences and follow their train of thought.

Summary Paragraphs

Summary, or *concluding*, **paragraphs** are found at the end of the chapter. They tell you, in effect, where your journey will end and summarize where you have been. Some texts make it easy for you by having a subheading, called *summary* or *conclusion*, at the end of a chapter.

Preview the introductory paragraphs of your chapter. From them, what do you expect to read about?

_____

_____

_____

Now preview the topic sentences of every paragraph. If the chapter is long, work with one section or approximately 10 pages, whichever is appropriate to your text. What kinds of specific information do they tell you to expect to read about?

_____

_____

_____

_____

Finally, preview the summary or concluding paragraphs of your chapter. What other information do they tell you that you will read about?

_____

_____

_____

_____

At this point, you have established the outline of the chapter and uncovered how the writer has sequenced his or her thoughts. This ability is useful in previewing as well as in taking notes from your texts (see Chapter 10). In addition to the organization pieces of the chapter, there are other pieces of information that can help you uncover clues to what will be discussed.

Boldface and Italicized Print

Boldface and *italicized print* are other ways that publishers indicate that something is important, such as a new vocabulary term, a person's name, a date, or an event. **Boldface** words, **dark print like this**, usually point out a new vocabulary term, while **italicized** words, *slanted printing like this*, usually indicate something important (See Figure 6–6).

Figure 6–6
Sample Page Illustrating Heads and Type Source: Kerley, Peggy et al. Civil Litigation for the Paralegal. *Delmar Publishers Inc. © 1992. Reprinted with permission*

Chapter 5 The Initial Pleadings 99

MARTIN REDSHAW, doing business as Marty's Diner, Plaintiff.

If the plaintiff is doing business under a fictitious name, before the lawsuit is filed you should verify that the plaintiff has complied with all local laws regarding such usage. Some states, for example, require that fictitious name statements be filed, and failure to do so can affect the right of a party to sue in some cases.

Where the defendant is doing business under a fictitious name, the true name of the party may be unknown to you when you are preparing the complaint. Your state may have various records that can be checked, but these are not always complete or accurate. It is therefore necessary to identify the defendant in the complaint by the fictitious name. In such a case, when the true name of the defendant or defendants is determined, the complaint can generally be amended.

Subheading →
boldface → **Fictitious Defendants.** Not to be confused with parties who use a fictitious name in business is a concept known as **fictitiously named defendants**, a procedure that is allowed in some jurisdictions. This term usually refers to defendants whose very identity is unknown. They are usually identified as "Does." In jurisdictions that allow their use, "Does" are commonly named as defendants in complaints to cover a situation where a new defendant is discovered after the statute of limitations has run. In such a case the attorney argues that the complaint was filed against the newly discovered defendant within the statute of limitations. He was just referred to by an incorrect name. The attorney then tries to amend the complaint to "correct" the name.

heading → Joining Multiple Parties

Many lawsuits involve disputes with multiple plaintiffs and/or defendants. The rules concerning joinder of multiple parties can be extremely involved and confusing. However, joinder of parties usually falls into two categories, joinder that is allowed but not required, known as **permissive joinder**, and joinder that *boldface →* is required, or **compulsory joinder**. Before drafting any complaint with multiple parties you may need to review these rules. For *italics →* example, in the *Hendricks* case described in the commentary, you may need to know whether the Hendricks can sue the realtor, the company for which she works, and the seller in the same lawsuit. This is determined by the rules of joinder, which are usually found in the appropriate state laws (or Rules 19–21 of the Federal Rules of Civil Procedure, if the case is in federal court).

Margin notes ↓

fictitiously named defendants
Defendants in a lawsuit who are not identified by their correct names; usually refers to the practice in some state courts of including several "Does" as defendants to provide for discovery of additional defendants after the statute of limitations has run.
permissive joinder
A concept allowing multiple parties to be joined in one lawsuit as plaintiffs or defendants as long as there is some common question of fact or law.
compulsory joinder
The required association of multiple parties as plaintiffs or defendants in a lawsuit; occurs when the court cannot render relief without the presence of all the parties.

If your chapter has a lot of boldface or italicized words, you might first make a list of them and then find their meaning, either in the paragraph you found the word or in the glossary, *before* you read. This will help you to become familiar with the new vocabulary and help you to read with greater understanding.

Look for the boldfaced and italicized words in your chapter. Write down any that you don't know. Then find their meaning. Use a separate sheet of paper if necessary.

Boldface/Italicized Words	Meaning

Margin Notes and Footnotes

Margin notes and **footnotes** are additional ways publishers indicate that something is important. (See Figure 6–6.) **Margin notes** usually indicate an important idea that the author wants you to be aware of. They may also be pieces of additional significant information related to the text. Margin notes are located in the space outside the written text on a page.

Footnotes are explanatory comments or reference notes that relate to a specific piece of text on a page. They are found either at the bottom of the page, end of a chapter, or end of a book. Footnotes are indicated by numbers. For example, if the author wanted to provide more information about *osmosis*[12], the number footnote you would look for would be number 12. By locating these *before* you read, you will know if the information contained in the footnote is needed to better understand the text *or* if it is just a reference that the author included for your information. Noting this before reading will facilitate your learning, make your reading easier, and help you to make the best use of your time.

Look for margin notes and footnotes in your chapter. Make note of any important information provided in the margins as well as where the footnotes are located, if there are any.

_____

_____

_____

_____

_____

_____

_____

Illustrations and Captions

The old saying that a "picture is worth a thousand words" is a good reason to preview illustrations and captions. **Illustrations** include any photos, figures, graphs, cartoons. **Captions** are the information below or alongside the illustration that explain its value. Publishers provide illustrations and captions to help the reader better understand the material being presented.

Look at the illustrations and captions in your chapter. What do they tell you about what you will be reading?

_____

_____

_____

_____

End-of-Chapter Questions

Also of value to you are the **questions at the end of the chapter**. Though not all nonfiction reading material provides questions, textbooks usually do. These questions are helpful in establishing your purpose in studying this material and in fulfilling your reading responsibility. They tell you what the author feels you should learn from the chapter and offer you a way to check your understanding of the material you've read. If you are assigned chapter questions, by previewing them you will know what you should be looking for while you are reading and you will be better prepared to answer the questions afterwards quickly and effectively.

Note that there may be different types of questions that are asked or information requested for an end-of-chapter review. A **vocabulary**, or **key term**, **list**, provides you with all the new vocabulary for the chapter. A **review** or **discussion section** asks you related questions about the information presented in the chapter. Sometimes you will be asked to discuss your answers either on paper or with another classmate. By answering these questions, you will have a clearer understanding of the material. **Activities** or **projects** are a way to learn firsthand about the information discussed in the chapter. They are active ways to apply the new information to the "real world." For example, a textbook on job hunting may describe classified ads and explain how to read them. You might then be asked to check your own newspaper, looking for samples of the required information.

Review the questions at the end of your chapter. How many different types of questions are there? Which type seems the easiest? Most difficult? Which are most time consuming?

Different Types:

_____

_____

Easiest:

_____

_____

Most Difficult:

_____

_____

Time Consuming:

_____

_____

At this point, you have spent some time becoming familiar with your assignment and have gained valuable background knowledge that will make your reading easier. Isn't it true that we read things we are familiar with faster and with better comprehension than things that are unfamiliar to us?

Figure 6–7 is a quick reference worksheet that you can use for previewing a chapter. It is meant to guide and remind you of what to look for. Copy it and use it before beginning your reading assignments. After locating the information for previewing a chapter several times, you will probably be able to preview without the worksheet. If you forget where to find any of the information, review this section as needed.

Figure 6–7
Previewing a Chapter

A Quick Reference Tool

The following is a list of information needed for previewing any chapter of nonfiction reading material. Before each item is a blank space for you to put a check mark once you have previewed it. After each item, fill in the information requested with any other information you feel appropriate or important. Once you feel comfortable with previewing, keep this list as a reminder tool.

The Reading Assignment: _____

_____ Purpose:

_____ Reading Responsibility:

_____ Chapter Title:

_____ Headings and Subheadings: (use a separate sheet if necessary)

_____ Length of material:

         How much time do I expect to spend on it?

_____ Introductory paragraphs:

_____ Topic sentences:

_____ Summary or concluding paragraphs:

_____ Boldface and italicized print:

_____ Margin notes and footnotes

_____ Illustrations and captions:

_____ Questions at the end:

You should now be able to *read actively* by knowing how to prepare a plan of attack, map out a direction, and create a course of action for using your time wisely. Since all nonfiction material is similar in structure, you can now approach any reading with confidence and assurance.

(For information about previewing fiction, see Appendix C.)

SUMMARY

1. Becoming an active learner means becoming an active reader. Active readers have a plan of attack, map out their direction, and create a course of action for using their time wisely.

2. Nonfiction material is factual in nature while fiction is made up or imaginative. Textbooks are nonfiction.

3. Previewing is looking over material before reading it to discover clues to its contents.

4. Having a reading purpose and responsibility is an active beginning for any reading assignment.

5. Previewing a textbook should be done when you first receive the text to familiarize yourself with exactly what kind of learning tool it is.

6. Previewing a text chapter provides you with the author's outline and other important information related to the topic. It also provides you with background knowledge about what you will be studying.

REVIEW

Answer the following questions using your own words and thoughts based on the information you learned in this chapter.

1. What is previewing?

_____

_____

_____

2. When previewing a textbook, what do you look for?

_____

_____

_____

_____

3. When previewing a chapter of a textbook, what do you look for?

_____

_____

_____

_____

4. What do you think are the benefits of previewing *every* reading assignment? Think of the differences between previewing and not previewing. List more than five if you can think of them.

Benefit #1:

_____

_____

_____

Benefit #2:

_____

_____

_____

Benefit #3:

_____

_____

_____

Benefit #4:

_____

_____

_____

Benefit #5:

_____

_____

_____

5. Can you think of any drawbacks to previewing? If so, what are they?

_____

_____

_____

_____

6. What reading material do you have that you will preview?

_____

_____

_____

_____

CHAPTER 7

RAISING YOUR READING SPEED

LEARNING OBJECTIVES

After studying and working with the information in this chapter, you should be able to:

1. Explain the unlearning to relearn concept.

2. Identify THE reason to read faster.

3. Describe the three tools for reading faster.

4. Identify the three factors that determine your reading speed.

5. Choose which reading tools work best for you.

6. Begin using the reading tools on your own reading activities.

. . . T he key is to use a tool or tools to help you read actively, not passively.

Speed reading courses became popular in the early 1950s. They are even more popular today for a number of reasons. First, there is an increasing desire to do more in less time. Reading has typically been a time consuming task that seems to take forever—especially for students.

Second, there continues to be an information explosion. Information is produced and processed much faster today than ever before due to computers and other high technology advances. Every time someone comes up with a new idea or way of doing something, it ends up being published in magazines, newspapers, or books. According to the American Booksellers Association of America, there were more than 133,000 new titles added to *Books in Print* in 1991 alone! This does not include magazines, newspapers, junk mail, and other forms of printed information!

Lastly, reading faster enables students and professionals to keep current in their fields of study or work and to advance in their careers. Reading is a form of communication, like television or radio, that many people do not take advantage of because their reading attitude or skills are not adequate enough.

In Chapter 6, you learned how to preview both a textbook and a textbook chapter. Previewing helps you to read faster because you become familiar with the material before you read. In this chapter, we continue to provide you with tools that you can use to read faster. In addition, you will come to understand that a student's goal is to read efficiently, not just for speed alone.

Today's information explosion makes increasing your reading speed essential to increasing your knowledge. What method have you already learned that can help you to read faster and more effectively? (Photo courtesy of Abby Marks-Beale, The Reading Edge)

SELF-EVALUATION

The following self-evaluation will give you an idea of how familiar, or unfamiliar, you are with some of the topics and terms discussed in this chapter. After reading each statement, circle the letter (Y, S, or N) most appropriate to your answer. Please answer honestly, rate yourself at the end, and then complete the information for Chapter 7 on page 374 in the Appendix A.

Y = yes; frequently   **S** = sometimes   **N** = no; never

1. I can handle my reading workload with ease.   Y S N

2. I wish there was more reading material in my areas
of interest.   Y S N

3. I read both for school/work *and* for pleasure.   Y S N

4. I know how to effectively increase my reading
speed when I want to or need to.   Y S N

5. I know how to look for and read key words.   Y S N

6. I know how to look for and read in phrases.   Y S N

7. I know how to use my hands or a white card to
help me increase my reading speed.   Y S N

8. I know how to adjust my reading speed according
to my purpose and background knowledge.   Y S N

9. I realize that learning to read faster takes an active
reading approach.   Y S N

10. I enjoy reading.   Y S N

<u>Rate Yourself</u>

Number of Ys _____ x 100=

Number of Ss _____ x 50=

Number of Ns _____ x 10=

Total =

LEARNING TO READ FASTER

Learning to read faster is a skill that is developed, like all other skills, over a period of time. Most students learn to read in the first grade at the age of six. Take your current age and subtract six years from it. The result is the number of years you have been developing your reading habits. If you are eighteen years old and subtract six years, you have been developing your reading habits for twelve years! If you start to change some of your reading habits now, you will probably not feel as comfortable with the habit as you once did because you are taking a new approach, not one that you have used for twelve years. BUT, with little effort practicing the new habits, you will gain comfort with better reading skills. *This is called unlearning to relearn.*

All things are difficult before they are easy.

*- Thomas Fuller, British clergyman
and author*

Unlearning to Relearn

Unlearning to relearn can only happen when you already have learned to do something. In this case, you have already learned to read. In order to improve your reading, you need to unlearn it first, then relearn it.

Let's take the example of an automatic car versus a manual stick shift. Say that you have learned to drive an automatic and become an excellent driver. You are both comfortable and capable behind the wheel. However, the first time you try to drive a stick shift, you no longer seem to be an excellent driver. You have trouble working the clutch, stall out in the middle of intersections, and grind the gears. You do not feel very comfortable or very capable. This is what unlearning can feel like.

At this point, it would be easy to give up and say that you are no good at driving a stick shift. On the other hand, if learning to drive the stick shift was necessary or important enough, you could practice with it a few more times to figure out how to best drive this car. Doing this means taking some time and energy to relearn the skill. Relearning means finding what works for you. With a little practice, you can master the stick shift and once again become an excellent driver.

What other skills do you think require unlearning to relearn? Brainstorm a list below:

_____

_____

_____

_____

_____

_____

While you are reading through this chapter, trying some of the new tools to raise your reading speed, keep in mind that feeling uncomfortable is a sign of breaking your old habit and beginning to create a new one. The key is to keep trying them until they can work for you. Not all of the tools work well for everyone, but by giving them a try you will find the ones that work best for you.

THE Reason to Read Faster

We have already mentioned some of the reasons why reading faster is important. We have not mentioned, however, THE reason. What do you think the relationship is between reading faster and your ability to concentrate? To read faster, you have to concentrate! Take, for example, a walk down the street. What can you do easily when you are walking down the street? You can window-shop easily. Think of five more things and write them below in the left column first. Then, if you can do the same activity as well while running, rewrite it on the right. If not, leave it blank as in the example.

While walking, I CAN:	While running, I CAN :
1. window-shop easily	- - - - - - - -
2.	
3.	
4.	
5.	
6.	

From this activity, you will see that when you run you cannot possibly do as many things as well at the same time as when you are walking. Speeding up anything forces you to focus on the activity and concentrate. With reading, you are forced to focus and concentrate, reducing your ability to daydream. With more concentration given to reading, you will be able to better understand what you are reading, learn more from everything you read, and finish it in a shorter amount of time. Sound like something you'd like to do? Read on!

HOW TO READ FASTER

The Active Learning Staircase in Figure 7–1 reminds you that just reading, or beginning at the first word and stopping at the last, is the most passive learning activity. By adding previewing to your reading habits (Chapter 6), you can move up to a more active level on the staircase. In this chapter, you will learn the next three steps toward reading actively: *reading in key words* and *phrases; using a pacer;* and *adjusting your speed.* These steps are also the tools for reading more efficiently.

Figure 7–1
The Active Learning
Staircase

The basis of any tool that helps you to read faster is a natural human visual ability called peripheral vision. Your **peripheral vision** is the wide distance you are able to see on your left and right while staring straight ahead.

Try this experiment: As illustrated in Figure 7–2A, stare straight ahead at a point on a wall or an object. Extend both arms out in front of you with your fingertips pointing up. While still staring straight ahead, spread your arms out and back to each side while still "seeing" your hands as in Figure 7–2B. Get to the point where you can still see your hands. If they disappear from sight, bring them back in a little, as in Figure 7–2C. Once you have found the farthest point back without them disappearing, look at how far

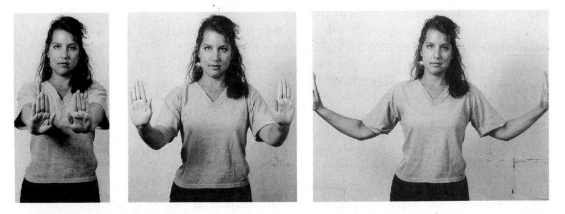

Figure 7–2A, B, and C
As shown in Figures 7–2A, B, and C, you can discover your peripheral vision distance by staring straight ahead at a point on a wall or an object, extending both arms out in front of you with your fingertips pointing up, spreading your arms out and back, and recognizing how far you are able to see before your hands seem to disappear. How wide is your peripheral vision?

apart your hands are. This is your peripheral vision ability. If your vision, for whatever reason, is mostly from one eye, you probably still have peripheral vision ability from that eye.

When you look down on a page, you cannot see a wide distance. What you do see is your *eye span*. Your **eye span** is how much information you see at a time when you look down at the page. Reading faster can be accomplished by working with your peripheral vision to increase your eye span.

There are three simple tools you can use to increase your eye span to read faster: *reading key words; reading phrases;* and *using pacers.* Reading in key words and reading in phrases are active reading tools for your eyes. Using pacers is also for the eyes and adds the use of your hands or a white card.

Reading Key Words

Key words are the more important words in text. They are *usually* longer than three letters in length and are considered to be those words that carry the most meaning in a sentence.

For example, most people read the following thirteen-word sentence word for word:

When you pick up a book, the world is literally at your fingertips.

However, by looking for and stopping your eyes only on the more important words, you can still understand the text while saving time. Read only the words in bold below:

When you **pick** up a **book**, the **world** is **literally** at your **fingertips**.

Now look at the words that are not in bold. Are you familiar with them? Have you seen them thousands of times? Are they as important as the words in bold?

When reading only key words, understand that you are *not skipping* the other words. You are simply spreading your peripheral vision to increase your eye span to see both the key word and the nonkey word(s) at the same time.

Read only the key words indicated in boldface in the following paragraph. See if you can spread your peripheral vision to see the unbolded words along with a bolded one. Try to understand the text without "reading" every word.

One of the **characteristics** of the **modern world** is the **ease** and **degree** of **travel. Historically, people** have **always traveled,** but **much** of that **travel** was **not** for **pleasure. While** the **terms "travel"** and **"tourism"** are **often used interchangeably** and the **terms** may **appear synonymous,** in the **past travel** was **generally undertaken** for **financial, military,** or **business reasons, while tourism** was **travel** for the **sake** of **recreation** and for the **enjoyment** of **new** and **different places** and **people. While people** have **always traveled** to **some extent** for the **thrill** of **travel** or **curiosity about other places, mass tourism** is a **modern phenomenon. Until** the **last few decades, only** a **select** few were **able** to **travel** for **tourism.**

Now is the time to remember the unlearn to relearn idea. Learning to read in key words is probably very different for you. If you feel uncomfortable, that's good! Recognize that this is the first step toward relearning. With a little practice, you will feel more comfortable and find that you are reading quicker than before with the same or better understanding than you had before using this method. Think about it: If you can learn to read and understand a ten-word sentence by only reading five key words, what will that do to your reading time?

Now it's your turn to practice finding key words. Try the following exercise.

Directions: You will be looking for the key words in the following paragraphs. DO NOT read each sentence first to figure out which word is more important to the meaning of the sentence. This will waste your time, rather than save it. INSTEAD, quickly underline *as you read* the words that are generally, but not always, three letters in length or longer and seem to carry some meaning. When you are done, reread the paragraph to see if reading your key words makes sense. Make changes as needed. The first sentences are completed for you. *There are no right or wrong key words as long as they make sense to you.*

Paragraph 1:

Once in a while you may think that a store or company you are dealing with has made a mistake. It could also give you some other reason to make a complaint. Maybe you bought something from a store and were told you would receive it in a few weeks. Months go by and you still do not have the item. Maybe you have received something damaged and you want the store to take it back. Getting big businesses to take care of complaints about such things is sometimes hard. Have faith; there are ways to register your complaint so that it will be taken care of.

Paragraph 2:

Cancer is the uncontrolled growth of abnormal tissue. In healthy tissue, body cells grow, die, and are replaced by new cells. This is a normal process that goes on day after day. Sometimes cells do not follow the rules of the body; they begin to grow quickly, steal nourishment from surrounding cells, and push normal cells out of the way. They prevent normal cells from doing their regular jobs. Finally, these cells cause changes in the body which produce signs that indicate something is wrong.

Paragraph 3:

There is strong evidence that suggests that the use of standardized tests, which assess abilities, personalities and integrity, are a valuable screening tool in the preemployment process. While initially many companies and selection experts were hesitant about the use of these tools, many hospitality organizations now use testing as a regular component in the selection process. We predict that testing will become both more sophisticated and widely used in our industry.

If you want more practice underlining key words, you can use newspapers, magazines, or your textbooks. Once you have begun to master the key word idea, practice reading in key words from a few paragraphs in this textbook or any other of your texts. Avoid using your pen to underline anymore because it will slow you down.

Keep in mind that reading key words is only one tool for increasing your reading speed. Just because you have learned it doesn't mean you have to use it. In the next section, you will learn about another tool called *phrasing*.

Reading Phrases

Most passive and unskilled readers read one word at a time. This is an inefficient and time consuming method. As you learned in the last section, not all words are equally important. Reading key words allows you to get the information you need without reading word for word.

Reading phrases is a way to make reading more effective for the reader. A **phrase** is a group of words that expresses a thought. If you can learn to read in thoughts instead of word for word, you will better understand what is written and be able to read faster. Read the following paragraph and notice that each phrase, or thought, is indicated between the slash marks.

Doctors have found/ that many people/ spend many hours/ in sleep/ for which /there is /no physical need./ When these habits/ are changed/ and these people/ try to do with less,/ they often find/ no difference/ in health/ or efficiency./ You might experiment/ with reducing your sleep time/ by half an hour./ Give yourself/ a few days/ to get adjusted/ to the new pattern./ If you are/ as effective/ as you were before,/ you will gain/ the equivalent/ of a week/ of Sundays/ in the course/ of a year./

Now it's your turn to practice finding phrases. Try the following exercise.

Directions: You will be looking for phrases, or groups of words that form a thought, in the paragraphs below. DO NOT read each sentence first to figure out where the thoughts are. This will waste your time, rather than save it. INSTEAD, quickly place a slash mark, *as you read,* where you believe one thought ends and another begins. Then reread the paragraph to see if reading your phrases makes sense. Make changes as needed. The first sentences are completed for you. *There are no right or wrong lengths of phrases as long as they make sense to you.*

Paragraph 1:

Once in a while/ you may think/ that a store/ or company/ you are deal-ing with/ has made a mistake./ It could also give you some other reason to make a complaint. Maybe you bought something from a store and were told you would receive it in a few weeks. Months go by and you still do not have the item. Maybe you have received something damaged and you want the store to take it back. Getting big businesses to take care of com-plaints about such things is sometimes hard. Have faith; there are ways to register your complaint so that it will be taken care of.

Paragraph 2:

Cancer/ is the uncontrolled growth/ of abnormal tissue./ In healthy tissue,/ body cells grow,/ die,/ and are replaced/ by new cells./ This is a normal process that goes on day after day. Sometimes cells do not follow the rules of the body; they begin to grow quickly, steal nourishment from surround-ing cells, and push normal cells out of the way. They prevent normal cells from doing their regular jobs. Finally, these cells cause changes in the body which produce signs that indicate something is wrong.

Paragraph 3:

There is strong evidence/ that suggests/ that the use of standardized tests,/ which assess abilities,/ personalities/ and integrity,/ are a valuable screen-ing tool/ in the preemployment process./ While initially many companies and selection experts were hesitant about the use of these tools, many hos-pitality organizations now use testing as a regular component in the selec-tion process. We predict that testing will become both more sophisticated and widely used in our industry.

If you want more practice slash-marking phrases, you can use newspapers, magazines, or your textbooks. Once you have begun to master the phrasing idea, practice reading phrases from a few para-graphs in this textbook or any other of your texts. Avoid using your pen to make slash marks anymore because it will slow you down.

What You Need to Know about Column Width. **Column width** is how wide or narrow the printed text is on a page. Newspapers and mag-azines are typically printed with narrow columns. Textbooks are printed in both ways as illustrated in Figure 7–3. Reading in key words works very well with all kinds of columns, but reading phrases works well only when reading wide column material. Because with phrasing you are looking to put words together, nar-row columns can be very frustrating and choppy to read.

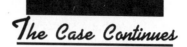

The Case Continues

In the chicken carry-out business a situation similar to the McDonald story occurred. In 1955, the Kentucky Fried Chicken franchise chain was begun by 66-year-old Colonel Harland Sanders. In 1964 John Y. Brown, later the governor of Kentucky, purchased the organization, and in 1974 he sold the operation to the giant distiller Heublein. Although Colonel Sanders was no longer a company official, he was retained by Heublein as a $200,000-a-year public relations figure. In contrast, when the McDonald brothers closed their deal with Ray Kroc, they completely dropped out of sight. What is the rest of the story regarding why the McDonalds never became spokespeople for the mammoth fast-food chain bearing their name?

Early in their negotiations, there was a personality clash between the reserved New England-reared McDonald brothers and the flashy Chicago salesman, Ray Kroc. When Kroc built his first restaurant in Des Plaines, Illinois, he discovered that in order to store potatoes, he needed to modify the building plan and construct a basement. For legal reasons, he required documentation from the McDonald brothers to alter the restaurant. Although Kroc made the alteration, the brothers refused to furnish him with the required written statement. Kroc confided to his friends that the McDonalds acted as though they wanted him to fail.

In another incident, after the McDonalds agreed to sell their organization to Kroc, they insisted at the last minute on keeping their original restaurant in San Bernardino. Kroc wanted this profitable outlet in order to generate necessary cash for the growing franchise chain. Kroc became extremely angry and disillusioned with the McDonalds when they would not budge from their position. Eventually, Kroc opened a restaurant directly across the street from the original one, and because he owned the McDonald name, the brothers were forced to rename their operation "The Big M." Kroc was greatly elated when he finally ran the brothers' restaurant out of business. Now you can understand why the McDonalds never became spokespersons for the worldwide restaurant organization that bears their name.

Sources: Adapted from Robert Johnson, "McDonald's Combines a Dead Man's Advice with Lively Strategy," *The Wall Street Journal,* December 18, 1987, pp. 1, 13; Ray Kroc with Robert Anderson, *Grinding It Out* (Chicago, Henry Regnery Company, 1977), pp. 69, 70, 115, 116; and "The Burger that Conquered the Country," *Time,* September 17, 1973, pp. 86, 87.

Nationalism is a political/economic attitude that encourages the development of stronger domestic industries, which results in greater self-sufficiency within the country.

Nationalism is a political/economic attitude that encourages the development of stronger domestic industries, and this results in greater self-sufficiency within the country. International events will probably cause nationalism to remain an important factor in overseas marketing activities. All countries seek a favorable balance of trade. This means that they want to export more goods than they import. Domestically produced goods are being heavily promoted in the United States for that reason. The labor union's national TV advertising campaign makes the point with the memorable "Look for the Union Label" song and other commercials featuring Bob Hope and other celebrities displaying "Made-in-the-U.S.A." labels.

Demographic Forces

Demography is the study of population characteristics, such as age, birthrate, education, geography, number of households, income, occupation, race, and the mix of women and men.

Demography is the study of population characteristics, such as age, birthrate, education, geography, number of households, income, occupation, race, and the mix of women and men. Astute marketers look

---

Figure 7–3 Example of Narrow and Wide Column Width on Same Page of a Textbook. *Source: Husted, Stewart, et al.* Marketing Fundamentals. © *1993 Delmar Publishers Inc. Reprinted with permission.*

Using Pacers

Pacers can be either your hands or a white card that you can use to help you keep your place while reading and/or to force you to move your eyes down the page faster. Learning how to use them correctly is very important because these tools, when used incorrectly, will slow you down.

Pacers as a Place Keeper.   Many readers have a hard time getting from the end of one line to the beginning of the next accurately. If you miss the next line, then you will have trouble understanding the author's ideas. You will also waste your time because you will have to go back to find where you were. Reading wide column material is especially challenging because the return distance from the end of one line to the beginning of the next is long. If you can use your hands or a white card to keep your place, you will be able to better understand your reading because the ideas will flow more smoothly. You will also save time because you won't be losing your place.

Pacers as an Eye Mover.   Pacers are also used to force the eyes to move faster, especially when you are tired or bored. If you are studying facing a window or an aisleway and a person walks by, your eyes will naturally be distracted and will follow the person for a moment. This is because *the eyes naturally follow movement.* If you can create movement on your page, your eyes will move faster down the page.

Pacer Rules.   To use a pacer correctly, there are two important rules you must try to follow. They are:

1. Keep the pacer moving forward.

2. Do NOT stop or go back.

   Notice we said "try to follow." Rules were made to be broken, but they should be used as important guidelines to help you learn how to best use these tools.

The Pacers.   In the following activity, you will find five different pacers to try. You will probably not like all of them, but try to find at least one of them that you are willing to make your own.

   Directions: Read each pacer description and study the accompanying figure. Then, using either this textbook or some other reading material, try using the pacer. Keep the pacer rules in mind.

#1: The Center Pull Method (Figure 7–4)

Figure 7–4
The Center Pull Method

The center pull method is done by placing the index finger of one of your hands under the first line of the text in the center of the column. While your eyes read from left to right, your finger "pulls" your eyes down the page. (This works best with narrow columns.)

#2: The Left Pull Method (Figure 7–5)

Figure 7–5
The Left Pull Method

The left pull is similar to the center pull. You place your index finger on the left margin or the beginning of the line. Your finger then "pulls" your eyes down the page while keeping your place. (This works well with all material.)

#3: The Two Finger Pull (Figure 7–6)

The two finger pull uses the index fingers of both hands. Place the left index finger on the left margin or the beginning of the line and place your right index finger at the end of the same line your left hand is on. While your eyes move from left to right, your hands should move down with your eyes. Your fin-

Figure 7–6
The Two Finger Pull
Method

gertips should be on the same line as your eyes most of the time. (This works with all material, especially wide columns.)

#4: The Thumb or Pen Push (Figure 7–7A and B)

The thumb or pen push is done from the top down. Place your thumb, or a closed pen, above the words you want to read. Start your thumb or pen moving down and try to read fast enough to keep your thumb or pen moving. (This works well with narrow columns.)

Figure 7–7A and B
The Thumb or Pen Push
Method

#5: The White Card Method (Figure 7–8)

The white card method begins by using any blank white card or blank piece of paper. It is important that there be no writing on it and *it should be equal in length to the size column you are reading*. A blank 3 x 5 index card can be used for both narrow and wide columns depending on which edge of the card you use. You can tape two cards next to each other for very wide columns.

Figure 7–8
The White Card Method

Though you can place a card either above or below the line of text, by far the most effective method is *above* the line. If you place the card *below* the line, it is easy to regress, or go back over material you have read. It also covers the text you are about to read. It is like placing a wall between you and the upcoming text. On the other hand, placing the card *above* the line covers what you have already read, which avoids regression. It also leaves exposed the text you are about to read. So to use the card effectively, place it <u>ON</u> <u>TOP</u> of the words you already read, leaving exposed the words you are going to read. Start moving the card down the page.

Combining Your Reading Tools

You now have three new tools to practice using on your reading material to help you read faster. As you get better with them, you may find, as do others, that combining them is very powerful. For example, reading key words with a pacer, or reading phrases with a pacer, or reading a combination of key words and phrases, is extremely helpful in increasing your reading speed. Remember, whatever you do, *that the key is to use a tool or tools to help you read actively, not passively.*

Nothing happens by itself . . . it will all come your way, once you understand that you have to make it come your way, by your own exertions.
- Ben Stein, lawyer, speechwriter, and contemporary author

ADJUSTING YOUR READING SPEED

When driving a car, a driver should not drive fast all the time. When driving on a highway, a driver is supposed to go fast. But when on city streets, a driver needs to slow down because pedestrians, stop lights, and other cars can get in the way. A driver needs to change driving speed according to the conditions of the road.

Similarly with reading, a reader should not read fast all the time.

Why do you think you should *not* read fast all the time?

_____

_____

Why do you think you should *not* read slowly all the time?

_____

_____

If you read fast all the time, you may miss important information. If you read slowly all the time, you will daydream more and waste your time. So how fast should you read?

Three Factors for Determining Reading Speed

Your reading speed mainly depends on the following three factors: your *reading purpose*; the *difficulty of the material*; and your *familiarity with the subject matter* or *background knowledge*.

Your reading speed depends first upon your reading purpose. In Chapter 6, you learned about reading purposes. Your *reading purpose* is basically why you are reading what you are reading. Let's say your reading purpose was to get the gist, or main ideas only, of your textbook chapter. In this case, you would read fairly quickly looking for the main ideas while not wasting your time on the details. If your reading purpose was to learn step by step how to put a faucet on a sink, then you would read more slowly.

Your reading speed can also depend upon *how difficult the reading material is*. If you are reading a book that has difficult vocabulary for you, or a lot of technical information, you would read it slower than if the vocabulary were easy and the information not technical.

Finally, your *background knowledge*, or what you already know, greatly affects your ability to increase your reading speed. The more you already know about the topic or material, the faster you can read; the less familiar you are with it, the slower you will read. By previewing a chapter, you will be able to increase your reading speed because you are familiar with the chapter contents before you actually read it.

When to Speed Up and When to Slow Down

Since reading fast all the time or reading slowly all the time are not efficient, you have to learn when to speed up your reading and when to slow it down.

While reading an article or chapter, your reading speed naturally goes up and down depending on a number of factors, such as how much you daydream and how familiar the material is. If you learn to change your reading speed *on purpose*, instead of accidentally, you will complete your reading in an efficient amount of time with good understanding.

In Chapter 3, you worked on the influences that affected your ability to study. Briefly review that chapter to help you complete this section. Most of these same factors come into play while reading as well as studying.

Let's take a closer look at these factors. Following are two columns: a speed-up column and a slow-down column. First write as many of the conditions or influences that help you to read faster on the speed-up side. Then write those that cause you to slow down on the slow-down side. (Important clue: There is usually an opposite relationship between one side and the other.)

Things that help me to SPEED UP	Things that cause me to SLOW DOWN
Reading for main ideas (purpose)	Reading for details (purpose)
Easy vocabulary	Difficult vocabulary
Some background knowledge	Little background knowledge
For class discussion (responsibility)	For quiz or test (responsibility)

In Appendix E, you will find one student's list for your comparison. Since readers are different, you may not always agree with this student and that is fine. What is essential is that you know what affects your ability to speed up or slow down. This is an important quality of an active, efficient reader!

Flexibility IS the Key

Being an active reader means being a flexible reader. A **flexible reader** is basically a reader who can adjust his or her reading techniques according to the reading purpose, difficulty of material, and background knowledge. In this chapter you discovered why it is important to adjust your reading speed. You also became aware of the factors that affect your reading speed. Additionally, you learned new tools to apply to your reading to increase your reading speed. This combination of awareness and skill is what makes you a flexible reader.

SUMMARY

1. Learning to read faster increases your concentration.
2. Unlearning is uncomfortable but important to improve a skill or habit.
3. Reading faster can be accomplished by working with your peripheral vision to increase your eye span.
4. The three tools for increasing your eye span are:
   ❏ reading in key words
   ❏ reading in phrases
   ❏ using pacers
5. The tool(s) you use can depend on the width of the column.
6. The three factors for determining reading speed are:
   ❏ reading purpose
   ❏ difficulty of the material
   ❏ background knowledge
7. Active readers are flexible readers.
8. The most important thing is for you to figure out what works best for you.

REVIEW

Answer the following questions using your own words and thoughts based on the information you learned in this chapter.

1. Why is it important to learn how to read faster? Give at least three reasons.

_____

_____

_____

_____

_____

2. Why is changing your reading habits challenging to do? What do you think you have to do in order to improve your skills?

_____

_____

_____

_____

3. How does your peripheral vision affect the way you read? What can you do to expand your peripheral vision while reading?

_____

_____

_____

_____

4. Which of the reading tools do you find most useful? Why?

_____

_____

_____

_____

_____

5. Which of the reading tools do you find least useful? Why?

_____

_____

_____

_____

_____

6. Why should you learn to adjust your reading speed? What can you do to adjust your reading speed?

_____

_____

_____

_____

_____

CHAPTER 8

LEARNING TO SKIM AND SCAN

After studying and working with the information in this chapter, you should be able to:

1. Identify the reading gears in being a flexible reader.
2. Describe the qualities of a flexible reader.
3. Explain the differences between skimming and scanning.
4. Describe skimming and discuss its benefits.
5. Describe scanning and discuss its benefits.
6. Begin to use skimming and scanning on your own reading workload.

T he hardest part about skimming and scanning is remembering to do it!

Have you ever seen a swimming pool with leaves floating on top of the water? A tool called a "skimmer" is needed to remove them from the pool. The purpose of a skimmer is to quickly pass over the surface of the water and collect the pieces on top. In reading, a reader can become a skimmer by reading quickly, staying close to the surface to get the main ideas.

Flexible readers are capable of skimming assignments like a skimmer collects debris in the water, and scanning what they read like a radar scans for fish underneath the water's surface. Skimmers and scanners are flexible readers. Are you a skimmer and a scanner?

Another tool called a "scanner" is commonly used by fishermen. The purpose of the scanner is to locate schools of fish underneath the water's surface. This gives the fishermen specific information as to where to drop their nets for the the best catch. In reading, a reader can become a scanner, reading below the surface of the main ideas looking only for the specific piece(s) of information they need.

Skimmers and scanners are flexible readers. They read according to their purpose and get what they need quickly without wasting time. Skimmers and scanners do *not* read everything. This is what increases their reading speed. Their skill lies in knowing when and how to read this way without missing what is needed.

In this chapter, you will (1) learn more about being a flexible reader by learning about the three main reading gears, (2) learn how and when to skim and scan, and (3) experience what your eyes are doing to use each of these important reading tools.

SELF-EVALUATION

The following self-evaluation will give you an idea of how familiar, or unfamiliar, you are with some of the topics and terms discussed in this chapter. After reading each statement, circle the letter (Y, S, or N) most appropriate to your answer. Please answer honestly, rate yourself at the end, and then complete the information for Chapter 8 on page 374 in the Appendix A.

Y = yes; frequently   **S** = sometimes   **N** = no; never

1. I know my reading purpose before I read. Y S N

2. I change reading gears according to my purpose and background knowledge. Y S N

3. I know the difference between skimming and scanning. Y S N

4. I know how to move my eyes when skimming. Y S N

5. I know how to skim effectively. Y S N

6. I am aware of how quickly my eyes and brain communicate while scanning. Y S N

7. I use a pacer to help me scan effectively. Y S N

8. I can scan accurately. Y S N

9. I know that reading everything all the time is not an efficient use of my time. Y S N

10. I am a flexible reader. Y S N

<u>Rate Yourself</u>

Number of Ys _____ x 100=

Number of Ss _____ x 50=

Number of Ns _____ x 10=

Total =

If you only care enough for a result, you will almost certainly attain it.

- William James, Harvard psychologist and philosopher

THE READING GEARS

In Chapters 6 and 7, you learned step by step how to move from being a passive reader to an active one on the Active Learning Staircase. In this chapter, you will complete the reading journey to reading actively by learning how to adjust your reading speed. (See Figure 8–1.)

Unskilled, passive readers are like a one-speed vehicle. They read their favorite magazine the same speed they do a textbook.

Figure 8–1
The Active Learning
Staircase

Skilled, flexible readers are like a multi-speed vehicle. They change speeds according to the type of material they are reading as well as their purpose and background knowledge.

In reading, there are basically *three reading gears*, or speeds, that a reader can use to be flexible (See Figure 8–2). *Low gear* ranges from about 100 words per minute (wpm) to 250 wpm. This

Reading Gear	Type of Reading	Reading Speed in Words-Per-Minute	Percent of Comprehension	
LOW	Difficult For studying For notetaking Unfamiliar	100–250	High (80%+)	Low Gear
MIDDLE	Everyday Reading Magazines Newspapers Somewhat familiar	250–500	Average (70%)	Middle Gear
HIGH	All kinds of material Purpose is to skim Purpose is to scan Very familiar	500–800	Lower (50%+)	High Gear

Figure 8–2
The Reading Gears

word-for-word reading is necessary only for studying or committing to memory the information you are reading. It may also be necessary for reading material that is fairly difficult or for material in which you have little or no background knowledge. In low gear, you look for a high level of comprehension, somewhere around 80 percent to 90 percent.

If you read everything in low gear, you are definitely a passive reader. Chances are you are also talking while you are reading— either physically moving your lips or hearing your voice reading every word in your head. Both of these forms of talking while reading slow you down (because you are reading every word), tire your eyes (because you are stopping your eyes on every word), and have a tendency to hinder comprehension (because you are reading one word at a time instead of focusing on the more important words or thought units). Reading in key words, reading in phrases, and using pacers, as described in Chapter 7, help you to avoid reading everything in low gear.

Middle gear ranges from 250 wpm to 500 wpm. Reading in the middle gear is appropriate for everyday reading like newspapers and magazines, and for material that you are familiar with or in which you have a fair amount of background knowledge. In this gear, you would be looking for a fairly good amount of comprehension ranging from 70 percent to 90 percent. You also cover more material in a given period of time. Reading in middle gear requires the application of the reading tools and practice.

High gear speed should be almost twice as fast as your middle gear, or from about 500 wpm to 800 wpm. Reading in high gear is appropriate for skimming where you are not reading everything, but still accomplishing your purpose. This is why the speed can increase so much. In high gear, your level of comprehension is expected to be lower than the middle gear.

Scanning is also a high gear speed, but because you are only looking for a piece of specific information the speed can go even higher than 800 wpm. With scanning, accurately finding what you are looking for means 100 percent comprehension.

There are times when a major shift, either up or down, has to occur during reading, either because the material becomes difficult or easy or because you change your concentration level. Before reading, it is a good idea to decide which gears are appropriate for your reading purpose and background knowledge. This will help keep you on track.

Which gear is appropriate for the following? Is one gear enough, or could it vary?

Type of Reading	Purpose	Background Knowledge	Gear
Newspaper	To keep current	Varies	Middle to High
Magazine	To build my background knowledge	Varies	_____
Magazine article	To do research for a paper	Little	_____
Textbook	To read my assignment	Some	_____
Textbook	To research Albert Einstein	None	_____
Instructions	To replace an oil filter	Some	_____
Newspaper	To track the stock market	Some	_____
Textbook	To locate a specific topic	Little	_____
Instructions	To format a computer disk	None	_____
Fiction book	To relax and enjoy	None	_____

WHAT IS SKIMMING?

Skimming is one of the tools you can use to read in high gear. Fortunately for you, you have some background knowledge in it though you may not realize it. In Chapter 6, we discussed a form of skimming called "previewing." **Skimming**, as with previewing, is reading in high gear looking only for the general or main ideas. It also means that your overall understanding is less because you are not reading everything. You get the comprehension you need by reading only what is important to your purpose. It does not mean reading everything in detail for as much comprehension as possible.

There are a few differences between skimming and previewing. Previewing occurs before the actual reading process and requires you to search only for the main ideas in the writer's outline. Skimming, on the other hand, takes place while reading and allows you to look for some detail in addition to the main ideas.

How to Skim

To skim, you read at a fast speed and do not read everything. *What you do read is more important than what you leave out.* So what material do you read and what material do you leave out?

Let's say you are doing some research and have a long chapter or article to review. By reading the first few paragraphs in detail, you will get a good idea about what will be discussed. Once you know where the reading is going, you do not have to continue to read in detail. You can begin to read only the first sentence, also called the *topic sentence*, of each paragraph. This will give you the main idea of that paragraph. If you do not get the main idea in the topic sentence, then you might have to skim more of the paragraph to find it.

At the end of each topic sentence, your eyes should jump down through the rest of the paragraph looking for important pieces of information, such as a name or date, but again not reading everything. Continue to read the topic sentences and jump down through the rest of the paragraphs until you are near the end. Since the last paragraph or more may contain a conclusion or summary, you should stop skimming there and read it in detail.

Remember that your overall comprehension will be lower than if you read in detail. If, while skimming, you feel that you grasped the main ideas, then you are skimming correctly.

Figure 8–3 provides an excellent example of what should be read while skimming. Review this figure now, moving your eyes to the words, ignoring the blank spots.

Figure 8–3 also provides an excellent example of what your eye movements feel like while skimming. While skimming, your eyes should move quickly as if they were sprinting on tiptoe down an obstacle course. Review this figure again, this time being very aware of where your eyes are going and how they are moving and feeling.

When to Skim

Because skimming is done at a fast speed with lower than normal comprehension, you would not want to do it all the time. There are many times, however, that it is useful. Say you were researching information about the first automobiles ever made for an oral report due in a few days. You go to the library and find six books and four newspaper articles about this topic. (Chapter 14 will provide you with information on how to do this.) Because you have to be ready in a few days, you do not have the time to read everything in detail, but you need a lot of solid information. Skimming will help you to quickly locate the information you need while making sure you use your time wisely. It will also increase the amount of material you can use for your research.

Let's say it is a few days before your final exam. You need to review the material you studied all term, but don't want to reread everything. By skimming it, you will quickly locate the information you do not know well so you can study *that* instead of the information you know well.

While reading, ask yourself the following questions to help you decide whether to skim. If you answer "yes" to any of these, then skimming will be a useful tool.

❑ Do I have only a small amount of time?

❑ Is a preview enough?

❑ Do I already know this?

Figure 8–3
How to Skim Source: Fry, Edward. Skimming and Scanning (2nd Ed.) © 1989 by Jamestown Publishers, Providence, R. I. Reprinted with permission.

HOW TO SKIM

Usually the first paragraph will be read at average speed all the way through. It often contains an introduction or overview of what will be talked about.

Sometimes, however, the second paragraph contains the introduction or overview. In the first paragraph the author might just be "warming up" or saying something clever to attract attention.

Reading a third paragraph completely might be unnecessary but . . . . the main idea is usually contained in the opening sentence . . . . topic sentence . . . .

Besides the first sentence the reader should get some but not all the detail from the rest of the paragraph . . . . names. . . . . dates . . . . Tells you nothing . . . .

. . . . hence sometimes the main idea is in the middle or at the end of the paragraph.

Some paragraphs merely repeat ideas. . . . .

Occasionally the main idea can't be found in the opening sentence. The whole paragraph must then be read.

Then leave out a lot of the next paragraph. . . . . to make up time . . . . Remember to keep up a very fast rate . . . . 800 wpm . . . . Don't be afraid to leave out half or more of each paragraph . . . . Don't get intersted and start to read everything . . . . skimming is work . . . .

. . . . Lowered comprehension is expected . . . . 50% . . . . not too low . . . . Skimming practice makes it easier. . . . . gain confidence . . . . Perhaps you won't get anything at all from a few paragraphs . . . . don't worry . . . . Skimming has many uses . . . . reports . . . . newspapers . . . . supplementary . . . text . . . . The ending paragraphs might be read more fully as often they contain a summary.

Remember that the importance of skimming is to get only the author's main ideas at a very fast speed.

The last question to ask is "Can it be skipped?" Believe it or not, sometimes the best use of your time is to *skip* material. That's right—not read it at all! If you have a lot of background knowledge or feel that you don't need the information, then by all means skip it! Just because someone wrote it doesn't mean you have to read it. *If you pick and choose carefully what you skim and skip, you will be pleasantly surprised at the large amount of information you can get in a short period of time.*

Now that you have begun to learn about how and when to skim, you are ready to experiment with the skimming exercises on the following pages. Please read the directions in detail before starting each exercise.

Before doing these exercises, read the Instructions for Timing in Appendix D. For each of these exercises, follow the order of activities as listed below:

1. Write down your Beginning Time.

2. Skim the article quickly but to your satisfaction.

3. Write down your Ending Time.

4. Answer the ten questions that follow without looking back to the reading.

5. Figure words-per-minute in Appendix D.

6. Figure your comprehension percentage by checking your answers to those in Appendix D.

You will now see short informational readings on several different topics. Without looking at the questions on the following pages, skim the information in the way you have just learned while timing yourself. Remember, skimming is done at a fast speed with lower than normal comprehension. *You are not required to get 100 percent comprehension, so do not read everything!* Read looking for the general ideas with a few specifics.

Skimming Exercise #1—"Labor Unions"

Begining time: _____
Ending Time: _____
Time: _____

A little less than twenty percent of the American workforce are members of labor unions. A labor union is a group of workers who have joined together to protect their rights. The two main types of unions are craft and industrial. A craft union is made up of skilled workers in a craft or trade, such as plumbers, musicians, or barbers. Workers in the same industry often belong to an industrial union. Perhaps you have heard of the United Auto Workers or the United Mine Workers. These are industrial unions.

Throughout its history, organized labor has fought for three main goals. These have been improvements in:

1) Wages, hours, and benefits

2) Job security

3) Safe and healthful working conditions

Unions do other things besides working for these goals. One is to provide apprenticeship programs that teach work skills to young union members. Some unions have hiring halls where workers can go to find out about job openings. Political involvement is often an important labor goal. Unions frequently give money to favorite candidates and provide campaign workers.

The presence and strength of unions varies among geographic areas. Most unions are in the Midwest and Northeast parts of the United States. These areas have large construction, manufacturing, transportation, and mining industries.

A company that has an agreement with a union is called a union shop. In a union shop, the employer can hire whomever he or she chooses. However, the employee must join the union within a certain period of time. About twenty states, most of them in the South, have so-called "right-to-work" laws that don't allow union shops. These states have open shops in which an employee doesn't have to join a union. Open shops may exist in the other thirty states as well, but employees are often under pressure to unionize.

When you start a job, a co-worker or supervisor may ask you to join a union. Members of the local union must vote on your membership. Usually, though, anyone who applies is accepted. You will proabably pay an initiation fee to join and you must pay regular dues.

Source: Bailey, Larry. The Job Ahead. *© 1992 Delmar Publishers Inc. Reprinted with permission.*

Without looking back at the information you just skimmed, answer the following ten questions to the best of your ability. Make a guess when you are not sure.

Decide whether the following statements are true (T), false (F), or not mentioned (N). A *true* statement is a fact based on the information you read. A *false* statement is one that is mentioned but not correct. A statement that is *not mentioned* was not discussed at all.

_____ **1.** Approximately 20 percent of the American work force are members of labor unions.

_____ **2.** A labor union is a group of workers who have joined together to protect their rights.

_____ **3.** There are craft unions and mine unions.

_____ **4.** A craft union member would be a machinist.

_____ **5.** Only men can be a member of a union.

_____ **6.** Unions seek to improve an employee's job security.

_____ **7.** Unions are strong in all areas of the country.

_____ **8.** A union shop is a company that has an agreement with a union.

_____ **9.** An employee must be a member of the union *before* working in a union shop.

_____ **10.** Union members are required to wear the union logo on their work clothes.

Once all ten questions are answered, turn to Appendix D to figure your skimming words-per-minute and percentage of comprehension.

Skimming Exercise #2—"The Changing Workplace"

Begining time: _____

Ending Time: _____

Time: _____

When this country was founded in 1776, most people lived and worked on small, family-owned farms. The farm family raised livestock, poultry, and grain. Surplus food was traded for other products.

As trading increased, small villages grew along rivers and other transportation routes. The growth of towns provided new jobs for shop owners, bankers, blacksmiths, and others. Employment in nonagricultural occupations grew steadily. Agriculture, however, still remained the base of the economy.

In 1876, the share of the labor force working in agriculture stood at about fifty percent. Gradually, the number of farmers decreased as more and more people moved to cities. Meanwhile, agricultural production increased due to better equipment, improved plant and animal strains, and new farming methods. By 1990, the number of workers employed in agriculture had shrunk to less than three percent of the labor force.

In the second half of the 1800s, U.S. industry expanded rapidly. Growing towns and cities needed more and more goods. Typical workers in the early

1900s had factory jobs. They produced steel, machinery, and other manufactured goods. By 1920, over sixty percent of all workers were employed in goods-producing industries.

Growing industry and a growing population needed many kinds of business, transportation, communication, personal, and government services. In response to these demands, service industries began to expand. About 1955, the number of workers providing services passed the number of workers producing goods. Typical service occupations included secretary, clerk, salesperson, and manager.

The shift to service industries and occupations has continued. In 1990, over seventy percent of all workers were employed in services. This service economy, however, is also undergoing change. A new economy is evolving based on knowledge and information.

New ways of dealing with information are changing many types of industries. Here are some examples. Not long ago, communications meant sending information through cable or between ground-to-ground stations. Now, orbiting satellites beam communications around the world.

The use of robots in auto manufacturing is another example. Before robots, skilled workers used hand-held spray guns to apply paint finishes. Now robots do this, receiving their instructions from computers.

Computers haven't just changed the communications and auto industries. Computers are influencing almost all industries and occupations. In many offices, for example, computers are replacing typewriters. Computers are the backbone of the information society.

Source: Bailey, Larry. The Job Ahead. *© 1992 Delmar Publishers Inc. Reprinted with permission.*

Without looking back at the information you just skimmed, answer the following ten questions to the best of your ability. Make a guess when you are not sure.

Decide whether the following statements are true (T), false (F), or not mentioned (N). A *true* statement is a fact based on the information you read. A *false* statement is one that is mentioned but not correct. A statement that is *not mentioned* was not discussed at all.

_____ **1.** In 1776, most people lived and worked on a farm.

_____ **2.** Small villages grew because the farming industry grew.

_____ **3.** One hundred years after the country was founded, about 3 percent of the labor force were working on farms.

_____ **4.** It can be assumed that advancements in technology have shrunk the farming work force.

_____ **5.** Industry grew because towns and cities needed more goods.

_____ **6.** Farmers were retrained to work in industry.

_____ **7.** The population has grown faster than industries.

_____ **8.** Service occupations have come about because of the growth of the population.

_____ **9.** Industries have basically remained the same over the years.

_____**10.** The economy of the 1990s is based on knowledge and information.

Once all ten questions are answered, turn to Appendix D to figure your skimming words-per-minute and percentage of comprehension.

Skimming Exercise #3—"The Attraction of Place"

Begining time: _____

Ending Time: _____

Time: _____

People have always traveled. Curiosity, a basic characteristic of humans, has led people of all eras to explore new environments, seek new places, discover the unknown, search for different and strange places, and enjoy other experiences. This suggests that one place is different from another place, or there would be no curiosity about other places. The *National Geographic* magazine, for example, is considered one of the truly fine magazines in the world today. It adorns many libraries, public and private. It expends considerable effort to illustrate the differences that exist in the world between places. Its popularity reflects people's curiosity about other places and cultures.

While people have always traveled, tourism as we know it today is a recent phenomenon. It has only been since World War II that tourism, particularly international tourism, has developed as a major activity in the world. Early travelers and early tourism were reserved for a few: for the rich or the very brave. One important impetus for tourism resulting from World War II was that the war brought many people in contact with other people and places. They became more interested in the world. The events in one part of the world have an important impact on residents in another part of the world. Growth and change in modes of transportation have also encouraged travel. Replacement of transatlantic ships by airplanes was followed by the jet age from the 1960s to today. Fast, cheap transportation has make world travel a possibility for millions of people.

There are well-developed links between tourism and geography, in that the uniqueness of a place (whether it be an Indian periodic market, a tremendous waterfall, a snowy mountain village, or a resort on a sunny sandy coast) is the result of the geographic relationships at that place. *Geography* is the study of the earth as the home of humans. It is concerned with the combination of factors that make each individual place on the face of the earth somehow unique. Study of geography represents an attempt to gain an understanding of the causes of the uniqueness that characterizes each place. Uniqueness results from the combination of the natural (or physical) setting of climate, landform, and resources, and the features created by the residents of that place such as buildings, economy, dress styles, or other cultural features. The combination of physical and cultural factors that make each place different is the basis for human curiosity about other places, which causes the growth and development of tourism.

The process of tourism itself has contributed to the uniqueness of place. Every place on the earth's surface changes over time. Changes in economy, political organizations, culture, population size, and the physical environment constantly alter the texture and fabric of the complex mosaic that makes up a place. The invasion or migration of large numbers of people from another place for a short period of time will have an impact on the visited place, changing the uniqueness, creating a new and different cultural, political, economic, and physical landscape.

Source: Hudman, Lloyd, and Richard Jackson. Geography of Travel and Tourism. © *1990 Delmar Publishers Inc. Reprinted with permission.*

Without looking back at the information you just skimmed, answer the following ten questions to the best of your ability. Make a guess when you are not sure.

Decide whether the following statements are true (T), false (F), or not mentioned (N). A *true* statement is a fact based on the information you read. A *false* statement is one that is mentioned but not correct. A statement that is *not mentioned* was not discussed at all.

_____ **1.** People travel when they get bored with their surroundings.

_____ **2.** The only magazine mentioned by name in this reading was the *National Geographic* magazine.

_____ **3.** Tourism as we know it today is the same as when traveling began.

_____ **4.** A benefit of World War II is that it brought many people in contact with other people and places.

_____ **5.** The cost of traveling has increased with the growth and change in modes of transportation.

_____ **6.** Women are better travelers than men.

_____ **7.** Geography, as it is defined in the article, is the study of earth as the home of humans.

_____ **8.** Detailed geographical maps tell a lot about a place.

_____ **9.** Human curiosity causes the growth of tourism.

_____ **10.** The uniqueness of each place is advertised in the travel brochures.

Once all ten questions are answered, turn to Appendix D to figure your skimming words-per-minute and percentage of comprehension.

Benefits of Skimming

Think for a moment about how skimming can be helpful to you. How can it help your reading speed?

_____

_____

How can it satisfy your reading purposes?

_____

_____

How can it help with your classwork and other educational reading material?

_____

_____

How can it help for doing research?

_____

_____

How can it help for reading the newspaper or magazines?

_____

_____

What other ways do you think skimming can be helpful to you?

_____

_____

If you haven't realized it already, skimming has a positive effect on more than just school work. It increases your overall reading speed because your eyes pick up only certain important material. You can satisfy your reading purpose quickly and efficiently. It helps you keep current with your classwork as well as with the world around you. Just imagine the amount of information you can get through!

When doing research or other reading, you will be able to weed out material that is not valuable to your research. This way you can spend your time on the valuable information only.

The most important benefit of skimming, however, is your added ability to be a flexible reader. This adds high gear to your reading abilities. Skimming is easy to do; the hardest part is remembering to do it. Use the questions that were listed in this section to help you decide when skimming is appropriate.

WHAT IS SCANNING?

Scanning is another tool for reading in high gear. Unlike skimming, **scanning** is looking only for a specific fact or piece of information without reading everything. You scan when you look for your favorite show listed in the television guide. You scan when you are looking for your friend's phone number in a telephone directory, and you scan when you are looking to define a word in a dictionary. Scanning requires that your comprehension be perfect because you have to accurately locate the specific information you need. Scanning also allows you to get details and other information in a hurry.

How to Scan

Because you already naturally scan many different types of material in your daily life, learning more details about it will be easy.

Establishing your purpose, using the appropriate material to find what you are looking for, and knowing how the information is arranged *before* you start is essential to scanning. For example, if you need to find the meaning of a word, then your purpose is to find the word. Using a dictionary is the most appropriate tool to accomplish this purpose. You know that a dictionary is arranged alphabetically, so if you are looking up the word *loquacious*, then you would immediately look for it under the "L" section. Starting from the beginning of the dictionary would be a huge waste of time! (*Loquacious* means very talkative, by the way.)

As a student and in day-to-day life, you will have many reasons to look for specific information. Before signing up for your courses, you had to scan the catalog looking specifically for the courses you wanted to take. What other specific information have you had to look for, or will you have to look for in the future? What material will you use to find it?

Information I need	Where to look for it
The meaning of an unknown word	In a dictionary
What course(s) to take	In the course catalog
What time a television show is on	
What page is information on Gandhi	
What is the zip code for Cary, SC	
What day is Christmas this year	
How to print labels on my computer	
What is the population of S. Africa	
What is the capital of Utah	

The material you can scan is typically arranged in the following ways. Like the dictionary, information can be arranged **alphabetically**, going in order from A to Z, or **chronologically**, going from beginning to end. Information can be also be arranged **nonalphabetically** like a television listing, or **by category**, like an auto parts catalog. Sometimes information you seek is located within the written paragraphs of your text, also known as **textually**, like an encyclopedia entry.

How do you think the following material is arranged?

Type of material	Arrangement of material
Dictionary	Alphabetically
Television listing	Nonalphabetically
Encyclopedia entry	Textually
Index	
History reading	
Zip code directory	
Magazine articles	
Sport pages of the newspaper	
Reference listings	
Newspaper articles	
Computer manuals	

Once you have established your purpose, know what material to use to accomplish that purpose, and know how the material is arranged, then you are about ready to scan.

Learning to use your hands while scanning is very helpful in locating specific information. Do you do anything with your hands to locate a word in a dictionary? To find the starting time of your class on a course schedule? To read a train or bus schedule? Using a pacer (see Chapter 7) is extremely helpful in focusing your attention and keeping your place while scanning down a column of material.

Your peripheral vision will also help you scan effectively. If your hand is running down a list of names, you are able not only to see the name your finger is pointing to, but also the names above and/or below. Let your eyes work for you when searching for information.

Keep key words in mind while scanning. Key words come from your purpose. Say you are looking for the time a train leaves from New York City going to Washington, D.C. The key words to keep in mind are "from New York City" and "to Washington, D.C." If you are looking for the amount of money the computer printer PX–710 costs from a list of many, the key word to keep in mind is "PX–710."

Now that you are familiar with the basics for scanning, try scanning in the following course listing. Time yourself to see how long this exercise takes. (See "Instructions for Timing" in Appendix D if needed.) First read a question below the listing and then search above, using your hands or a white card pacer, looking for the correct answer. When you have found the correct answer, write it down in the blank provided next to the question. Notice how quickly your eyes and brain are communicating to each other to eliminate the incorrect information and focus on the correct information.

Begining time: _____

Ending Time: _____

Time: _____

Nursing

NUR 216 Health & Physical Assessment in Nursing ....3.0 cr

Prerequisite: NUR 215

6860	70	04:00p-06:50p M	Staff	****	01/25-05/22
		Special Information: Meets Lawrence & Mem. Hosp.			
8389	71	04:00p-06:50p M	Staff	****	01/25-05/22
		Special Information: Meets Hosp. of St. Raphael			
5180	72	04:00p-06:50p M	Staff	****	01/25-05/22
		Special Information: Meets Manchester Hospital			
2959	73	04:00p-06:50p M	Staff	****	01/25-05/22
		Special Information: Meets St. Francis Hospital			
9958	74	04:00p-06:50p M	Staff	****	01/25-05/22
		Special Information: Meets St. Mary's Hospital			
0315	75	04:00p-06:50p M	Staff	****	01/25-05/22
		Special Information: Meets Central CT ST Univ			
5400	76	04:00p-06:50p M	Staff	****	01/25-05/22
		Special Information: Meets Backus Hospital			

1. What is the name of the course listed?_____
2. What is the course number?_____
3. What time and day does Section 75 meet?_____
4. How many class sections are there?_____
5. Where does Section 72 meet?_____
6. Where does Section 76 meet?_____
7. How many credits does this course offer?_____
8. What is the prerequisite to this course?_____
9. From what date to what date do all the classes meet?_____
10. Where does Section 75 meet?_____

(To check your answers, see Appendix D.)

When to Scan

Because scanning is looking for a specific piece of information only, you will want to do it only when you need it. Say you were doing the research mentioned in the skimming section of this chapter for your oral report. Before you skim, you could scan the index of the book or reference material looking to find, first, if the book even had any information you would want and, second, if it did, what pages you could find it on.

There are many other times when scanning is appropriate. Most have already been mentioned in this chapter.

In the past, you scanned without knowing that you were doing it. Now, with the information provided in this section, you are more aware of what you are doing. This awareness and practice of this information will make your scanning ability more effective.

Now that you have more specific information about scanning, you are ready to practice with the scanning exercises on the following pages. Please read the directions in detail before starting each exercise.

For each of the following exercises, you will be able to practice your scanning ability. Time yourself to see how long each exercise takes. (See "Instructions for Timing" in Appendix D if needed.) Though there are no words-per-minute to figure, the quicker you locate the information with accuracy, the better!

First read a question below the table or listing and then search above, using your hands or a white card pacer, looking for the correct answer. When you have found the correct answer, write it down in the blank provided next to the question. If you have trouble locating an answer, go on to another question and come back to it later.

Scanning Exercise #1—Telephone Listing

Begining time: _____
Ending Time: _____
Time: _____

555–7998 **Williams Anne M Mrs** 80 Henry Hudson
555–1022 **Williams Antique Shop** 179 Bayshore Rd
555–2933 **Williams B E** 7 Eastern Ave
555–9016 **Williams Barbara S** Westbury
555–4810 **Williams Basil & Christine** 10 Freeland
555–8993 **Williams Beryl** 296 Palmer Farms Rd
555–1248 **Williams C** 790 Lake Rd
555–4208 **Williams C Webb** Taconic Rd
555–9084 **Williams Christopher B** 4 Eastern Ave
555–7379 **Williams Claude H** 92 Pickford
555–0225 **Williams & Co** 251 Waller
555–7561 **Williams David** 5 Pilot Rock Rd.
555–1114 **Williams Elizabeth C** North Pine
555–1286 **Williams Francis S** 35 St Andrews Rd.
555–0635 **Williams George & Kathi** 24 Lake Drive N
555–7175 **Williams Geo R D** 133 Prospect Dr
555–4228 **Williams Gwynne** 43 Bloomfield Rd
555–8993 **Williams Howard O Jr Dr** 296 Palmer Farms Rd
555–0848 **Williams** - Children Phone 296 Palmer Farms Rd
555–2331 **Williams J Bryan III** 10 Stansbury Pl
555–1766 **Williams J R** 34 Covert
555–7187 **Williams John F** 102 Calvert Dr
555–1391 **Williams John I** 91 Cedar Dr
555–1995 **Williams Joseph L III** 50 Cleveland Ave
555–9283 **Williams Jos L Jr** 141 Dairy Rd
555–6800 **Williams Joseph L Jr** rl est 32 Park Pl
555–2892 **Williams Joseph S** Parsons Dr
555–6800 **Williams Josephine C** rl est 32 Park Pl
555–5061 **Williams K & R** 171 Versailles Ave
555–8376 **Williams K R** 182 Lake Rd
555–3800 **Williams Karen L** atty 100 Kuntsler Rd
555–1941 **Williams Keith** 40 Dairy Rd
555–9443 **Williams Ken** 16 Madison Ave
555–1687 **Williams Lincoln A** 44 Hudson
555–0870 **Williams Lou** 5 Kings Rd
555–2341 **Williams Philip** 155 Taconic Rd
555–0671 **Williams Philip J** 2 Mendota
555–3383 **Williams R E** 140 Westbury
555–5061 **Williams R & K** 171 Kingsway Plaza Dr
555–8570 **Williams Richard A** 6 Allwich Ave
555–1012 **Williams Richard A** atty 1 Belli Blvd
555–7282 **Williams Roger J** 15 Prospect Park Dr
555–9198 **Williams Staunton Jr** 184 Eastern Ave
555–4826 **Williams Sydney M** 795 Leslie Lane
555–6233 **Williams Thos R** 205 S Maine Maid Rd

1. Whose phone number is 555–7379?_____
2. Who lives at 2 Mendota? _____
3. How many listings does 296 Palmer Farms Rd. have?_____
4. What is the business phone of Joseph L. Williams, Jr.?_____
5. Whose phone number is 555–3383?_____
6. Who lives at 182 Lake Rd.? _____
7. What is the phone number of 205 S Maine Maid Rd.?_____
8. What is the business address of Richard A. Williams?_____
9. Whose phone number is 555–1391?_____
10. Who lives at 795 Leslie Lane?_____

(Check your answers in Appendix D.)

Scanning Exercise #2—Cable TV Listing

Begining time: _____
Ending Time: _____
Time: _____

Wednesday Basic Cable Programs December 16											
P.M.	**6:00**	**6:30**	**7:00**	**7:30**	**8:00**	**8:30**	**9:00**	**9:30**	**10:00**	**10:30**	**11:00**	**11:30**
A&E	Rockford Files		Wilderness	Search	Our Century		Justice	Spies	1st Flights	Travel	Evening at the Improv	
AMC	Movie: "Mississippi"		Movie: "Tail Spin"			Reflections	Movie: "The Fall of the Roman Empire"					"Tail Spin"
BET	Video LP	Screen	Triple Thr't	Desmond's	Sanford	Comicview	Video Soul				Generation	Desmond's
CNBC	Money Pol.	Business	Portfolio	Money T'lk	Money	Steals	Real Story	D. Cavett	McLauglin	Personal	Steals	Real Story
CNN	The World Today		Moneyline	Crossfire	Primenews		Larry King Live		Year in Review: Sports	Sports		Moneyline
CSPAN	Moscow	Call-In			Event of the Day							
DISC	Nature	Wildlife	Search for Adventure		Mac/Mutley	Animals	Wings of the Luftwaffe		Beyond 2000		Mac/Mutley	Animals
ESPN	Ski Believe	Up Close	SportsCtr.	College Basketball			College Basketball: North Carolina St./Princeton					SportsCtr.
FAM	Rin Rin Tin	New Zorro	The Waltons		The Young Riders		Father Dowling Mystery		The 700 Club		Scarecrow & Mrs. King	
LC	Cuisine	Peasant	Renovation	Do It	Beakman	The Stars	Archaeol.	Beakman	Black Forest Journey		Beakman	The Stars
LIFE	Supermkt.	Shop/Drop	Unsolved Mysteries		L.A. Law: El Sid		Movie: "Bay Coven"				thirtysomething	
MSG	Powerboat Racing		Yankees	Forum	Page One	Basketball	March/Dimes Holiday		College Bowl Games		Boxing: Gibbins/Vice	
MTV	Classic	The Grind	MTV Jams	Comedy	Sports	Prime Time With Duff			Style	U2: Zoo TV		
NICK	You Do?	Crazy Kids	Looney	Bullwinkle	Get Smart	Superman	M.T. Moore	Van Dyke	Dragnet	Hitchcock	Lucy Show	F Troop
SC	Racing	Thor'bred	Medicine	NHL Hockey: Washington Capitals at Hartford Whalers					Tennis		Tuesday Night Football	
TBN	Praise the Lord				TBN Today	Footsteps	M. Murillo	J. Van Impe	Praise the Lord			
TBS	3's Comp.	A. Griffith	Hillbillies	Sanford	Movie: "The Gambler II" (Part 2)				Movie: "The Legend of the Golden Gun"			
TNN	VideoPM				Crook & Chase		Nashville Now			C. Daniels	Club Dance	
TNT	B. Bunny	Captain	Jetsons	B. Bunny	Movie: "Honky Tonk"				Movie: "Somewhere I'll Find You"			
UNI	G'raciones	Noticiero	Baila Conmigo		Maria Mercedes		Cara Sucia		Portada		Noticiero	Perez
USA	MacGyver: Countdown		Quantum Leap		Murder, She Wrote		Movie: "Past Midnight"				MacGyver	

1. What time is "Larry King Live" on? _____
2. On what station can you see the movie *The Legend of the Golden Gun?* _____
3. "MTV Jams" is on at what time? _____
4. Which station has programs in Spanish? _____
5. How long is the NHL hockey game? _____

(Check your answers in Appendix D).

Scanning Exercises #3A-E—Scanning Text

For each of the following paragraphs, there is one or two questions to answer. Read the question(s), then scan through the paragraph looking for the answer(s). When you find the answer(s), write it in the blank next to the question. Time yourself once for all five questions.

Begining time: _____

Ending Time: _____

Time: _____

#3A: What is the function of the eyelashes? _____

Hair protects the body in several ways. The eyebrows keep sweat from falling into the eyes. The tiny hairs inside the nose and ears stop small particles from entering and causing damage. The eyelashes keep small objects from getting into the eye. These hairs all act very much like a screen door on a house in keeping out unwanted organisms. The skin itself screens out harmful rays from the sun which may cause burns and harm the body.

#3B: What is being described in this paragraph? _____

Picture an immense room, segmented by brilliant blue draperies, flashes of color, neon lights, video presentation, models in sequined gowns, men and women in business attire and in the aisles, crowds of people of all ages in varied attire strolling and stopping frequently to view the booths. This would be a typical trade show. What is seemingly a random gathering of action and bodies, is in reality a carefully choreographed production. An air of excitement is deliberately created by the exhibit management company and exhibitors are encouraged to present a show.

#3C: How many types of cancer are there? _____

#3D: What is the leading cause of death in the United States? _____

It has been estimated that in the United States alone over 1,000 people a day die from some form of cancer. Since 1949 there has been a sharp rise in the number of men who develop cancer. Cancer of the lung has risen sharply in men. Cancer of the breast, colon and rectum occur most often among women. There are over one hundred types of cancer. Cancer is second only to heart disease as the leading cause of death each year. However, statistics also show that deaths due to cancer are increasing whereas those due to heart conditions are decreasing. Research continues into the cause and cure for cancer.

#3E: Where is optical center? (be specific) _____

When someone looks at a page, two things happen. First, the reader's eye will automatically go to the optical center. The optical center is defined as the place on the page where one's eye falls naturally. This is considered to be about three-eighths of a page from the top. Second, the reader's eye scans a page in the shape of a Z. This means that the eye moves across the top, diagonally down the page from right to left, and then across the bottom.

For this reason, illustrations placed at the tops and bottoms of pages make them look appealing. Understanding and remembering these two ways in which the eye naturally sees a page are critical to the page makeup.

(Check your answers in Appendix D).

Benefits of Scanning

Because scanning is a survival skill in daily life, finding specific information quickly and accurately can make your life easier.

Think for a moment about how scanning can be used and helpful to you.

How can scanning be used to increase your reading speed?

_____

_____

How can it be used to satisfy your reading purposes?

_____

_____

How can it be used to help with your classwork and other educational reading material?

_____

_____

How can it be used for doing research?

_____

_____

How can it be used for reading the newspaper or magazines?

_____

_____

What other ways do you think scanning can be used or helpful to you?

_____

_____

_____

_____

Finally, let's not forget that probably the most important benefit of scanning is your ability to be a more flexible reader. Scanning adds another high gear to your list of abilities.

Because you may be used to reading every word and may be uncomfortable not reading everything, know that you now have permission to not read everything by effectively skimming, scanning, and skipping material according to your reading purpose. Figure 8–4 is your permission slip; complete the blanks to make it yours.

Figure 8–4
Permission Slip from the Author

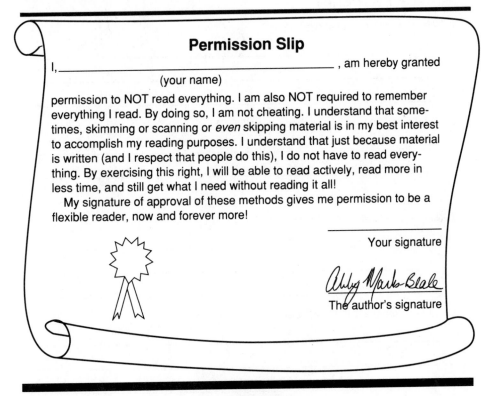

Permission Slip

I, _____ , am hereby granted
          (your name)

permission to NOT read everything. I am also NOT required to remember everything I read. By doing so, I am not cheating. I understand that sometimes, skimming or scanning or *even* skipping material is in my best interest to accomplish my reading purposes. I understand that just because material is written (and I respect that people do this), I do not have to read everything. By exercising this right, I will be able to read actively, read more in less time, and still get what I need without reading it all!

   My signature of approval of these methods gives me permission to be a flexible reader, now and forever more!

_____
Your signature

Ahly Marks-Beale
The author's signature

SUMMARY

1. There are basically three reading gears: low, middle, and high.
2. Flexible readers shift their reading gears depending on their purpose and background knowledge.
3. Skimming is looking for the general or main ideas. It is similar to previewing and is to be used when your purpose is to get an overview of the reading.
4. Skimming can help you get what you need quickly without wasting time.
5. Scanning is looking for a piece of specific information like a topic in an index. Using a pacer and your peripheral vision can help you find what you need quickly.

REVIEW

Using your own words, answer the following questions based on the information you learned in this chapter.

1. What are the three reading gears?

    _____

    _____

    _____

2. Why should a reader use these gears?

    _____

    _____

    _____

3. How can a reader use these gears?

    _____

    _____

    _____

4. What is the difference between skimming and scanning?

    _____

    _____

    _____

5. What would you tell another student about how to skim?

    _____

    _____

    _____

6. What would you tell another student about how to scan?

    _____

    _____

    _____

7. What are the benefits of learning to skim effectively?

    _____

_____

_____

8. What are the benefits of learning to scan effectively?

_____

_____

_____

9. How are you going to learn to skim and scan more effectively?

_____

_____

_____

PART 3
TAKING NOTES

CHAPTER 9
TAKING EFFECTIVE
NOTES IN CLASS

CHAPTER 10
TAKING EFFECTIVE
NOTES FROM TEXT-
BOOKS

CHAPTER 9

TAKING EFFECTIVE NOTES IN CLASS

After studying and working with the information in this chapter, you should be able to:

1. Identify THE reason for taking notes in class.
2. Summarize effective notetaking habits.
3. List and identify instructor personality clues.
4. List and identify instructor verbal clues.
5. Explain how to take notes and study with the Cornell Method of Note Taking.
6. Describe how to take notes and study with Mind Mapping®.
7. Begin to develop effective notetaking skills.

Learning to take good notes is like learning to take a photo on notebook paper of what happens in class on a particular day.

How many times have you written down a list of things to do? Or a shopping list for the grocery store? Or written down a telephone message for someone? Believe it or not, these common activities are notetaking activities. Writing things down is an effective yet simple means of remembering what you need to remember.

Let's take, for example, a telephone call. Imagine that while you were out you received a phone call from a potential employer. The person taking the message wrote down the name of the company the caller was from, but did not write down the person's name or phone number. This is an example of poorly taken notes. There is not enough useful information. If, however, the message had also included the name of the caller and his or her phone number, then the message would be useful. This is an example of good notes.

Good notetakers are usually successful students, since class lectures are often the basis for an instructor's tests. Are you an effective notetaker? What is your method of taking notes in class?

In your classes, taking good useful notes is extremely important to your success as a student. The content of lectures often becomes the content of exams. Learning to take good notes is like learning to take a photo on notebook paper of what happens in class on a particular day. Without it, you can never go back to get that picture again, and it would also make studying very difficult without all of the pieces of the picture.

Throughout this chapter, please remember that no two students take notes exactly the same way. Your notes, whatever way you choose to take them, must be useful and complete enough for you to succeed in your classes. *The key is to use the information provided in this chapter and adapt it to your own style of learning and notetaking.*

In this chapter, we would like to help you improve your notetaking skills in the classroom by focusing on the tools and skills needed to be an effective notetaker. You will learn (1) to know how and what to listen for, (2) to know what method(s) you can use and how you can write the information down, and (3) how to use your notes for effective studying.

SELF-EVALUATION

The following self-evaluation will give you an idea of how familiar, or unfamiliar, you are with some of the topics and terms discussed in this chapter. After reading each statement, circle the letter (Y, S, or N) most appropriate to your answer. Please answer honestly, rate yourself at the end, and then complete the information for Chapter 9 on page 375 in the Appendix A.

Y = yes; frequently   **S** = sometimes   **N** = no; never

1. I use a three-ring binder, not a spiral notebook, to take notes.   Y   S   N
2. I can pick out the information that is important to write down.   Y   S   N
3. I avoid writing down unimportant information.   Y   S   N
4. I take notes using key words, not full sentences.   Y   S   N
5. I abbreviate a lot when I take notes.   Y   S   N
6. I frequently use my own words when taking notes. Y   S   N
7. I take notes in every class.   Y   S   N
8. My notes are easy to study from.   Y   S   N
9. I know that taking good notes helps me do well as a student.   Y   S   N
10. I know how to take good notes.   Y   S   N

<u>Rate Yourself</u>

Number of Ys _____ x 100=

Number of Ss _____ x 50=

Number of Ns _____ x 10=

Total =

T here is always a better way . . . your challenge is to find it.
- Anonymous

WHY TAKE NOTES IN CLASS?

I n the past, many of your teachers encouraged you to take notes in their classes while others preferred that you did not. Some, perhaps, did not concern themselves with what you did so you were on your own. What is important to know now is that more learning takes place when you use various step-by-step activities that reinforce the learning:

Activity #1. Hear the instructor, then

Activity #2. Write down the information, then

Activity #3. See the information on the page, and then

Activity #4. Review it when you study.

If you do not write down the information in activity #2, then you can not see the information on the page in activity #3 or review it when you study in activity #4. This leaves hearing the information as the only way of learning. For many students this is not enough to learn from.

You know that notetaking is a good way to reinforce learning. What other reasons can you think of for taking notes in your classes?

1. _____

2. _____

3. _____

4. _____

5. _____

Imagine that you are in one of your lecture or discussion classes without a pen or notepaper to take notes. All you are doing is listening. Would you be concentrating on what was being said or would your mind be wandering more often than not? Now imagine that you are in your class and you have a pen and notepaper in front of you and were going to take notes. Would you be concentrating more this way?

The most important reason to take notes in any class is to improve your concentration. If you are a student or business professional in a classroom or meeting room, the more you concentrate, the more successful you will be at learning and understanding the information you are hearing. Taking notes, an active learning skill, is the best way to increase your concentration in class.

Using your notes to learn from is another important reason to take notes in class. Having them *to review and study from* will help you learn a lot and ace your tests at the same time. They also help you to *organize the information and to establish main ideas.* Your notes will help you *to remember the information longer* than if you did not have them and they sometimes serve as a visual reminder of exactly what was said that day.

PREPARING TO TAKE NOTES

You have been taking notes in your classes for years in a way that you have found to work best for you. In this chapter, we will provide you with some valuable information that can help make your notetaking as easy and effective as possible.

Throughout the rest of this chapter, when notetaking is discussed, we mean good, useful notetaking. The first step is to be prepared to take notes.

The Tools for Notetaking

Before you can take good notes, you need to be prepared with the appropriate tools for the job. The first tool you need to have is a *three-ring binder notebook*, not a spiral. In contrast to a spiral notebook, the three-ring binder gives you the ability to remove or add any extra pages or handouts where you want while maintaining the order in which your notes were taken. If you lend your notes to someone, you can take out only those they need instead of lending them the whole notebook. The plastic or hard cover of a three-ring binder provides more protection for your notes than the spiral paper cover, especially during wet weather. And if you take good care of your three-ring binder, you may be able to use it for more than one term. Depending on the size of the notebook, you can have one notebook for each one of your classes, or one for several classes. The only consideration is to keep your notes from each class together. If you have already bought your supplies for this term and are not able to change them, adapt this information as best you can until you can start fresh next term.

Another tool you need is the appropriate paper for the job. All notetaking paper should be 8 $1/2$ x 11 inches because smaller paper won't hold enough information and it tends to get lost or get out of order. For the first notetaking method discussed, you will be asked to use *summary paper*. Summary paper is not usual notebook paper. Instead of having a one-inch line margin on the left side, summary paper has a three-inch margin. In Figure 9–1, you will see a sample of what this paper looks like. You can make this paper yourself by taking a ruler to a one-inch margin paper and marking off with your pen a three-inch margin instead. If you want to buy paper with the three-inch margin already on it, you can get it through most college book stores or office supply stores. You will probably *not* find it at your local drugstore or other discount stores. For the second notetaking method discussed, you will be asked to use plain, unlined white paper, preferably three-hole punched.

Figure 9–1
Summary Paper

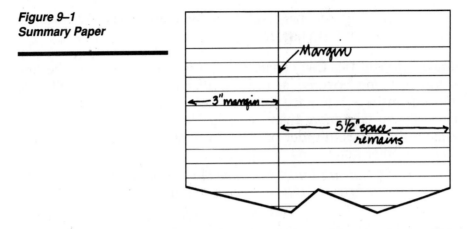

Another tool you need to have is an *erasable pen*. An erasable pen allows for mistakes and gives you the flexibility to make changes or additions to your notes as needed. Though both the summary paper and the erasable pen are a little more costly than other products, they are well worth the investment in your education.

If the tools you have in your hands right now are not exactly as described above, set yourself up as close to it as possible to continue to learn more about notetaking.

Draw a three-inch margin on your note paper and keep your pen handy.

Effective Notetaking Habits

Now that you have the tools necessary for taking good notes, there are some effective notetaking habits that you should be aware of that are very easy to use.

Preview Reading Assignments before Class. If, according to your syllabus or your instructor's comments, you know that Chapter 4 will be discussed in your next computer programming class, it is an excellent idea to spend a few minutes previewing or skimming the chapter *before* class. This will give you some background knowledge about the topic, which will help you to take good notes. You will also understand the information better, which helps you learn the material more easily.

Start Each Day with a Fresh Piece of Paper. Every page of your notes is like a photo of what happens on a given day. By starting each day with a fresh piece of paper, you will keep your photos separate and leave yourself room to add information as the term goes on.

Write on Only One Side of Your Paper. Writing on one side of your paper gives you open space on the other side to summarize the notes on the opposite page or draw mind maps that we will be discussing later in this chapter.

Always Date and Title Every Page.   If you write the date and the title of topics being covered at the top of each page, you will give yourself an easy reference guide to follow when you study your notes. If you take more than one page of notes in the same class, number the pages in order on the top right-hand side as pg. 1, pg. 2, etc. or other numbering you prefer.

Date and title your note paper right now.
Use the title of "Notetaking in Class"
(See Figure 9–2)

Figure 9–2
Dated and Titled Note
Paper

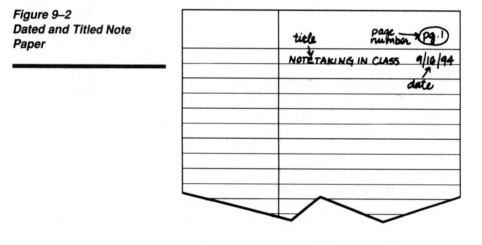

Write in the Shortest Form Possible.   When taking notes from an instructor, you do not have a lot of time to write down everything that is said, nor should you. Since we do not remember complete sentences, it is a waste of time to write them down. Instead, by using abbreviations and key words, you will be able to get the important information in a shortened form.

Use Abbreviations.   Using **abbreviations**, or shortened words or phrases, makes notetaking easier. They are easy to use once you establish your own style of abbreviating. You are already familiar with some abbreviations, but you will want to create some of your own. A simple way of creating your own abbreviations is to either *shorten the word, use a symbol,* or *omit vowels.* For example, if you are discussing "forms of communication" and the word "communication" is often repeated in your notes, you can shorten the word to "comm." If you are discussing a topic having to do with money, you can use the symbol "$" in your notes. If you are discussing "management," you can omit vowels and use "mngmnt" or an even shorter term "mgmt."

In the following list, the left side gives you a common word and the right side is for your shortened version of the word. Some are very simple while others will make you think. Use your imagination and creativity as long as you can remember what you have written.

Common Word or Term	My Abbreviation	Common Word or Term	My Abbreviation
abbreviation	abbrev.	decrease	
communication	comm.	equals	
money	$	and	
management	mgmt	definition	
chapter		plus	
North		with	
South		without	
East		therefore	
West		for example	
pages		percentage	
and so forth		number	
government		computer	
introduction		important	
association		building	
paragraph		something	
greater than		business	
less than		employer	
increase		employee	

Can you think of any other abbreviations you can use in your area(s) of study? List them below.

_____   _____

_____   _____

_____   _____

_____   _____

Use Key Words.   Using *key words*, as you learned in Chapter 7, is another good way of taking notes in a short form. Key words are the larger, more important words in a sentence. By looking to write only key words, you save time, concentrate on the main ideas, and end up with fewer words to study.

Read the following complete sentence. Then read the key words that could serve as your notes. Notice how easy it is to go from writing seven words to only three without losing meaning.

<u>Complete Sentence</u>:

The results of the test were conclusive.

<u>Key Words</u>:

Test results conclusive.

Now it's your turn to try to come up with your own versions of the following sentences. You can use abbreviations to make your notes as short as possible. After you have written your notes, reread them to see if they are understandable. If not, make changes.

Example:

Sentence: Advertising is the most expensive part of a new business venture.

My Notes: <u>Advrtsng = most $ new business</u>

An encyclopedia article is the best place to start researching a topic.

_____

Daily sales figures need to be completed by closing time.

_____

Computers have eliminated many jobs, but also made people work longer hours.

_____

Your most important job-hunting tool is your resume.

_____

As a secretary, you will have to take notes of important meetings and type them up for the record.

_____

_____

When making airline reservations, be aware of "black-out" periods. These are times when discounts and special fares are not available.

_____

_____

After you write a check, you should record the details of each transaction including the date, check number, to whom the check was written and for how much, in your bank transaction book.

_____

_____

_____

Learning to write in key words definitely takes concentration as well as some practice, but the time and energy you use to learn this will save you time and energy when you review your notes and study for exams.

Use Your Own Words. Whenever you take notes, there is rarely a need to write word for word what the instructor says. If you are instructed to write something exactly as it is said, then use your instructor's words. If you are writing notes on your own based on the information in the lecture, learn to use your own words instead of the lecturer's. Abbreviations and key words help make this possible. Writing your own words forces you to understand what is said before you write.

IDENTIFYING WHAT IS IMPORTANT

Being a good notetaker means being an active and skilled observer and listener. Finding and writing the appropriate information is easy once you know what you are watching and listening for. *Know that there is no right or wrong information to write down, only too much or too little.*

If you watch and listen carefully to your instructors, their actions and words will help you to quickly identify the important information.

Instructor Personality Clues

Almost everything an instructor says is important, but there are specific actions that an instructor takes to let you know that the information is important enough to write down. Think about some of the teachers you have had in the past. What did they do or say to let you know that something they said was important enough to write down?

1. _____
2. _____
3. _____
4. _____
5. _____

The most obvious clue is when they *tell you it's important.* They may say something like "This will be on the test," or, "You need to know this." Unfortunately, they don't always make it this easy.

If you listen carefully, you will sometimes hear your instructor repeat the information. *Repetition* is another easy clue for identifying the important information to write down. The use of repetition is common when describing a new vocabulary term, when there is an important name or date to be remembered, or when there is a difficult concept being presented. Listen carefully to your instructors and learn to identify their repetition.

Another clue is when they *write information on the board or overhead.* Do you think that you will have good notes by only writing what the instructor puts on the board? Many students believe that these are the only notes they need. Typically, though, what instructors put on the board is mostly supplementary, or supporting information, to their lectures. It does not usually represent all of the important information. As a result, learn to use the notes on the board as supporting information to the day's lecture topic.

If you watch and listen to your instructors carefully, you will be able to hear *changes in their voices and see changes in their facial expressions.* Because your instructors are human, when they are describing something exciting or of high interest to them, their voices and facial expressions will change. Think about your instructors and what they do. Do their voices get louder or softer? Do they speak faster or slower? Do their faces and eyes "light up"? Do their eyes become intense and stare more than usual? Do their faces get flushed with color? Some instructors actually get so excited about their topic that they perspire and breathe heavily! If any of these changes occur, it is in your best interest to pay close attention to what they are saying and take some notes. If your instructor is excited about something, or finds an idea interesting, chances are pretty good you will see it again, most likely on a test.

Sometimes you discover too late that an idea is important to write down when the instructor uses "the pause." A *pause* is when an instructor stops speaking for a few moments; it is used to give you time to write down what he or she just said. If you were paying attention and the instructor paused, then the pause would be welcome as a time to write. If you were not listening, however, or daydreaming, then the quiet in the room will capture your attention. Other students will be furiously writing while you are wondering what you just missed. If this happens to you, use the active learning technique of asking your instructor to repeat what he or she just said.

Many instructors will provide you with *handouts* related to the topic you are discussing in class. These handouts are important to make note of so that you remember to review them while you are studying. A simple note such as "review handout mgmt styles—9/16 class" is sufficient for this purpose.

Now that you have learned more about an instructor's personality clues, photocopy Figure 9–3 and answer the questions on this form in several of your next classes as an exercise in developing your listening and notetaking skills.

Figure 9–3
Getting to Know Your Instructor's Personality Clues

Your Name _____

Class Name _____ Instructor's Name _____

Today's Topic (s) _____ Today's Date _____

This form is to be used after you have completed reading and learning about your instructor's personality clues. Photocopy this form as many times as you need and complete it in its entirety. Use one form for each class you attend.

Getting to Know Your Instructor's Personality Clues

Did your instructor use any of the common personality clues? Check those that apply and give examples of how they used them. If they use other clues not already discussed, include them at the end.

_____ They Tell You It's Important _____

What did they say? _____

What did you do? _____

_____ Repetition _____

What did they say? _____

What did you do? _____

_____ Write Information on the Board or Overhead _____

What did they say? _____

What did you do? _____

_____ Voice Changes _____

What did they say? _____

What did you do? _____

_____ Facial Expressions _____

What did they say? _____

What did you do? _____

_____ Pauses _____

What did they say? _____

What did you do? _____

_____ Handouts _____

Were they related to your topic? _____

What did you do with them? _____

_____ Other _____

What did they say? _____

What did you do? _____

Based on the information you wrote on this sheet, what are some possible test questions that your instructor could ask? Do you have enough information to answer them in your notes?

Possible Test Questions:

1. _____

_____

2. _____

_____

3. _____

_____

4. _____

_____

5. _____

_____

Instructor Verbal Clues

Not only is the way an instructor delivers the information important, but also what the instructor specifically says. What follows are descriptions of some of the common important verbal clues that an instructor uses to tell you something is important enough to take notes on. This information is also commonly found on tests.

Definitions.   When an instructor is teaching you about a new topic, chances are there are new terms that go with it. For example, let's say today's topic is automation. "Automation" as defined by your instructor is "mechanical tools that do a job with less human effort." Your instructor gives you an example of a computer. Your notes could look similar to this:

Automation = mechanical tools that do job w/ less human effort (e.g., a computer)
new word   *what is it?*   *example*
or concept

What are some of your definition examples based on the classes you take? Use a similar format to the above for writing your examples. Refer to your notebook or textbook for definitions if necessary.

1. _____
2. _____
3. _____
4. _____
5. _____

Description.   Continuing with the same automation topic, the instructor may now describe in more detail what is meant by automation. "Automation was developed to make work more efficient. If a secretary makes a mistake on a letter typed on a typewriter, then the letter would have to be retyped in its entirety. With a word processor computer, the secretary only has to recall the letter in the computer and make necessary changes, which saves time and increases the amount of work that can be done in a day."

Your notes could continue to resemble these:

computer = > efficient than typewriter, saves time & ↑ amt of work in day.
description   *what are its qualities?*

Can you think of several examples of when your instructor has described information? Refer to your notebook or textbook if necessary.

Write your examples below using the good notetaking ideas suggested in this chapter.

1. _____

_____

2. _____

_____

3. _____

_____

Compare and Contrast.   **Comparing** is used when looking at things that are similar and **contrasting** is used when looking at things that are different. Continuing with the same example, suppose your instructor went on to say, "There are some obvious similarities between a typewriter and a computer. They both have keys that produce typed information, they are both found in offices, and they are commonly used by secretaries and typists. But this is where the similarities end. Computers produce information much faster than the typewriter. Their 'brains,' called memory, can be programmed to do many more functions than a typewriter and can save the information for future use."

Your notes need to reflect these similarities and differences because they are fair game for a test. You could expect this instructor to ask on a test "What are some similarities and differences between a typewriter and a computer?" or "Compare and contrast the typewriter and the computer."

There are many ways to write these notes. Your notes should answer the question "What is it like and what is it unlike?" One good example is as follows:

Typewriter vs. Computer
    Similarities
        —keys produce typed info
        —found in offices
        —used by secretaries and typists
    Differences
        —Comp's faster
        —Comp's have a memory for programming
        —Comp's can save info for future

These notes are written in an informal outline that is explained in more detail in the next section of this chapter.

Can you think of an example of when your instructor has compared and/or contrasted information? Refer to your notebook or textbook if necessary. Write your examples below using the good notetaking ideas suggested in this chapter.

_____

_____

_____

_____

Chronological Order. **Chronological order** is the same as *time order* and *step-by-step order*. In this class discussion on automation, the instructor may tell you the date of when the first typewriter was created and then continue giving you dates through the development of automation and computers. Your notes would need to accurately document the dates and what happened during each one.

1867 = 1st manual typewrtr

1956 = 1st electronic typewrtr

1964 = 1st word-processing computer

Your instructor could tell you step by step how to turn on a computer. Your notes should include all of the steps of the process.

How to turn on a computer

Step #1—Turn on hard drive. Wait 5 seconds

Step #2—Turn on monitor

Step #3—Turn on printer

Can you think of an example of when your instructor has used chronological order in a lecture? Refer to your notebook or textbook if necessary. Write your example below using the good notetaking ideas suggested in this chapter.

_____

_____

_____

_____

Classification. **Classification** means what class, group, or category your subject is in. An easy example is that a college student in the first year of study is in the freshman class. In the second year, he or she is in the sophomore class, and so on. Computers belong in the category of automation. Almost every concept you learn about belongs to a class, group, or category of information. Your notes should be able to answer the question "To which class, group, or category does this information belong?"

Can you think of an example of classification from the classes you take? Refer to your notebook or textbook if necessary. Write your example below using the good notetaking ideas suggested in this chapter.

_____

_____

_____

_____

Cause and Effect. **Cause and effect** information is described as if something happens (the _cause_), and then something happens as a result (the _effect_). If you don't turn the lights out when you leave a room (the cause), your electric bill will increase (the effect). If you put your finger into a live electrical socket (the cause), you will get an electrical shock (the effect). If you try to mix water with oil (the cause), they will not mix (the effect).

Can you think of an example of cause and effect from the classes you are taking? Refer to your notebook or textbook if necessary. Write your example below using the good notetaking ideas suggested in this chapter.

_____

_____

_____

_____

Now that you have learned more about an instructor's verbal clues, photocopy Figure 9–4 and answer the questions on this form in several of your next classes as an exercise in developing your listening and notetaking skills.

Figure 9–4
Getting to Know Your Instructor's Verbal Clues

Your Name _____

Class Name_____ Instructor's Name _____

Today's Topic (s) _____Today's Date _____

This form is to be used after you have completed reading and learning about your instructor's verbal clues. Photocopy this form as many times as you need and complete it in its entirety. Use one form for each class you attend.

Getting to Know Your Instructor's Verbal Clues

Did your instructor give you any information from his or her verbal clues? Check those that apply and give examples of how he or she used them.

_____ **Definition**

What needed to be defined?	What is it?
1._____	_____
2._____	_____
3._____	_____

_____ **Description**

What was described?	What are its qualities?
1._____	_____
2._____	_____
3._____	_____

_____ **Compare and Contrast**

What was compared and/ or contrasted?	What is it like or unlike?
1._____	_____
2._____	_____
3._____	_____

_____ **Chronological Order**

What order was given?	How did it develop?
1._____	_____
2._____	_____
3._____	_____

_____ **Classification**

What was being discussed?	To what class, group, or category does it belong?
1._____	_____
2._____	_____
3._____	_____

_____ **Cause and Effect**

What was being discussed?	What was the cause and what was the effect?
1._____	_____
2._____	_____
3._____	_____

Based on the information you wrote on this sheet, what are some possible test questions that your instructor could ask? Do you have enough information to answer them in your notes?

Possible Test Questions:

1. _____
   _____
2. _____
   _____
3. _____
   _____
4. _____
   _____
5. _____
   _____

HOW TO TAKE NOTES

Notice that up to this point, you have not been instructed in any specific notetaking method; rather, we have spent time on what all good notetakers do. Now you will be given more information on what form to write your information. Hopefully you will find these proven methods useful. *Remember, though, that you are to use and adapt the information to your own style of learning and notetaking.*

Before writing anything down, it is helpful to know your instructor's lecture style. If your instructor is sequential in his or her lecture style, like they are speaking from an outline, it will be fairly easy to take organized and logical notes. If your instructor is random, it will be more challenging to keep organized, logical notes, but still possible to write down the important information in a more random format. (For more information on identifying teaching styles, see Chapter 2.)

Both sequential learners and random learners need to take good notes from these styles of instruction. Here are two recommended methods to choose from. The first method, *The Cornell Method of Note Taking*, will probably be favored by a sequential learner while the second method, *Mind Mapping* will probably be favored by the random learner. Both learners, however, can learn something from both methods depending upon the style of the instructor.

The Cornell Method of Note Taking

The Cornell Method is a unique notetaking format that has been proven highly effective by college students for over forty years. It was developed by Walter Pauk, a professor at Cornell University (Ithaca, NY) in the early 1950s. He found that many students were not doing well on their exams, even though they were doing everything students are supposed to do, including attending classes, doing their assignments, and taking their tests. He found that the students were lacking notetaking skills and an effective method for taking good notes.

Look at Figure 9–5. Notice the labels that have been added to indicate the parts of your summary paper: "body" on the right side of the margin and "recall column" on the left. Each of these two columns is used in a specific way.

Figure 9–5
Labeling the Parts of the
Summary Paper

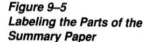

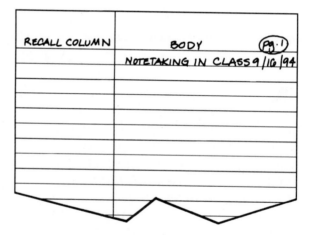

The Body. The **body**, or the right-hand side of the margin, is where you want to write the bulk of your notes. These notes should be in an *informal outline* that organizes your thoughts on the page. Outlines make it easy for you to study from and quickly let you know which ideas are more important than others. An informal outline looks like Figure 9–6.

Figure 9–6
An Informal Outline

Informal Outline	= Organizes thoughts
They look like →	Theme, Topic, or Main idea
	- supporting idea or info.
	- detail
	- example
	- detail
	- example
	- supporting idea or info.
	- detail
	- example
OR numbered →	Theme, Topic, or Main idea
	1. supporting idea or info.
	a. detail
	example
	b. detail
	example
	2. Supporting idea or info.
	a. detail
	example

Learning to take notes in informal outlines becomes easier with practice. Notice that the most important ideas are closer to the margin, while the supporting ideas and details are indented and farther away. Be careful not to indent too much because you will quickly run out of space to take your notes. You can use a symbol like a dash to indicate a new detail or you can use numbers and letters. If an idea needs to be continued to the next line, keep similar items lined up. This keeps your notes easy to read. If all of your notes were lined up next to the margin, it would be impossible to quickly decide which ideas are more important than others.

Skipping lines between main ideas gives you the flexibility to add or change your notes.

Figure 9–7 contains texts of information for you to begin practicing your own informal outlines. Use summary paper and write your notes *only* on the right side of your margin. You can work individually or with other classmates. While you are working, ask yourself which ideas seem to be the most important? Which are less important? Why? What do *you* think is the best way to write the notes? (Keep in mind that no two notetakers are the same.) By sharing your ideas with others, you may get ideas that will help make your notetaking easier.

Figure 9–7
Sample Paragraphs for Practicing Informal Outlining

Using the following paragraphs and several pieces of summary paper, begin practicing taking notes in informal outlines like Figure 9–6. Read each text *first* before writing anything. This will help you decide which ideas are more important than others and what information you actually want to take notes on. This is similar to what you have to do in a classroom—listen first, then write. Remember to use as many effective notetaking techniques as possible.

Text #1

Learning is an activity of one who learns. It may be intentional or random; it may involve acquiring new information or skills. It is usually accompanied by change in behavior and goes on throughout life.

Text #2

Success in your classes depends upon effective notetaking and study techniques. To be successful, you must be able to record and to study a variety of lecture information. Lecture information is presented in many different formats. Some instructors prefer giving main ideas with details, others prefer a lot of vocabulary building with related examples. Some enjoy using a variety of visual aids, like handouts or overheads, while some just use the blackboard. The Cornell Method of Note Taking can be used with all lecture formats. It helps students simplify their record of the lecture material, while providing a simple study technique at the same time.

Text #3

American public schools did not always exist. Education actually began in the home with the mother being the first teacher. Mothers taught their children reading, writing, and arithmetic as well as Bible education. They were also in charge of teaching their children discipline. As the youngsters grew, the mothers continued teaching their daughters in sewing, cooking, and homemaking, while the sons learned the apprenticeship of their father.

Text #4

People are not born with background knowledge. Background knowledge accumulates starting at birth and is the result of whatever the person is involved in, who influences them, what they learned in school, what they read, what they see on television, who their friends are, and so on. This background knowledge is a valuable tool, especially for reading. Possessing background knowledge helps readers read faster. They also read with higher levels of concentration and comprehension.

To build background knowledge while reading, good readers ask themselves three simple questions before getting started. The first question is

"What do I need to know?" If readers can answer this question, then there is a purpose in mind. The second question is "How well do I already know it?" or "How much background knowledge do I already have?" A lot of background knowledge means faster reading with greater interest than if they had none. The last question is "What do I need to know?" It is the responsibility of the reader to seek out information he or she is unfamiliar with. This is the key to building background knowledge.

Text #5

What makes people successful? The behavior most common to successful people is that they listen respectfully to everyone. Close observation reveals that listening is a set of behaviors that involves more than simply hearing another's words. Making eye contact with the speaker is important for making a person believe you are hearing what he or she is saying. Responsive facial expressions, such as a quizzical look when you don't understand what the person is saying or widening your eyes when you are in disbelief, are appropriate and let the speaker know you are listening. Nodding your head and saying "Uh-huh" or "I see" from time to time lets the speaker know you are hearing him or her. Sitting or standing in attentive postures tells the speaker you are prepared and receiving his or her message. Avoiding distractions like a telephone ringing makes the speaker feel important. Asking the speaker questions will help clarify your understanding as well as let the speaker know you really heard what was said.

The Recall Column. The **recall column** is the most important part of this method. This left-hand column is used for any information you want to recall or remember based on the notes you took on the right side. Information in the recall column can be simply a word, like a vocabulary word, or a name, or a date. It can also be a mathematical formula or the number of details you want to remember. One of the best uses of the recall column is to make up your own question about your notes on the right that will help you predict what may be on a test.

Read the notes in Figure 9–8. Imagine that you are the student who took these notes and you have a test on them next class. Look specifically at the recall column and the notes in the body directly across from it. These notes demonstrate four examples of how the recall column can be used. The first example begins with the word "Lectures." This is a *vocabulary term* to know for your test, so it is set apart in the recall column for you to recall.

The second example, reading down the recall column, is the *question format.* A question, created to reflect the information in the body, is your best tool for knowing what may be on the test. Based on the notes you took, would it be fair for the instructor to ask on your test, "What are five things you can do in class for taking good notes?" If you can answer this question while you are studying, then you will easily answer it on the test.

Figure 9–8
Student's Notes Using the Recall Column

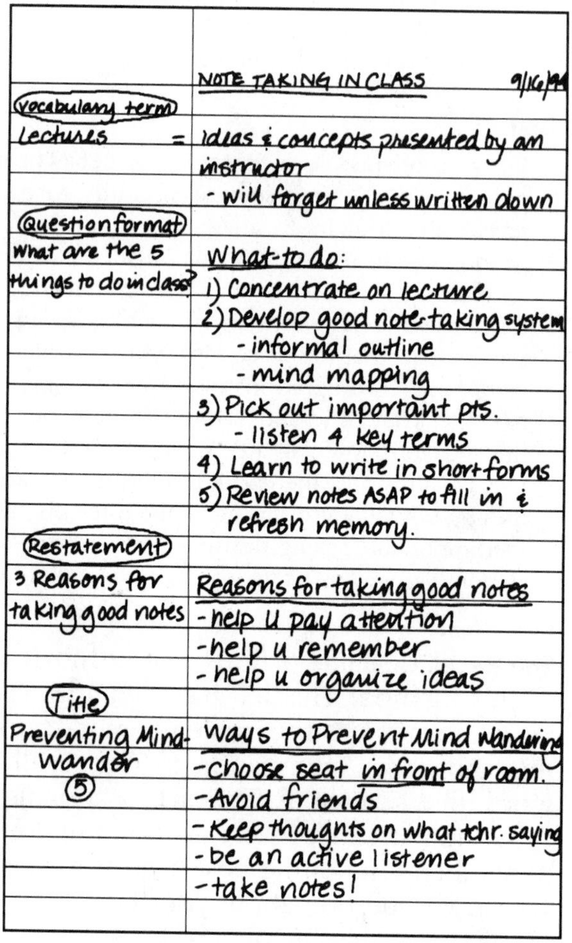

	NOTE TAKING IN CLASS 9/16/94
(Vocabulary term)	
Lectures =	ideas & concepts presented by an instructor
	- will forget unless written down
(Question format)	
What are the 5 things to do in class?	What to do:
	1) Concentrate on lecture
	2) Develop good note-taking system
	- informal outline
	- mind mapping
	3) Pick out important pts.
	- listen 4 key terms
	4) Learn to write in short-forms
	5) Review notes ASAP to fill in & refresh memory.
(Restatement)	
3 Reasons for taking good notes	Reasons for taking good notes
	- help U pay attention
	- help u remember
	- help u organize ideas
(Title)	
Preventing Mind-wander (5)	Ways to Prevent Mind Wandering
	- choose seat in front of room.
	- Avoid friends
	- Keep thoughts on what tchr. saying
	- be an active listener
	- take notes!

The third example is the *restatement*, where you rephrase what is in the body of your notes such as "three reasons for taking good notes." If you can remember all three reasons while you study, then answering them on a test is easy.

The fourth example is creating a *title*, based on the notes in the body, and writing it in the recall column. The circled number "5" under this title indicates that you have five things to remember about preventing mind wandering according to your instructor's lecture.

The recall column is usually filled in *after* class, preferably the day of the class or at the latest, the day after. This is so that you don't forget what happened in your class. It is quite challenging to fill in the recall column while you are in class because taking notes in the body takes most of your time.

You can, however, learn, while in class, to take notes using the recall column for information such as a name, date, event, etc. If you are taking notes on anything that needs to be defined, you can immediately place the word on the left side and then define it on the right. You can put topics that are being described on the left and their descriptions on the right. You can write topics that are being compared and contrasted on the left and what it is like and/or unlike on the right. You can write a math formula on the left and how to figure it out on the right. And instead of writing topics and other main ideas in the body of your notes, you can immediately use the recall column to avoid rewriting them there later.

Before completing your recall column, add missing information and cross out the unimportant information in the body of your notes. Then look at your notes and decide what word, question, restatement, or title you need to put in your recall column that will help you to remember everything that is important on the page.

Using the recall column makes studying easy. It is an active way of reviewing your notes and making your learning more effective. Cover up the body of your notes with a blank piece of paper and begin testing yourself based on the information you wrote in the recall column. You can recite it aloud or write the information on the blank paper to compare with your actual notes when you have finished quizzing yourself. The goal is to recall all of the information accurately. Keep working at it until you get it all. As another way to ensure you know the notes, place your blank paper over your recall column and test yourself on the information in your recall column.

Using the recall column means you should never have to rewrite your notes again. Even if your notes are messy, you can neaten them by using the recall column to organize and clarify. The recall column also acts like a flash card, giving you an active way to review your notes.

In what ways do you think you can use the recall column in the classes you are currently taking?

Recall Column	Body
vocabulary term	its definition

Mind Mapping

Mind Mapping is a creative way to take notes that organizes ideas through visual patterns and pictures. For some of us, worrying about an outline or any other form while taking notes can keep us from focusing on getting the information from the lecture. Mind Mapping allows flexibility for jotting down the information that we need. When you first look at a Mind Map, the information doesn't seem to be organized at all. At a closer look, you will see that it is very organized with a natural association of ideas in clusters or groups. Each cluster of ideas creates a visual picture, which helps you remember the ideas better.

To create a Mind Map, start in the center of your plain, unlined white paper with your main idea or topic and branch the supporting ideas and details in various directions, as in Figure 9–9.

If you are a sequential learner in a random instructor's class, Mind Mapping will help you get the ideas of the instructor down on paper without worrying about the proper order. Because there is little order in the random instructor's lecture anyway, it is best not to try to put order into the lecture during class. Try jotting your thoughts down in this form, and then for review make an outline from the mapped notes later. It is for this outline that summary paper is useful when creating a Mind Map.

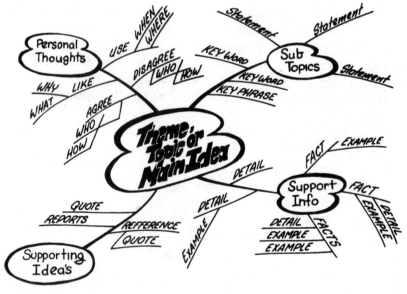

Figure 9–9
The Creation of a Mind Map

The extra step of restructuring your notes into a more sequential order is a good review, essential for learning success. By taking notes in this form, you will also be better able to see the "big picture," the connections and the relationships, all to be asked for by the random instructor on tests.

If you are a random learner in a sequential instructor's class, Mind Mapping will ensure that you are able to get all the details and facts down quickly during the lecture because the sequential instructor will be testing you on all those details and facts. When you, as a random learner, review your notes, you can add more details to the map, color code the main ideas, and number items in terms of importance. You can outline the information if you wish.

Look at Figures 9–10 and 9–11. These particular Mind Maps contain all the key ideas that were discussed in Chapter 2 about identifying teaching styles. Figure 9–10 is a sequential approach to Mind Mapping while Figure 9–11 is a more random approach. Though the styles look different, they are both considered to be Mind Maps.

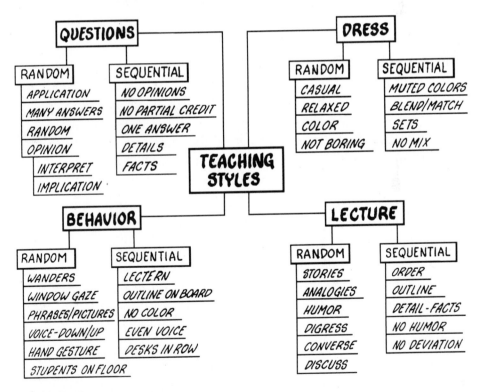

Figure 9–10
Sequential Approach to Mind Map of Chapter 2

Figure 9–11
Random Approach to Mind Map of Chapter 2

Follow the flow of ideas in these Mind Maps by connecting one idea to the next. Compare these notes to the information you read and remember the different styles of the random and sequential instructor in Chapter 2. Then answer the questions that follow:

What do you notice about the Mind Maps?_____

_____

Could an informal outline be created from the maps?_____
If so, how would you do it?_____

_____

Are all the main ideas and details contained on the maps?_____
Are the main ideas separated from one another?_____
Are small words such as "of, at, the, a, when" and other unimportant words omitted?_____
Is it easy to determine relationships, connections, similarities, and differences about the information by looking at these maps?_____
Is there space to add more information or details later if necessary?

_____

In Figure 9–11, the added pictures will also help your memory. This is because we remember pictures better than words. If you enjoy doodling, you may find this method an outlet for what you do naturally.

Adding different print sizes, shapes, and colors to your Mind Map is an easy and fun way to review your notes. This personalization will improve later recall of the information. If you have notes in an outline, you can create a Mind Map from your outline as a study tool. And when you have finished creating your Mind Maps, you can put them up around your study area like you would a picture. The more you look at something, the more you learn.

By choosing and working effectively with a notetaking method that fits your learning style, you will possess a valuable tool for your learning success. Using the other methods will also help you succeed with instructors whose styles are different than yours. The most important thing to remember about notetaking is to use whatever method(s) works best for you.

SUMMARY

1. Of the many important reasons to take notes in class, by far the most important is to improve your concentration.

2. Getting prepared to take notes includes having the appropriate tools for the job. Without them, the job cannot be done well.

3. The basis of good notes is having effective notetaking habits. They include using abbreviations, key words, and your own words.

4. Learning to watch for your instructor's personality clues will provide you with information about what is important enough to write down and what you might be tested on.

5. Learning to listen for your instructor's verbal clues will also provide you with information about what is important enough to write down and what you might be tested on.

6. The Cornell Method of Note Taking is an effective method for taking sequential notes. Learning to use the recall column will not only aid in organizing your thoughts but also give you a tool to study from.

7. Mind Mapping is an effective method for taking random notes. It is a creative way to organize ideas through visual patterns and pictures.

REVIEW

Using your own words, answer the following questions based on the information you learned in this chapter.

1. In your view, what are the most important reasons for you to take notes in your classes?_____

_____

_____

2. What tools do you need to take good notes and why?_____

_____

_____

_____

_____

3. What are some effective notetaking habits? Write as many as you can remember. _____

_____

_____

_____

_____

_____

4. What are some personality clues that your instructors use in class? What do you think they mean?

Clues	Meaning?

5. What are some verbal clues that your instructors use? What do you think they mean?

Clues	Meaning?

6. Of the two methods recommended in this chapter, is there one that you think will work better for you? If so, why? If not, why not?_____

_____

_____

_____

_____

7. If you are a sequential learner in a random instructor's class, what would you suggest in order to take good notes?_____

_____

_____

_____

_____

8. If you are a random learner in a sequential instructor's class, what would you suggest in order to take good notes?_____

_____

_____

_____

_____

9. From everything you read about and learned in this chapter, what pieces of information are the most valuable to you and why?_____

_____

_____

_____

_____

CHAPTER 10

TAKING EFFECTIVE NOTES FROM TEXTBOOKS

LEARNING OBJECTIVES

After studying and working with the information in this chapter, you should be able to:

1. Identify THE reason for taking notes from your textbooks.

2. Differentiate between just reading and reading actively.

3. Define highlighting and explain the most effective way to use it.

4. Distinguish between two types of margin notes and explain how to use them.

5. Describe full notes and discuss when to use them.

6. Begin taking effective notes from your own reading assignments.

T aking notes from your textbooks is a way to organize and remember what you read.

At this point, you already have quite a bit of background knowledge on how to become actively involved in your learning. In order to fully understand this chapter, several chapters are worth recalling to refresh your memory or to preview if you have not worked with them yet.

In Chapter 1, you learned about the differences between an active and passive learner and what you can do to become more active. In Chapter 3, you started thinking about the relationship between mind-wandering and concentration. It was suggested that you begin keeping a list of "Things I Can Do to Reduce Mind-Wandering While I Study." Finally, you focused on how you can increase your concentration while reading by previewing in Chapter 6 and by applying simple techniques for reading faster in Chapter 7.

In this chapter, you will once again focus on how to improve your concentration while reading, but this time through notetaking. In Chapter 9, you learned what all good notetakers do as well as several ways that you can use these methods for your own style. In this chapter, you will build on that knowledge by adding information on (1) using a highlighter effectively, (2) using margin notes to make studying easier, and (3) taking full notes from your more complicated or technical texts.

Effective notetakers are more successful learners. Are you an effective notetaker? What methods do you use to capture the key concepts and information from your reading?

SELF-EVALUATION

The following self-evaluation will give you an idea of how familiar, or unfamiliar, you are with some of the topics and terms discussed in this chapter. After reading each statement, circle the letter (Y, S, or N) most appropriate to your answer. Please answer honestly, rate yourself at the end, and then complete the information for Chapter 10 on page 375 in Appendix A.

Y = yes; frequently   **S** = sometimes   **N** = no; never

1. I take some form of notes from my textbook
   reading assignments.   Y S N
2. I know how to use a highlighter effectively.   Y S N
3. I know how to create margin notes in my texts.   Y S N
4. I can find the author's outline in my text and can
   take effective notes from it.   Y S N
5. I take notes from my texts using key words.   Y S N
6. I abbreviate words when I take notes from my texts. Y S N
7. I mark areas I don't understand in my text so I can
   ask my instructor about it.   Y S N
8. I know how to study from my texts without a lot
   of rereading.   Y S N
9. When I read my texts I use note taking as an active
   way to concentrate and learn.   Y S N
10. I learn more when I take effective notes from
    my texts.   Y S N

<u>Rate Yourself</u>

Number of Ys _____ x 100=

Number of Ss _____ x 50=

Number of Ns _____ x 10=

Total =

. . . **R**ead, mark, learn and inwardly digest them.

- Book of Common Prayer

WHY TAKE NOTES FROM YOUR TEXTBOOKS?

Taking notes in your classes is a way to organize and remember what is discussed. Taking notes from your textbooks is a way to organize and remember what you read. Without notetaking during both of these activities, your learning is more passive than active.

Most textbooks are nonfiction. Nonfiction, or factual, reading is more difficult to follow than fiction. Typically, there is no story or characters to follow, just a lot of facts and information. When you sit down to read your nonfiction textbooks, how good is your concentration? Can you concentrate easily or are you constantly fighting your wandering mind? If you are like most readers, you may have trouble keeping your concentration on textbook material, especially if it is unfamiliar or new information.

If you remember the section in Chapter 9 on notetaking in your classes, *the most important reason* to take notes in class is to improve concentration. So in order to improve your concentration while reading, once again, taking notes is the answer.

Since a lot of your background knowledge is gained from the textbooks you read, it is to your advantage to use as many tools as possible to make your learning effective.

LEARNING FROM YOUR TEXTS

When you are given a textbook reading assignment, knowing you will be tested on it later, what do you do to learn the information on the page? Be specific. _____

_____

_____

_____

_____

_____

In your opinion, and based on what you wrote above, what activities do you do that are shown in Figure 10–1? Circle the activity or activities that you feel your reading and study habits most closely resemble. [Note: The staircase on the right is for passive readers and notetakers while the staircase on the left is for active readers and notetakers.]

Now that you have established what you currently do, let's take a closer look at the learning habits of the passive and active learners.

Just Reading versus Reading Actively

On the Active Learning Staircase in Figure 10–1, *just reading* is the most passive way to learn. It means that you read from the begin-

Figure 10–1
Active versus Passive
Learning Staircases for
Notetaking

ning to the end of your assignments without previewing. It also assumes that you do not take notes. Your mind wanders frequently and you lose your concentration easily.

Reading actively is much more than "just reading." It means that you are using some or all of the following reading efficiency tools (see Chapters 6, 7, and 8 for more information):

❏ Previewing the chapter—to gain background knowledge

❏ Reading in key words—to read faster and concentrate more

❏ Reading in phrases—to read faster and concentrate more

❏ Reading with a pacer—to read faster and concentrate more

❏ Adjusting your reading speed—to not waste time

By reading actively, you are reducing mind-wandering while learning at the same time. Notice how reading actively starts you higher up on the Active Learning Staircase. When you add active notetaking activities like highlighting, writing margin notes, and/or taking full notes effectively, you climb even higher on the staircase. Reading actively with effective notetaking is certainly a powerful learning combination!

Highlighting

Highlighting is a step up the Active Learning Staircase. *Highlighting* means using a yellow (or pink, or blue, or green, etc.) highlighter pen to highlight, or underline, the important information in your texts. The reason it makes you a more active learner is that you are actively looking for, or concentrating on finding, the important information. It leaves you less time and energy to mind wander.

Highlighting, the way that a passive student does it, is *not* effective. Passive students find too much information to highlight. They often waste their time highlighting whole paragraphs and pages. When it comes time to study for a test, they again waste time because they end up having to reread everything they highlighted. Some use a fancy color-coding system that makes it more difficult to remember what color they used for what than to keep track of the important information.

Professor Claude Olney, the author of the study skills program "Where There's a Will, There's an A," said it best: "Highlighting postpones learning." What do *you* think he means by this statement?

_____

_____

_____

_____

When a passive learner highlights a paragraph, this action says, "This is important information but I am too lazy to learn it now. I will come back to it and reread it again at another time." Active learners highlight less and try to understand and learn as much as possible while they are reading. This avoids rereading it all and wasting their time later.

Highlighting effectively means to:

1. *Read the complete paragraph or section before highlighting anything.* This avoids highlighting too much. When you read, everything sometimes seems important because it is new or unfamiliar. If you can be patient and finish reading the paragraph or section, you will have a better understanding of how the ideas are related and what is really most important to highlight.

2. *Never highlight more than a few words or a phrase at a time.* Highlighting too much is a waste of time and not very effective as a study habit. Learning to highlight less can mean more learning. Within an important paragraph, you will find key words such as a vocabulary term, a name, an event, a dollar amount, a date, etc. Rarely is it necessary to highlight more than that. At most, you might highlight a phrase.

3. *Decide what is most important.* Keep in mind that what may be important to one student may not be to another. If you are worried that you did not highlight the "right" information, know that *there is no right or wrong highlighting, only too much or too little.*

When you buy your textbooks for the term, it is a good idea to avoid purchasing books with highlighted areas. Though it may mean buying a new book instead of a used book, it is an investment in your active learning process. What may have been important to the former owner of the book may not be to you. It also makes it difficult for you to read and make your own highlights.

Look at Figure 10–2A and then Figure 10–2B. These are examples of Brian's and Jake's use of highlighter.

Figure 10–2A

Brian's Highlighting Example Source: Joyce, Marilyn. Ergonomics: Humanizing the Automated Office. © 1989 South-Western Publishing Co. Reprinted with permission.

Ergonomics ["ergon" (work) + "nomos" (natural laws)] is the science of work. Specifically, it is the science that addresses people's performance and well-being in relation to their job tasks, their equipment, and their environment. The key to understanding the true value and role of ergonomics is knowing that an organization's most important resource is people. Therefore, anything that contributes to the performance, health and well-being, and commitment of the workforce is important to both the employer and the employee.

ERGONOMICS IN THE OFFICE ENVIRONMENT

As you might expect, ergonomics has become increasingly important in automated office environments where more and more workers are using computers as a tool for completing job tasks. Recently, several important organizations have endorsed ergonomics as a means of meeting the needs of workers in automated offices. For example, ergonomics has been endorsed as a solution to the problems of VDT* users by the Occupational Health and Safety Administration (OSHA), the American Medical Association (AMA), and the World Health Organization (WHO).

In a 1987 directive, OSHA made ergonomics and ergonomic training a priority. OSHA states," . . . the most fundamental strategy is to promote workplace education and awareness programs aimed at the maintenance of musculoskeletal health and the prevention of injuries." In addition, the OSHA model curriculum now includes ergonomics as one area to be included in a course of study on both the graduate and undergraduate levels.
* VDT = video display terminal

Figure 10–2B

Jake's Highlighting Example Source: Joyce, Marilyn. Ergonomics: Humanizing the Automated Office. © 1989 South-Western Publishing Co. Reprinted with permission.

Ergonomics ["ergon" (work) + "nomos" (natural laws)] is the science of work. Specifically, it is the science that addresses people's performance and well-being in relation to their job tasks, their equipment, and their environment. The key to understanding the true value and role of ergonomics is knowing that an organization's most important resource is people. Therefore, anything that contributes to the performance, health and well-being, and commitment of the workforce is important to both the employer and the employee.

ERGONOMICS IN THE OFFICE ENVIRONMENT

As you might expect, ergonomics has become increasingly important in automated office environments where more and more workers are using computers as a tool for completing job tasks. Recently, several important organizations have endorsed ergonomics as a means of meeting the needs of workers in automated offices. For example, ergonomics has been endorsed as a solution to the problems of VDT* users by the Occupational Health and Safety Administration (OSHA), the American Medical Association (AMA), and the World Health Organization (WHO).

In a 1987 directive, OSHA made ergonomics and ergonomic training a priority. OSHA states, " . . . the most fundamental strategy is to promote workplace education and awareness programs aimed at the maintenance of musculoskeletal health and the prevention of injuries." In addition, the OSHA model curriculum now includes ergonomics as one area to be included in a course of study on both the graduate and undergraduate levels.
* VDT = video display terminal

Which one will spend more time learning?_____

Which one will spend less time?_____

Why?_____

_____

_____

Using Brian's and Jake's examples as well as your own highlighting experiences, what are you going to do to make your highlighting effective?

_____

_____

_____

_____

_____

Creating Margin Notes

Margin notes are yet another step up the Active Learning Staircase. **Margin notes** are either summary notes or questions you create in the margin of your text based on the information you need to know. It is used just like the recall column in the Cornell Method of Note Taking.

Creating margin notes is an active form of notetaking because, once again, you are actively looking for, or concentrating on finding, the important information. You then take a step closer to learning the information by forcing yourself to either summarize the information or create a question and then write it in the margin. When it comes time to study, you will spend most of your time studying from your margin notes. As a result, you will have less information to reread as well as an effective, time-saving method for review.

Some of your textbooks may already have preprinted notes in the margins. There may be some important information from the text reprinted there. There may be vocabulary words and their meaning. Or there may be just white space on either the left or the right side of the text so you can create your own. Some texts do not have a lot of space in the margin, making it challenging to write as many margin notes as you might like. (If this is the case, you can instead write your margin notes in the recall column of a piece of summary paper. Indicate what page the notes are referring to in the body of your notes for later reference if needed.) Take a look through your own textbooks, including this one, and see how the margins are used, if at all.

It is best to use an erasable pen when you write in the margin of your texts. This will give you the flexibility to erase, change, or add to your notes. Avoid using pencils, as they have a tendency to smear and regular pens do not erase.

Margin notes are most effective if you:

1. *Read the complete paragraph or section before writing anything.* As discussed with highlighting, when you read, everything sometimes seems important because it is new or unfamiliar. If you can be patient and finish reading the paragraph or section, you will have a better understanding of how the ideas are related and what is really most important to summarize.

2. *Decide what is most important.* In some paragraphs, you may think everything is important to make a note about. In others, you may not think anything is important. Here again, *there is no right or wrong information to create margin notes about, only too much or too little.*

To select which information to write notes about, consider the following guidelines. Write margin notes if:

❑ You think you are going to be quizzed or tested on it

❑ You think you may need to know it for a class discussion or essay

❑ If the information is new or unfamiliar to you

3. *Write using your own words, key words, and abbreviations.* If you rewrote exactly what was printed in the text in your margin, you would be wasting your time and cluttering your margin with unnecessary words. Margin space is limited, so learning to write less is more effective. Learn to write margin notes using your own words, key words, and your own abbreviations. Other markings that you can add to your margin notes can include:

❑ Placing a question mark (?) in the margin next to information you do not understand to remind you to ask your instructor about it, or

❑ Placing an asterisk (*) next to very important information.

Can you think of any others?_____

Look at Figure 10–3A, Sandy's summary-in-the-margin notes, and 10–3B, Catherine's question-in-the-margin notes. These are two different ways that you can use the margin for notes.

Figure 10–3A
Sandy's Summary-in-the-Margin Notes Source: Joyce, Marilyn. Ergonomics: Humanizing the Automated Office. © 1989 South-Western Publishing Co. Reprinted with permission.

def. ergonomics

Ergonomics ["ergon" (work) + "nomos" (natural laws)] is the science of work. Specifically, it is the science that addresses people's performance and well-being in relation to their job tasks, their equipment, and their environment. The key to understanding the true value and role of ergonomics is knowing that an organization's most important resource is people. Therefore, anything that contributes to the performance, health and well-being, and commitment of the work-force is important to both the employer and the employee.

People = organize most imp asset

3 imp Contribution to employers & employee

ERGONOMICS IN THE OFFICE ENVIRONMENT

Ergon ↑ important
– computers
3 organizations endorse ergon. as way to meet office works med

As you might expect, ergonomics has become increasingly important in automated office environments where more and more workers are using computers as a tool for completing job tasks. Recently, several important organizations have endorsed ergonomics as a means of meeting the needs of workers in automated offices. For example, ergonomics has been endorsed as a solution to the problems of VDT users by the Occupational Health and Safety Administration (OSHA), the American Medical Association (AMA), and the World Health Organization (WHO).

1987 OSHA directive

In a 1987 directive, OSHA made ergonomics and ergonomic training a priority. OSHA states, " . . . the most fundamental strategy is to promote workplace education and awareness programs aimed at the maintenance of musculoskeletal health and the prevention of injuries." In addition, the OSHA model curriculum now includes ergonomics as one area to be included in a course of study on both the graduate and undergraduate levels.

* VDT = Video display terminal

Summary-in-the-Margin Notes. A **summary** is a brief statement or restatement of main points. It is a shortened version of what you find to be important in the text.

In the first paragraph of Sandy's text, you will see that there are three separate summaries in the margin. The information in each one could possibly show up on a test. The first one indicates

Figure 10–3B
Catherine's Question-in-the-Margin Notes Source: Joyce, Marilyn. Ergonomics: Humanizing the Automated Office. © 1989 South-Western Publishing Co. Reprinted with permission.

What is ergonomics?

What is an organization's most imp. resource?

What is imp. to both employer and employee? ③

Ergonomics ["ergon" (work) + "nomos" (natural laws)] is the science of work. Specifically, it is the science that addresses people's performance and well-being in relation to their job tasks, their equipment, and their environment. The key to understanding the true value and role of ergonomics is knowing that an organization's most important resource is ① people. Therefore, anything that ② contributes to the performance, health and well-being, and ③ commitment of the workforce is important to both the employer and the employee.

ERGONOMICS IN THE OFFICE ENVIRONMENT

Why is ergo. increasingly important?

What organizations endorsed ergon...? ③

As you might expect, ergonomics has become increasingly important in automated office environments where more and more workers are using computers as a tool for completing job tasks. Recently, several important organizations have endorsed ergonomics as a means of meeting the needs of workers in automated offices. For example, ergonomics has been endorsed as a solution to the problems of VDT* users by the Occupational Health and Safety Administration (OSHA), the American Medical Association (AMA), and the World Health Organization (WHO).

What happened in 1987? By whom?

What was said?

In a 1987 directive, OSHA made ergonomics and ergonomic training a priority. OSHA states, " . . . the most fundamental strategy is to promote workplace education and awareness programs aimed at the maintenance of musculoskeletal health and the prevention of injuries." In addition, the OSHA model curriculum now includes ergonomics as one area to be included in a course of study on both the graduate and undergraduate levels.

* VDT: Video display terminal

---

a definition she needs to remember. There is also a bracket surrounding the text that includes the definition in case she needs to quickly review it. *Using a bracket is a simpler and time-saving form of highlighting.*

The second summary indicates another important idea. Notice that the margin note is written in Sandy's own abbreviated language. Sandy does not think that the third note is as important as the others, but she expects she may be tested on it. Notice the numbering in the text to indicate each of the ideas she wants to recall. This type of numbering is effective when you have a series of related ideas to remember.

Question-in-the-Margin Notes. In the margin of Catherine's text, you will find questions. She prefers to summarize the important ideas as a question, similar to the questions her instructor may give on a test. The answer to each question is easily found by rereading the text next to the question. Notice that she uses her own form of abbreviation. Notice also that she indicates exactly how many things she needs to recall when there is more than one answer ("What is imp. to both the emplyer and the emplyee?" 3).

Combining Margin Notes and Effective Highlighting. Effective highlighting can be added to your margin notes to help quickly identify important ideas or reinforce others. Highlighting several words or phrases in addition to your margin notes can make for good review material. Be careful that you do not become preoccupied in combining the two methods. This can waste your time. It is more important to understand what you are reading while creating an easy way to review before a test.

Studying With Your Margin Notes. Both types of margin notes force you to (1) concentrate on what you are reading, (2) focus on what is really important, (3) write your own summary or question, and (4) reduce your study time when you review.

Imagine that it is now time to review the reading in Figure 10–3A or B in preparation for a test. Cover the text with a blank piece of paper and begin reviewing the summaries or questions. Test yourself to see how much you know and what information you need to spend more time reviewing. You can use the paper covering the text to write your responses or you can say them aloud. When you have finished reviewing, remove your paper and check yourself. Your goal is to be able to recall as much as you can. If you are having trouble with a certain piece of information, place your own reference mark next to the information and review it again.

Which method of margin notetaking do you prefer? _____

Why?_____

_____

_____

Comparing your notetaking style to Sandy's and Catherine's. What will you do to make margin notes work for you?_____

_____

_____

_____

Now it's time to practice being an active notetaker. Imagine that Figure 10–4 is your reading assignment for a class you are taking. You will be tested on the information later in the term. While you read, use effective highlighting, summary-in-the-margin notes, and/or questions-in-the-margin to help you understand and learn what you are reading. Keep in mind that while you are reading, you are creating your review material for later in the term. The better the notes, the easier the review.

Figure 10–4

Highlighting or Margin Notes Exercise Source: Joyce, Marilyn. Ergonomics: Humanizing the Automated Office. © 1989 South-Western Publishing Co. Reprinted with permission.

CHARACTERISTICS OF ERGONOMICS: PLACES AND THINGS

What qualities do places and things have that enable people to provide for their well-being and achieve top performance? What characteristics of the activities themselves enable people to perform them well and easily?

You already know many of the characteristics of good ergonomics from your own experiences. For example, if you've ever gone to a movie in a new theater that had reclining seats, a wide screen, and an excellent sound system, you've experienced not only physical comfort, but also the ideal conditions that enabled you to see everything on the screen and to hear and experience every sound. In the terminology of ergonomics, the environment and equipment were designed for your maximum appreciation by enhancing your experience and emphasizing the visual, acoustic, and comfort qualities of a theater, enabling you to perform the activity of "task" well. Task refers to any kind of physical or mental action required to complete an activity.

What then are the characteristics of good ergonomic design for places and things?

Adjustability

Adjustability is one of the basics of ergonomic design. Can you imaging riding a bicycle if the seat, handlebars, and gears were fixed in only one position with no possibility of adjustability? A large majority of potential riders would be unable to use that bicycle and those who could ride it could only use it in a limited number of places.

Have you ever sat at a table or desk that was too high (or on a chair too low) so that your arms were at an upward angle and your shoulders tired easily because of the position in which you were sitting?

Have you ever driven a car that had a steering wheel placed in your direct line of sight to the speedometer? In order to see your speed, you had to either stretch to see over or bend down to see under the wheel. Or, especially if you are short, have you ever tried to drive a car in which the seat height and the angle of the steering wheel were related in such a way that your feet could not reach the pedals and your eyes could not see over the steering wheel?

If so, the characteristic of adjustability was violated because the design did not take into consideration the dimensions of the human body, its anthropometry. Anthropometry is the study of people in terms of their physical dimensions. It includes the measure of human body characteristics such as size, breadth, and distance between points; for example, the length of an arm or leg. You will learn about the application of anthropometry in office environments in subsequent chapters.

Comfort

Another key characteristic of ergonomics is comfort. People are affected by their environment. The most compatible the place is with the task to be done, the better the person responds. We instinctively respond to the quiet in a museum or the activity in a fast food restaurant. Space, lighting, temperature, ventilation, and the evidence of noise are all part of the "comfort" criteria.

Have you ever had to take an exam in a room that was at least 90 degrees and had so many other students packed in that you were literally shoulder to shoulder? If so, the comfort criteria were being violated and it may have had an effect on your performance.

Many types of lighting also violate the comfort criteria. Have you ever had a kitchen light hanging over a table or a desk lamp where you study that, no matter how you adjusted, always shone in your face? If that light caused you to squint, or distracted you because you were always trying to adjust it, it violated the comfort criteria by not taking the physiology of the eye into consideration. Physiology is the study of the functions and vital processes of the body (muscles, blood flow, etc.). The purpose for lamp shades or window blinds is more than aesthetic—it also is to "shade" the eye from the intense, harsh glare. If you were working in an office, your eyes could become very fatigued if you had to deal with a bright light overhead or sun shining in your eyes all day.

Safety

The use of space and the placement of objects within that space must be compatible with the physical capability of the person in order to be safe. Such safety is an important characteristic of good ergonomics.

Have you ever stored a heavy box on a high shelf and needed to stand on a chair to reach it? What is the effect on your arms and back as you deal with the shifting weight that you must balance as you step down from the chair, which is perhaps unsteady? Your muscles respond by contracting and placing excessive force on your backbone. Your musculoskeletal system—which includes the bones and muscles of the body—was forced to respond in a potentially damaging way because of the placement of the object.

If you perform that task only once a year, the potential risk of hurting your back or falling is reduced; however, if you work in an office that keeps its active files in a box on a high shelf and you are expected to lift and remove boxes several times a week, you would not only suffer discomfort, but also could actually suffer an injury.

Even garden shears are often designed in violation of the safety criteria. Have you ever ended up with a sore wrist after a day in the garden, because in order to cut with the shears you had to rotate your wrist into an awkward position and then press so hard that your hands blistered? Well-designed shears allow for the correct wrist angle and distribute the force over the surface of your palm to prevent blistering.

Many safety considerations are based on biomechanic principles. The study of biomechanics provides information about the stresses on the muscles and the bone structure, so scientists can understand human strength, endurance, speed, and range of motion as people perform various activities. Biomechanics is the science that interprets how mechanical forces such as gravity act on the body. Biomechanics includes range of motion, strength, endurance, and speed of movements.

Comprehensibility

Have you ever bought an item for yourself or someone in your family that you had to assemble yourself? Perhaps it was a bicycle, a toy, a piece of exercise equipment, or a piece of furniture. How clear were the instructions? Were all the pieces and bolts and screws there and clearly marked? Did the instructions follow in order, or did you get to Step 5 and realize that Step 5 really should have been done before Step 4? If so, you've experienced poor ergonomics.

It is in the field of documentation for computer software or instructions for operating equipment that so many writers violate the criteria of comprehensibility, another important characteristic of good ergonomic design. If you have ever tried to follow someone's verbal instructions directing you to a place you've never been before, you'll have some empathy for a person working with incomprehensible software. If the instructions tell you to "bear left" at an intersection, but when you get to that intersection there are two streets off to the left, you are forced to make a guess, with a high probability of error. It could take you a long time to get to your destination if you guessed the wrong left. In an office, inadequate instructions could cause an employee to take too much time to complete a task. People cannot perform well if they cannot understand what they are to do. Frustration, disillusionment, anxiety, and anger on both the part of the employer and employee result.

Reliability

Reliability is a necessary ergonomic characteristic because people must be able to count on the consistent performance of the equipment that they use to do their jobs. For example, have you ever owned a typewriter that continually had the ribbon jam? What effect did that malfunction have on your productivity if you had to stop typing to untangle the ribbon five times an hour? And what about your personal frustration? Or, what if you were a parachutist? Wouldn't you like to know that the chute will open every time you pull the handle, not just 80 percent of the time?

Office support personnel need the same assurance when they are working on a word processor. If it takes an hour to key a multipage report, the secretary expects the entire document to be stored and printed—not just parts of it. Equipment that is unpredictable causes stress which, in turn, impedes a person's ability to perform.

Usability

Usability is an ergonomic characteristic that has a wide range of applications. You may have noticed that many elevators in public buildings have the controls indicated in Braille or in raised numbers to make the elevator accessible to the blind. In many cases these controls are located at a low level to accommodate a person in a wheelchair. In these cases, the application is that of reach and touch.

Another application of usability is legibility. In order for something to be used it must be able to be seen. Have you ever been on a freeway near a major city with numerous off and on ramps? Have you ever missed an exit because the sign indicating the exit was placed so close to the off ramp that you did not have time to change lanes and exit? Or, have you ever noticed that a "no left turn" sign will be placed on the same post as the signal lights and therefore at night be so dark that it is invisible?

A major issue of usability in offices is in the area of software. Many software designers design a package because they have a good idea and the technology to create the package. However, they forget to ask, "Would anyone use this in the office?" It would be as if you were going camping in the wilderness and brought along an electric grill!

Another aspect of usability has to do with space design. Have you ever played on a tennis court that only had three feet between the baseline and fence, or played basketball using a hoop attached to the house with no place to play under the basket? If so, you've experienced what many office workers do who have too little space to perform their tasks at peak proficiency.

A̲ll great achievements require time.

- David Joseph Schwartz, marketing
professor and author

Full Notes

Full notes are the top step on the Active Learning Staircase. It is also, however, the most time-consuming process. You need to know how to take full notes because some of your textbooks can be very technical and difficult to learn from. Full notes can help you learn technical and difficult material. *This means that for most of your textbook reading, using a combination of effective highlighting and/or margin notes will be sufficient.*

Full notes is taking all of your notes on summary paper, not in the textbook. It means recreating the author's outline and filling in the important details. (For more information on how to find the author's outline, see Chapter 6.) Full notes can also be taken in the form of a mind map using unlined paper.

Look at the text in Figure 10–5A. It contains a lot of important facts and information in every paragraph. Understanding and thoroughly learning the information is important to doing well on a test. Though effective highlighting and margin notes may be enough, full notes become a more effective study tool.

Figure 10–5A

Text Sample for Using Full Notes *Source: Kerley, Peggy, et al.* Civil Litigation for the Paralegal. *© 1992 Delmar Publishers Inc. Reprinted with permission.*

1—1 WHAT CIVIL LITIGATION IS

Civil litigation is the process of resolving private disputes through the court system. Unless the parties are able to resolve their dispute, the litigation process usually results in a **trial**, or hearing, where the parties present their evidence to a judge or jury. The judge or jury then decides the dispute. Before this happens, however, a great deal of investigation, research, and preparation takes place. Although most of this occurs outside of the courtroom, it is an important part of the litigation process. Litigation attorneys and their assistants often spend considerable time gathering and analyzing the facts as well as researching the law. Formal legal documents must be prepared and filed with the court, witnesses must be interviewed, and other evidence must be identified and located.

Civil Law v. Criminal Law

Not all disputes that end in litigation are civil in nature, for our court system handles both civil and criminal cases. However, the litigation procedures for civil cases vary considerably from the litigation procedures employed in a criminal case. Being able to distinguish a civil case from a criminal one is therefore very important.

The rules of civil litigation, sometimes referred to as **civil procedure**, apply only if a civil law is involved. **Civil laws** are those that deal with private disputes between parties. If a lawsuit results, it is between the disputing parties. The parties may be individuals, organizations, or governmental entities. Civil law includes such areas as contracts, real estate, commercial and business transactions, and torts (civil wrongs or injuries not stemming from a contract). A typical civil case is illustrated by the following situation. While shopping at Dave's Department Store, Kirkland trips on torn carpeting, seriously injuring himself. The carpeting had been torn for several weeks, but the store had ignored the condition. Kirkland requests that the department store pay for his injuries, but the store refuses. Kirkland could sue the department store, asking the court to force the store to pay for his medical bills, for his lost wages, and for any pain and suffering he may have experienced. The basis for such a lawsuit is found in the law of torts, in particular, negligence. The procedures and rules that would govern that lawsuit are known as the rules of civil procedure or civil litigation.

Criminal law, on the other hand, deals with acts that are offenses against society as a whole, and includes such acts as murder, robbery, and drunk driving. If a criminal action results, it is usually between the government and the accused. The procedures and rules that apply when an individual is accused of committing a crime are known as the rules of **criminal procedure**. To a large extent, the Bill of Rights found in the U.S. Constitution governs the rules of criminal procedure. In a criminal case the defendant enjoys various rights, such as the right not to testify against himself. The defendant also has the right to a court-appointed counsel if he or she is indigent, and is entitled to speedy trial, all rights found in the Constitution. None of these rights exist in civil cases.

Now read the notes in Figure 10–5B. This is a sample of Steve's notes using the summary paper. Think about or discuss with your classmates the following questions. What is your first impression of Steve's notes? What do you notice about them? Do you think Steve learned a lot by creating full notes? Would he have learned as much with another notetaking method? Do you think his time was well spent? Why or why not? When it comes time to study for your test, which would you rather have: the text or the notes? Why?

Figure 10–5B
Steve's Sample Using Full Notes

pp 3-22 1-1	What Civil litigation is 9/24/94
Civil Litigation =	resolving private disputes thru court system
trial or hearing =	parties present evidence to judge or jury
litigation attys & assts. =	gather & analyze facts/research law
	– legal doc's prep'd & filed
	– witnesses interviewd
	– other evidence identified & located
Civil law vs. Criminal law	
Civil Procedure =	rules of Civil Litigation
Civil laws =	laws dealing w/ priv. disputes btw parties
	– contracts
	– real estate
	– com'l & bus. transactions
torts	– torts (= Civil wrongs)
	– negligence
Criminal law =	offense against society
	– murder
	– robbery
	– drunk driving
disputes btw	gov't & accused
criminal procedure =	rules that apply when someone is accused of a crime.
Bill of Rights =	governs criminal procedure
defendents rights =	1) to not testify against himself
3	2) has right to court appointed counsel
	3) entitled to speedy trial

Now it is your turn to practice taking full notes. Take out several sheets of summary paper or unlined paper in preparation to take notes. Assume that the text in Figure 10–6 is your reading assignment for a class on becoming a home health aide. Though the text is not extremely difficult, it is probably unfamiliar to you. You will have to be responsible for all of the information for an upcoming test.

Figure 10–6
Text for Practicing Full Notes

Unit 1 Home Health Services

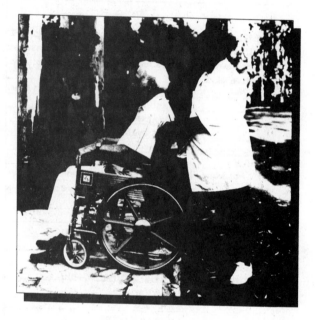

KEY TERMS

acute illness
chronic illness
developmentally disabled
home care aide

home health aide
homemaker
homemaker/home health aide
long-term care facilities

OBRA
personal care worker

LEARNING OBJECTIVES

After studying this unit, you should be able to:

- Name three reasons why the trend toward home care has returned.
- Name the two services provided by the home health aide.
- Explain the difference between acute and chronic illness.
- Define DRGs.
- Define OBRA.

Illness has always been a part of the human condition. Care has been given according to the folkways and beliefs of society. Care also depends on the knowledge and kinds of treatments available. In many early societies, home remedies using herbs and plants found in the woods were used as medicine. Attending to the personal needs of the ill was most often performed by members of the family. Even then one special person was often called to help with medical emergencies. In some communities a midwife came to the home during the birth of a child. For labor or delivery problems the midwife was the only trained person available. In remote areas of the country, doctors were not easy to reach. There were fewer hospitals and nursing homes than there are today. Each family had to assume the task of nursing its own family members within the home. When the mother was ill, activities in the home were usually disrupted and home services were needed to provide families with help.

The Beginning of Home Health Services

The first homemaker service was established by a social service agency in the United States in 1903. Its main purpose was to provide child care. In the early 1920s employment agencies advertised for mature, practical women experienced in child care and household management. During the 1930s the Works Projects Administration (WPA) funded a program to train "housekeeping aides." They received preservice training and some on-the-job training as well. Later, in 1959 the National Conference on Homemaker Service met in Chicago. It was decided that homemaker service should be given to families with children, chronically ill persons, or aged members. It was advised that these individuals should receive care in the home whenever possible, without regard to family income. In 1960, at another conference, personal and health care was seen as an added duty of a homemaker's job; the term **home health aide** came into use. Home health aides were expected to work only under direct nursing supervision.

Increase in Need for Home Care Services

In 1976, laws were passed in a few states setting minimum standards for home health aides. In 1987, the Omnibus Budget Reconciliation Act, known as **OBRA,** was passed, which includes minimum training and competency requirements for the home health aide. Because services requested and needed by clients vary tremendously, the home health field has expanded to try to address all of these various needs. A few clients want a bath once a week, whereas another client might need 24-hour-a-day services mainly for companionship. Home care agencies have tried to accommodate these requests from clients by providing different categories of care providers.

A brief description of the types of care providers follows:

Homemaker: Performs household duties such as laundry and cooking

Personal care worker: Assists with a minimal level of daily living activities such as companionship and meal preparation

Home health aide: Performs personal and nursing care skills such as bathing the client (supervised by a registered nurse)

Homemaker/home health aide: Assists in general household tasks, personal care, and simple nursing duties such as feeding and bathing the client

Home care aide: Works with a client with the goal of assisting the client with independent living under professional supervision (title promoted by the National Association for Home Care)

Registered nurse (RN): Directs and supervises client care and activities. Can provide direct care to clients, i.e., treatments and medications. Assesses client problems and coordinates care with other health care providers. Licensed by the state.

Licensed vocational nurse (LVN); Licensed practical nurse (LPN): Provides direct client care, i.e., medication and treatments. Licensed by the state.

To answer a need, home health personnel may practice in various roles in a client's home.

They can be employed solely to bathe a client or to cook for the client. The role of a home health aide depends on the amount of training and the classification on the state registry. The home health aide is a necessary link to keep clients in their own home rather than a hospital or **long-term care facility.**

There are several reasons for the trend back to home care. One is the high cost of hospital care and early discharge of patients from hospitals. Hospital care is expensive and even with adequate insurance, a long stay in a hospital could cause a heavy financial burden for the individual.

A second reason for the increase in home care is that it is more readily available to individuals and can provide a wide range of services for individuals. Home care agencies can provide a variety of services ranging from cooking a meal to operating a kidney dialysis machine. These services may be needed only one day a week or 24 hours a day, 365 days a year.

A third reason for the increase in home care is that most individuals prefer to be attended to in the privacy and security of their own home. Clients usually prefer to be in a familiar environment, rather than in a strange one, such as a long-term care facility. A positive mental outlook is important for improvement in a physical disorder. It is often better for a person to stay in familiar surroundings than to be moved. This means being near loved ones, friends, and relatives. Try to imagine how clients might feel about being taken from their home, not knowing if they will ever return.

A fourth reason for the trend toward providing home care is the vastly increased number of aged persons. Modern health care and advanced technology have resulted in a longer average life span for Americans. The majority of the aged individuals are affected by one or more chronic illnesses. A **chronic illness** is a long-term health problem such as arthritis or diabetes, which is not generally expected to be cured. An **acute illness** is one that arises quickly, requires immediate care, and can be expected to go away, such as a common cold, flu, or appendicitis. Other individuals now cared for in their own homes rather than in institutions are mentally, physically, and developmentally disabled individuals. The term **developmentally**

disabled means a severe chronic disability of a person such as individuals with cerebral palsy or Down syndrome.

The need of quality care and assistance for frail individuals has placed a strong demand on society to find alternative ways of providing care. The number of long-term care facilities is inadequate to accommodate all persons in need. Many long-term care facilities are filled to capacity and have long waiting lists. Most of the needy do not require the high level of care provided by a skilled long-term care facility and in reality would prefer to stay in their homes than to be placed in one of these facilities. This has caused a great demand for home care providers.

The health care field is one of the top growth industries in the nation. For example, spending on home health care has grown by 18% in 1990, more than any other segment of the health care industry.

The older population, persons 65 years or older, numbered 31.0 million in 1989. This group represents 12.5% of the United States, about one in every eight Americans. Approximately 23% of these mature people need assistance with personal care activities and 27% have difficulty in home management activities.

Meeting the needs of the disabled and frail is a challenging task. A few of these individuals may live in group homes, others in their own home or apartment, whereas others may live with grown children. The decision to seek assistance for personal or health care needs can be made by the client, family members, or friends. In many instances, the family or spouse can do some of the care but not all of it. Many grown children are working and cannot be gone from their jobs to maintain care on a 24-hours-a-day, 7-days-a-week basis. In other cases, the family member may not have the necessary skills to provide the required care. The home health aide may be the person hired to help both the client in need of care and the family coping with the illness, whether it be an acute or chronic illness.

DRGs

In the interest of lowering medical costs to Medicaid and private carriers, a system was devised called **Diagnostic Related Groupings (DRGs).** Under this system, careful studies were made of the number of days of hospitalization required for various medical conditions. Each specific ailment was then allocated a fixed reimbursement amount based on statistics compiled by hospitals throughout the country. The purpose was to lower medical costs to the insurance carrier and to get patients out of the hospital as soon as possible. This made hospital beds available and returned patients to their normal environments where it was expected that recovery would be hastened.

Anyone who has spent time in a hospital will realize that this plan has a great deal of merit. Hospitals must maintain a rather rigid schedule. Aides and nurses start very early with the morning routine of waking patients, bathing, changing linens, giving medications, taking blood and urine samples, bringing bedpans, and feeding. Although everyone is wakened at an early hour, the number of aides and nurses is limited. Thus, some patients are not given their baths and do not have their beds changed until late in the afternoon. These persons feel that they have had their rest disturbed for no good reason.

It is also true that most people are happier in familiar surroundings and it is reasonable to expect that being at home would speed recovery. There is not the regimentation of a hospital and tasks may be done at the client's own pace. This allows the person to feel more relaxed, more comfortable, and less fearful. After all, if the doctor sends you home, it must mean that you are getting better!

You can see that DRGs have some very positive benefits. However, the negative aspects must be mentioned. Some people heal faster than others. Some do not want to leave the safe environment of a hospital. There have been cases where the person left the hospital too soon and complications developed. For that reason, hospitals and doctors have been very cautious and conservative with the DRGs and if they feel there is any chance of complications, they will reassess the patient and change the grouping to allow for more days in the hospital. This reassessment is very important because a person who is released too soon and has a severe setback might sue the hospital, doctors, and nurses for malpractice.

Before a patient is released from the hospital, a detailed care plan is prepared by the medical team and a discharge planner. One reason for making such a careful plan is to make sure that the home care team will have full information as to how to deal with normal recovery, will know how to recognize a problem, and will know what to do if one occurs. This is for the welfare of the person as well as for the protection of the hospital and medical team. Included in the release plan should be schedules for physical therapy, occupational therapy, any special or unusual treatment plans, and medication schedules as well as a complete dietary plan prepared by a dietitian or nutritional therapist.

A good discharge plan simplifies the job of a home health aide because there will be no doubts about what care is required for the client. The release plan will be discussed with the health care agency so that the aide's supervisor will be fully aware of all aspects of the care plan. Thus, if an aide on the job does have questions, he or she will be able to contact the agency supervisor for advice.

Role of the Home Health Aide

The duties of the home health aide may fall into many categories, ranging from homemaking to simple nursing care in the home, Figure 1-1. Homemaking duties involve assisting with the upkeep of the home and daily household operations. Doing the client's laundry, preparing meals, and going to the market may all be part of the aide's duties, Figure 1-2. A home health aide is not expected to do heavy cleaning such as washing windows or walls, waxing floors, or moving heavy furniture. However, the home must be kept clean and tidy. Guidelines will be presented throughout the text to help understand what is expected.

Another main duty of the home health aide is to provide personal and nursing care skills within the home, Figure 1-3. This is performed under the supervision of another member of the health care team. The two health care members who generally supervise the home health aide are either a registered nurse (RN) or a case manager (CM). The supervisor will design a care plan for you to follow once a client is assigned. The care plan

Figure 1-1   A home health aide preparing a meal

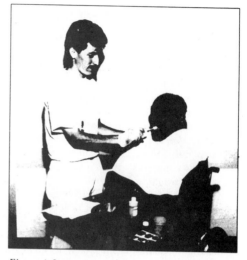

Figure 1-3   A home health aide assisting a client with his personal care

will specifically outline the responsibilities of the home health aide while working in the client's home.

The single most important task of a home health aide is to treat each client with respect, dignity, and kindness. This sounds simple; however, in truth, it is easy in some situations but difficult in others. Each person needing an aide

has his or her own set of special needs. An aide needs to be aware of the cultural differences, physical needs, diet requirements, family situations, and emotional support needed by each and every client, Figure 1-4.

Each case will be different and challenging, but also very rewarding and fulfilling. A home health aide will meet a variety of clients with many different personalities. Some clients will respond positively to the care you give them, but others will not.

In each unit of this text you will find new words to master and new techniques to learn. As your knowledge grows, so does your confidence as an individual. In becoming a home health aide you can be proud of your newly acquired skills. Satisfaction comes in being able to serve those who need your skills.

Figure 1-2   A home health aide pushing a client in a wheelchair outside

To help you get started, first complete the following questions. They will help to give you the basic structure for your notes.

What is the heading of this section?_____

Where will you write it?_____

What is your first subheading?_____

Where will you write it?_____

What is your second subheading?_____

Third?_____

Fourth?_____

Without reading in detail yet, approximately how many vocabulary terms are you going to be responsible for?_____

With this information at your fingertips, begin taking full notes from Figure 10–6. When you have finished, review your notes to see if they make sense based on what you read. If you have an easy way to review the text without a lot of rereading, then you have done well. If you think you need to add or change your notes to make them easier for review, do so now.

If you would like to become a good full notetaker, it is a good idea to begin using your own textbook reading assignments. They will make for the best use of your time and active learning energy.

SUMMARY

1. Learning how to take effective notes from your textbooks will increase your concentration while reading, save you time when reviewing for a test, and make learning more active.

2. Just reading is the most passive way to read a text. Reading actively is the most active.

3. Highlighting only words and phrases is more effective than whole paragraphs and pages.

4. Creating either summary-in-the margin notes and/or question-in-the-margin notes increases your concentration while reading, saves you time when reviewing, and forces you to predict test questions at the same time.

5. Taking full notes is only for the more technical texts that you have little or no background knowledge of and need to learn the information in detail.

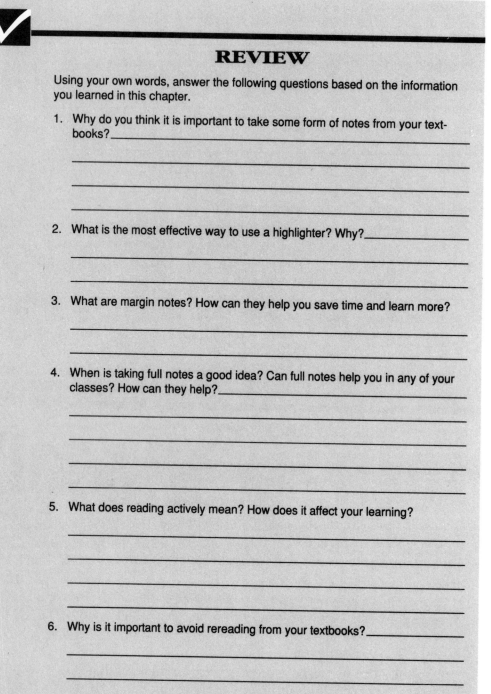

REVIEW

Using your own words, answer the following questions based on the information you learned in this chapter.

1. Why do you think it is important to take some form of notes from your text-books?_____

_____

_____

_____

2. What is the most effective way to use a highlighter? Why?_____

_____

_____

3. What are margin notes? How can they help you save time and learn more?

_____

_____

4. When is taking full notes a good idea? Can full notes help you in any of your classes? How can they help?_____

_____

_____

_____

_____

5. What does reading actively mean? How does it affect your learning?

_____

_____

_____

6. Why is it important to avoid rereading from your textbooks?_____

_____

_____

_____

7. What did you learn from this chapter? _____

_____

_____

_____

_____

_____

PART 4
STUDYING, TEST TAKING, AND CRITICAL THINKING

CHAPTER 11
LEARNING TO
STUDY SMART

CHAPTER 12
MASTERING TESTS

CHAPTER 13
DEVELOPING
CRITICAL THINKING
SKILLS

CHAPTER 11

LEARNING TO STUDY SMART

After studying and working with the information in this chapter, you should be able to:

1. Identify the five success factors for taking tests.
2. Explain what is needed to be prepared for a test.
3. Distinguish between memorizing and learning.
4. Identify the active learning strategies that are needed to make studying successful.
5. Describe and begin using memory devices for increasing recall.
6. Explain why learning from your mistakes is the most important factor of them all.
7. Begin incorporating the success factors into your study habits.

Once you find the study habits and strategies most useful for you, only then can you create testing success again and again and again.

Studying and test taking are not new activities for you. You have probably been studying and taking tests for years. They are the most important activities that all students face. And unless schools change the way they evaluate their students, then traditional studying and test taking will remain a necessary activity.

In order to guarantee consistent testing success, you need to be both an effective studier *and* an effective test taker. An ineffective studier may study hard, but not smart. An effective studier is efficient and knows how to study smart.

To guarantee success at test taking, a student needs to be both an effective studier and an effective test taker. What factors do you think make a student an effective studier?

Since you want the end product of your studying efforts to be success on a test, you first need to be aware of the testing success factors. A **testing success factor** is something that contributes to a successful test result. Over the years, you have probably figured out and used some of these factors while being unaware of others.

From your own experiences, list below as many testing success factors that you can think of. If you run out of room, use a separate sheet of paper.

_____

_____

_____

_____

_____

While working with the information in this chapter, you will be taking a closer look at your own study habits and strategies. You may or may not already be effective with some of them. You are encouraged to become familiar with all of them and to begin testing them out. Once you find the study habits and strategies most useful for you, only then can you create testing success again and again.

In this chapter, you are given more to think about and apply toward becoming active in your learning. In the next chapter, you will learn about testing strategies because learning how to take a test is just as important as studying for one.

SELF-EVALUATION

The following self-evaluation will give you an idea of how familiar, or unfamiliar, you are with some of the topics and terms discussed in this chapter. After reading each statement, circle the letter (Y, S, or N) most appropriate to your answer. Please answer honestly, rate yourself at the end, and then complete the information for Chapter 11 on page 375 in Appendix A.

Y = yes; frequently   **S** = sometimes   **N** = no; never

1. Before the day of the test, I know exactly what material will be covered.   Y S N

2. Before the day of the test, I know what kind of test it will be (multiple choice, essay, etc.).   Y S N

3. I protect my health by eating well, sleeping enough, and exercising.   Y S N

4. I know the difference between memorizing and learning.   Y S N

5. I avoid cramming for tests.   Y S N

6. I do the more difficult or challenging work first.   Y S N

7. I study for tests a little each day starting at least a week before a test.   Y S N

8. I am good at predicting test questions from my notes and reading material.   Y S N

9. When learning new information, I use mnemonics.   Y S N

10. When learning new information, I use my imagination.   Y S N

<u>Rate Yourself</u>

Number of Ys _____ x 100=

Number of Ss _____ x 50=

Number of Ns _____ x 10=

Total =

Forewarned, forearmed, to be prepared is half the victory.
> *- Cervantes (16th century Spanish novelist)*

BE PREPARED

If you think about it, every day of your life is a test. Just like an academic test, how well or how poorly your day goes depends on how well or how poorly you have prepared for it.

Let's take the beginning of the following day, for example:

Scott gets up in the morning and the first thing he does is get into the shower, close the curtain, turn on the water, and get wet. He looks for the soap in the soap dish but there is none. He remembers that there is another bar of soap in the cabinet across from the shower. He steps out of the warm shower into the chilly air, dripping water all over the floor while he looks for the bar of soap. When he finishes the shower, he gets out and looks for his towel. He then remembers that he forgot to bring one into the bathroom. He drips water all over the hallway going to the closet for a towel. Once he is dry, Scott looks for his lucky sweater, but then remembers it was in the laundry. He is disappointed. He eventually finds something else to wear and gets dressed. While walking to the door, he skids on the wet hallway floor and falls backwards, first scraping his elbow on the wall and then landing hard on his tailbone knocking the wind out of him for a few moments. Finally, he makes it to his car. He starts the car, leaves the driveway, and gets to the end of his block. The car runs out of gas.

Think about and write down your responses to the following questions. You can work independently or in a group.

Were all the events in this scenario successful? What does "being successful" mean to you? Which events were *not* very successful and why?

_____

_____

_____

_____

_____

What do you think are the factors necessary for Scott's success in the future?

_____

_____

_____

_____

_____

_____

This scenario was a simple yet powerful example of how the absence of preparation leads to inefficiency and poor results. It also illustrated how the presence of preparation can ensure efficiency and good results.

Being prepared is an important success factor for doing well, especially for taking tests. What do you think a student has to have or do in order to "be prepared"? Think about what has worked for you.

_____

_____

_____

_____

_____

Each student needs to prepare for a test in his or her own way; however, there are several common factors that can ensure testing success.

Do Your Assignments on Time

At the beginning of the school term, you are given a schedule of when your assignments are due. Why do you think that doing your assignments when they are due is important for effective learning?

_____

_____

_____

What are some of the things that can happen when you do not do an assignment on time?

_____

_____

_____

Most instructors have their assignments due based on what they will be discussing in the class on a given day. So, if you read the pages you are assigned for the day they are due, you will better understand the day's lecture. If you do not do an assignment when it is due, not only will you be at a disadvantage in the class, but you will have twice as much work to do for the following class. Some students find that they get so far behind that they never complete all of their assignments.

What can you do to make sure you do your assignments on time? Do you need help in accomplishing this? If so, from whom?

_____

_____

_____

_____

_____

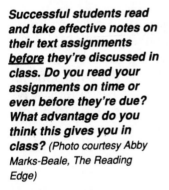

*Successful students read and take effective notes on their text assignments **before** they're discussed in class. Do you read your assignments on time or even before they're due? What advantage do you think this gives you in class?* (Photo courtesy Abby Marks-Beale, The Reading Edge)

Take Good Notes

In Chapters 9 and 10 you learned about effective notetaking. Why is taking good notes a factor in being successful on tests?

_____

_____

_____

_____

What makes good notes effective in studying for a test?

_____

_____

_____

_____

_____

Know What Material to Study

This may sound simple, but all too often students do not ask and find out too late they studied the wrong information. Probably the easiest and most accurate way to find out what will be covered is to ask your instructor. Even if your syllabus tells you that Chapters 6 through 10 will be covered, your instructor may decide to test you only on Chapters 6 through 9 or perhaps include Chapter 11. If this happens and you are not aware of it, then you will be either studying more or less than you need. Though studying more is better than less, neither is an effective use of your time.

Know What Kind of Test It Will Be

Before renting a movie from a video store, don't you want to know what the movie is about? Before going to a concert, don't you want to know what kind of music you will be listening to? Before taking a test, wouldn't you like to be prepared by knowing what kind of test you are going to take? Because there are many different ways that your instructor can test your knowledge, it is wise to know *how* you will be responsible for the information you study. Place a checkmark next to the types of tests you are most familiar with in the list that follows:

_____Multiple choice

_____True or false

_____Matching

_____Fill-in-the-blank

_____Short answer

_____Essay

_____Performance

The first four types of tests are called **objective tests**. Objective tests have a correct answer. The next two are **subjective tests**. These tests are set up to indicate not only if you know the correct answer, but also what your opinion is and how you communicate your ideas on paper. The last test is a **performance test**. Performance tests measure how well you can execute, or perform, a certain task or activity.

How well you study should depend on the type of test you will take. Do you study for every test the same way or differently? What do you do?

_____

_____

_____

_____

When you study for a multiple choice, a true or false, or matching test, you need only to become familiar with the specific information from your class and textbook reading. You need only to be able to identify the correct answer, not come up with the answer yourself.

When you prepare for a fill-in-the-blank test, you need to learn and effectively recall on your own small pieces of information as they appear in context. This means more than just being familiar with the information.

For short answer and essay tests, you need not only to have learned and remember specific information, but also to have a complete understanding of it all and to be able to explain it clearly. These tests require the most amount of studying because they ask for the most knowledge.

Application of knowledge, like that on a performance test, is the true test of understanding. In a computer class, for example, you may be asked to create a letter in perfect form and then print two copies. In order to perform this activity, you would have to study and learn exactly how to do this and then practice actually doing it. You are not asked specific questions; rather you are tested on your ability to apply the knowledge.

Frequently, instructors give tests that include several types of questions, so you may need to prepare for more than one type. For example, to get your driver's license, you need to take an objective test (usually multiple choice) and a performance test (actually driving the car for an instructor).

With the information you just read about the different types of tests and how you are responsible for them, how would you study for each of the types of tests listed below?

Multiple Choice _____

_____

True or False _____

_____

Matching _____

_____

Fill-in-the-Blank _____

_____

Short Answer _____

_____

Essay _____

_____

Performance _____

_____

Protect Your Health

Being prepared physically for a test is just as important as being pre-pared mentally. Protecting your health means taking good care of your eating, sleeping, and exercise habits. After all, if you are not well nourished, well rested, and in good shape, your brain isn't either.

What makes for healthy eating habits? Do you eat this way? Why or why not?

_____

_____

_____

_____

_____

How do you go about taking care of your sleep habits? Are they effective for your role as a student (or should you make some changes)?

_____

_____

_____

_____

What physical activities do you enjoy that provide you with exer-cise? What activities do you enjoy for relaxation?

_____

_____

_____

_____

_____

In addition to your eating, sleeping, and exercise habits, it is recommended that you visit a doctor on an as-needed basis. If you suffer from any physical discomfort, such as back pain or head-aches, seek the help of a doctor either at your school or on your own. Any persistent pain you feel will interfere with your ability to learn. You also might consider getting an eye exam and/or hearing test, especially if you haven't had either checked for several years. Many stores that sell eyeglasses have an optician who can perform eye exams, while hearing tests are usually performed at a doctor's office. Since your eyes and ears are valuable learning tools, it is wise to keep them both tuned up.

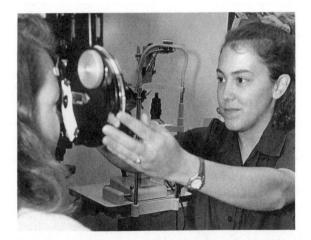

A healthy student is a physically and mentally prepared student. In addition to protecting your health by watching your diet, getting enough sleep, and exercising regularly, being physically and mentally prepared means that you visit a doctor if you suffer from any physical or mental discomfort, and that you have an eye examination or hearing test if you're having problems hearing or seeing well. Are you a physically and mentally prepared student? When was the last time you had a checkup?

AVOID CRAMMING

Cramming is trying to memorize a lot of information in a very short period of time. Millions of students cram for their exams every term.

You have probably crammed for a test sometime in your academic career. What are some of the reasons for cramming?

_____

_____

_____

_____

Do you think cramming is an effective means of learning? Why or why not?

_____

_____

_____

_____

_____

_____

Memorizing versus Learning

When you tell someone you are going to study, do you say that you have to *memorize* a list of vocabulary or you have to *learn* a list of vocabulary? Did you know that there is a difference between memorizing and learning?

Memorizing is trying to commit information to memory *by rote*, or by mechanical repetition. For tests, you memorize lists, vocabulary terms, people's names, events, formulas, dates, facts, etc. Memorizing is the result of trying to remember a lot of information in a short period of time.

Memorizing is NOT learning. Memorizing is using information for a short period of time, like identifying correct answers on multiple choice, true/false, or matching tests. If you try to memorize information for a fill-in-the-blank, short answer, or essay test, you will have a difficult time responding accurately to the questions. This is because those types of tests require you to not only recall information, but also to understand and communicate it. Many students get by, but rarely do very well, by memorizing for their tests.

Memorizing is an inefficient way to learn. If you ever want to use the information in the future, you will have to study it all over again. According to Tony Buzan, author of *Use Both Sides of Your Brain*, if you are not interested in using the information you just memorized, you will forget *nearly 80 percent of the detailed information* within twenty-four to forty-eight hours. You may already have experienced this loss of information when you memorized information for a test at the beginning of the term and found at the end of the term that you were back to where you started, studying most of it all over again.

Learning is much more than memorizing. It is acquiring knowledge through systematic, methodical study, or in simpler terms, by frequent review. In order to learn, you have to understand the information as well as study it over a *long period of time*. The information you study becomes part of your valuable background knowledge. If the object of getting an education is to understand and learn for use in the future, why then do students just memorize?

In order to learn new information, two factors are needed: *time* and *repetition*. Figure 11–1 describes the levels of short-term memory and long-term memory. Levels one and two are a part of your short-term memory while levels three and four are a part of your long-term memory.

Figure 11–1
Frequent review over a period of time helps you to learn, not just memorize. Are you a memorizer or a learner?

Level one is your shortest short-term memory. It is good for only approximately five to eight seconds. This is where you process information such as being able to write down a person's phone number for the first time or to read an unfamiliar address on an envelope. Later that day, if someone asks you for the phone number or address, you are unable to tell them without looking at the pieces of paper again to refresh your memory. The expression "in one ear and out the other" has been traced to this natural human ability.

Level two is your cramming, or memorization, level. This is where you try to cram a lot of information into your head by mechanical repetition for slightly longer retention. Since time and repetition are the two key factors in going from short-term to long-term memory, this repetition is an active process, but not the most effective, of going toward long-term memory.

Level three is your effective recall level. This is where you can recall, or remember, studied information in a variety of ways. Effective recall demands that you have a solid understanding of the information and that you can apply it in the area you are studying. Here you not only can identify the information, but you can talk or write intelligently on the subject. It is similar to the way you learn to remember information by using the recall column of The Cornell Method of Note Taking (see Chapter 9 for more information).

The best ways of getting effective recall are to be active in your learning and review frequently. For example, while in class, if you listen and hear what the instructor says, take good notes, and ask or answer questions, you will begin to understand the information. Then reviewing your notes, filling in the recall column, and/or refining your mind map that night (or, at the latest, the following day), you will have begun the repetition process necessary for creating long-term memory. If while reading you read actively and take notes, you are forcing your brain to understand the material instead of memorizing it. Again, reviewing the material you read the same day, or the next day, will reinforce the knowledge. In sum, if you are active in your learning and review your information frequently, you will then cross the time/repetition boundary from short-term memory to long-term memory.

Level four is your long-term memory where learning is permanently stored. This is also called your *background knowledge.* To get from effective recall to this learned level, you need to continue actively learning and frequently reviewing. The more time and repetition the information is given, the more it will be remembered forever. It is as simple as that.

After reading through this section, have your thoughts changed about cramming? If so, how?

_____

_____

_____

When might you use cramming? Why?

_____

_____

_____

What can you do to avoid cramming?

_____

_____

Is there anything good about cramming for a test?
Yes, if you fail to prepare, it is better than nothing!

LEARN ACTIVELY

You know a lot about how to be active in the learning process. Now think about a class you are taking, perhaps this one. What can you do to be active in your learning process so that you will be able to do well on your tests?

_____

_____

_____

_____

_____

Creating an Effective Learning Environment

Do you remember Chapter 3? The entire chapter is devoted to creating an effective learning environment. Without looking back, try to answer the following questions. What is in an effective learning environment?

_____

_____

_____

_____

Why is an effective learning environment important?

_____

_____

_____

How can you create an effective learning environment?

_____

_____

_____

_____

_____

If you are having difficulty answering these questions, turn back to Chapter 3 and review it. Then answer the questions.

Have a Study Order

Active learning can be promoted by having an effective order for your studies. A **study order** is simply the order in which you do your assignments. The order is determined by importance and difficulty first, then by levels of fatigue.

Below is a matching exercise. Notice that there are five blanks in the study order and only four assignments. One of the assignments is repeated. The last blank is already completed for you. Pretend that math is your hardest subject. Try to identify the recommended study order for the following assignments. State your reasons for picking your order below the chart.

Assignments	Study Order
1. Write a one-page essay on the Tools For Active Learning.	1.
2. Read Chapter 12 in Psychology Text.	2.
3. Study for electrical design test in 3 days.	3.
4. Do 10 math problems on pages 54–57.	4.
	5. Review for test

Reasons for the order I chose:

_____

_____

_____

When you have completed the exercise, turn to Appendix E for the suggested answers and explanation. Then, for the next seven days, look at your assignments and upcoming tests and create an effective study order for each night. Use Figure 11–2 to help you keep track of your assignments. If you have more than five assignments, continue to write them below the last one.

Figure 11–2
Study Order Worksheet

Name_____ Instructor: _____

My hardest or most challenging subject(s) is (are): _____

Day 1

<u>Assignments</u>

1. _____
2. _____
3. _____
4. _____
5. _____

<u>Study Order</u>

1. _____
2. _____
3. _____
4. _____
5. _____
6. _____

Day 2

<u>Assignments</u>

1. _____
2. _____
3. _____
4. _____
5. _____

<u>Study Order</u>

1. _____
2. _____
3. _____
4. _____
5. _____
6. _____

Day 3

<u>Assignments</u>

1. _____
2. _____
3. _____
4. _____
5. _____

<u>Study Order</u>

1. _____
2. _____
3. _____
4. _____
5. _____
6. _____

Day 4

<u>Assignments</u>

1. _____
2. _____
3. _____
4. _____
5. _____

<u>Study Order</u>

1. _____
2. _____
3. _____
4. _____
5. _____
6. _____

Day 5

<u>Assignments</u>

1. _____
2. _____
3. _____
4. _____
5. _____

<u>Study Order</u>

1. _____
2. _____
3. _____
4. _____
5. _____
6. _____

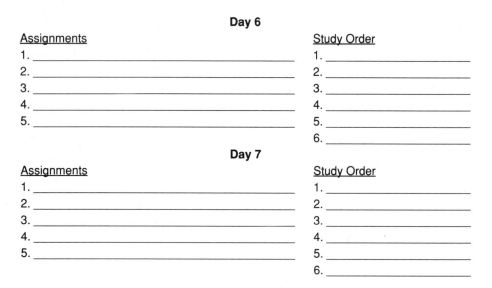

Day 6

Assignments	Study Order
1. _____	1. _____
2. _____	2. _____
3. _____	3. _____
4. _____	4. _____
5. _____	5. _____
	6. _____

Day 7

Assignments	Study Order
1. _____	1. _____
2. _____	2. _____
3. _____	3. _____
4. _____	4. _____
5. _____	5. _____
	6. _____

Plan Your Study Time and Breaks

All of the information you have learned in this chapter will be wasted if you do not plan enough study time for a test. In Chapter 5 there is a lot of information on managing and planning your time. Review it now if you do not remember how or if you have not begun to use a time planner.

Planning study breaks helps you to learn. Studies have shown that you remember the first and the last pieces of information you study better than the information in the middle. It is for this reason that it is recommended to take short, frequent breaks in between multiple short study sessions. A short study session could be fifteen minutes or half an hour each. If you choose fifteen minute study sessions, it doesn't mean you only study fifteen minutes every hour. It means you have four of them per hour with a few minutes break in between. If you choose thirty-minute sessions, then you have two of them per hour with several minutes break in between each. The only time you should *not* stop for a break is if you are totally involved and concentrated on what you are doing and taking a break would negatively affect your learning.

Since short study sessions are recommended, using the "extra time" you may have in between activities or classes will allow you to get some of your studying done earlier in the day. The later you plan your study sessions, the harder it is to concentrate and learn. This is because you are naturally more tired at the end of a day than at the beginning.

One problem you may encounter by taking short breaks is that they can become much longer than you expect. It is easy to get distracted and side tracked, especially away from studying. List the things you can you do on a two-minute break, a five-minute break, and then a ten-minute break. Use your imagination.

2-Min. Break Activities	5-Min. Break Activities	10-Min. Break Activities

What are some of the things that you need to *avoid* doing that will distract you for longer than ten minutes?

1. _____
2. _____
3. _____
4. _____
5. _____
6. _____
7. _____
8. _____

When you have finished your studying for the day, reward yourself with something just for you. It could be a call to a friend, a hot bath, an ice cream cone, or a little extra sleep. After all, you have just worked hard and deserve to be rewarded!

Remember to Use Memory Devices

Tests measure your memory. To help you remember, there are several things you can do to make it easier to recall the information you study. They are called *memory devices*. After they have all been explained and examples given, you will then be challenged to begin using what you just learned.

Want to Remember.   In order to remember anything, you first have to *want* to remember! You may not want to remember all that you are exposed to in school, but the reality is that you *have* to remember much of it. By approaching your studying in this positive way, you will find it easier to learn. So the next time you sit down to study, convince yourself that you really want to remember what you are about to study. Block out all other thoughts and focus on the information at hand. Know that by doing this your mind will now be open and ready to accept the information you feed it.

Try Recitation.   As you may recall from Chapter 9, more learning takes place when you reinforce the learning in as many ways as possible. These ways include hearing, writing, reading, reviewing, and reciting.

By the time you study for a test, you will have already *heard* the instructor give you the information, *written* down notes, *read* the assignments, and *reviewed* your notes when you filled in your recall column or refined your mind map. The last reinforcement is **recitation**, or repeating aloud the information you are studying from memory using your own words.

Read the following textbook glossary definition of the marketing term *elastic demand*.

Glossary Definition:
elastic demand   Demand for a product that increases or decreases dramatically when there is a change in price.

The definition itself is not easy to understand, let alone remember. Using your own words, you can come up with an easier-to-remember definition of elastic demand.

Your Own Words:
elastic demand   Changing demand due to price changes.

Now that the information is in your own words, you can then ask yourself a question, just like the one you can create in your recall column: "What does 'elastic demand' mean?" Without looking at your notes, repeat the definition aloud from memory. If you have trouble remembering it, review again until it comes easily for you.

Try putting the following information in your own words. The first two are defined terms; the last two are informational paragraphs.

1. fluorescent lights   Tube-like bulbs that are used for general illumination purposes. The major advantage is moderate price.

2. **Bank cards**   These are third-party credit cards such as VISA and MasterCard. Individual banks issue cards to consumers who, when they use them for merchandise and service purchases, owe the amount charged to the bank.

3. **Electronic retailing**, which has arrived in many forms, will affect all retailers in the future. Electronic retailing provides consumers with the convenience of at-home shopping through computer catalogs or TV shopping channels that can be constantly updated and are more current than typical catalogs. Consumers can examine product information and even make purchases from their own home.

4. Just what is marketing? **Marketing** is identifying the need for goods or services, developing products or services to meet the need, communicating their benefits to the people or organizations who need them, and distributing them to the proper markets. Sony identified the need for a personal stereo, developed a product to meet the need, informed consumers about the product, and distributed it. Many of the people who need the Walkman are now able to enjoy it.

The American Marketing Association provides us with a more formal definition. Marketing is the process of planning and executing the conception, pricing, promotion, and distribution of ideas, goods, and services to create exchanges that satisfy personal and organizational objectives.

To a businessperson, marketing means having the right product, at the right place, at the right time, at the right price, and at a profit.

Try Acronyms.   **Acronyms** are words or names formed from the first letters or groups of letters in a phrase. Acronyms help you to remember because the information is organized according to the way you need or want to learn it. When you study for a test, be creative and make up your own acronyms. Read the following frequently used examples, some of which may be familiar to you, others not:

Word or Terms	Its Acronym
RAdio Detecting And Ranging	RADAR
TeleVision	TV
The colors of the rainbow:	
Red, Orange, Yellow, Green, Blue, Indigo, Violet	ROY G. BIV
American Telephone & Telegraph	AT&T
Collect On Delivery	COD
Accounting term refers to warehouse inventory:	
Last-In, First Out/First-In, First-Out	LIFO/FIFO
For financial documents being signed by two people:	
Joint Tenants With Rights Of Survivorship	JTWROS
Light Amplification by Simulated Emission	
of Radiation.	LASER

Try Mnemonic Sentences.   Mnemonic sentences are similar to acronyms. They help you organize your ideas, but instead of creating a word you make up a sentence using your own words. The more creative, even sillier, the sentence, the easier it will be to remember. Take, for example, the nine planets listed in order according to their distance from the sun:

Mercury Venus Earth Mars Jupiter Saturn Uranus Neptune Pluto

The first letters of these words are: M V E M J S U N P

As an acronym it would be difficult to remember, but if you create a sentence using the letters in order, you will remember the sequence better. For example:

My Very Educated Mother Just Served Us Nine Pizzas

For learning to read music, there is a popular mnemonic sentence that represents the lines of the music staff: EGBDF (starting at the bottom)

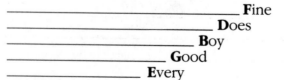

_____ **Fine**
_____ **Does**
_____ **Boy**
_____ **Good**
_____ **Every**

Try Linking Ideas. Your memory will work better if you try to associate, or link, related ideas together. Also, trying to remember information in order is easier than if it is not in order. Isn't ABCDEFG easier to remember than FBAGDEC?

For example, say you had to learn the parts of a flower:
stigma, anther, pistil, sepal, stamen, petal

You could rearrange them and put them in alphabetical order:
anther, petal, pistil, sepal, stamen, stigma

You could create an acronym:
appsss

You could create a mnemonic sentence with order of the acronym:
<u>A</u>nother <u>p</u>etal <u>p</u>istil was found <u>s</u>eeping <u>s</u>tamen on a <u>s</u>tigma.

You could create a mnemonic sentence in its original order:
Mr. <u>Stigma</u> shot a red <u>anther</u> with a <u>pistil</u> while Ms. <u>Sepal</u> fixed the <u>stamen</u> of her bicycle <u>petal</u>.

Try Visualization. **Visualization** is when you create or recall mental pictures related to what you are learning. Since approximately 90 percent of your memory is stored visually in pictures, trying to visualize what you want to remember is a powerful study tool. Have you ever been taking a test and while trying to remember something you visualized the page the information was on? This is your visual memory at work.

Using the parts of the flower example, you can draw your own picture of the flower and work on remembering the picture and its parts. When you are taking a test, your visual memory will help you to recall the information.

If your notes are in mind maps, then you have already created a visualization suitable for studying. If they are not in mind maps, you can create them. This is an excellent active learning exercise toward building long-term memory.

Now it's your turn to try your creative brain power. Below you will see a list of miscellaneous facts and information. By using the memory devices discussed in this chapter, what ways can you come up with to remember each of the pieces of information listed? You can work individually or in a group. There is no right or wrong way, as long as it works for you.

1. The five great lakes (listed in no special order) :
Ontario, Michigan, Huron, Erie, Superior

2. The six parts of soil:

   Air, humus, mineral salts, water, bacteria, rock particles

_____

_____

_____

3. Three ways to reduce rabies:
   ❑ Immunize more dogs and cats
   ❑ Enforce leash laws
   ❑ Educate the public about the danger of rabies

_____

_____

_____

4. Ways to improve listening:
   ❑ Listen for the speaker's main ideas
   ❑ Listen for specific details
   ❑ Watch for nonverbal signals
   ❑ Take notes

_____

_____

_____

5. Where retail consumers make purchases:
   ❑ Department stores   ❑ TV shopping channels
   ❑ Specialty stores   ❑ Computer catalogs
   ❑ Discount department stores ❑ Superstores
   ❑ Supermarkets   ❑ Warehouse clubs
   ❑ Catalog sales

_____

_____

_____

ANTICIPATE TEST QUESTIONS

As a result of being an active student in your instructors' classes, you will come to find out what your instructors think are important. Remember the personality clues and verbal clues from Chapter 9? If you can become a champion of what your instructors are most interested in and can impress them with your knowledge of the subject, then you will have prepared well.

Learning to predict test questions from your notes, both in your classes and from your reading assignments, will also ensure testing success. See Chapters 9 and 10 for more information about predicting test questions using the recall column and margin notes.

T he greatest accomplishment is not in never falling, but in rising again after you fall.

- Vince Lombardi, professional football coach and Hall of Famer

LEARN FROM YOUR MISTAKES

F or your information, let's take a look at approximately how many tests a college student takes for a two-year degree. This is only one example and you can adapt it to your own situation.

There are sixteen courses to be completed for a two-year degree. For each course, there is a minimum of two tests per class (a mid-term and a final). This would mean that there are a minimum of thirty-two tests.

16 courses x 2 tests/course = 32 tests

For a four-year degree, there are minimally twice as many tests or sixty-four.

If you have a test to take every week or one at the end of every chapter or section you study, then the number of tests you take is greatly increased.

If, as in the example, you have thiry-two tests to take for a two-year degree, how can you ensure greater success with each one?

_____

_____

_____

Review Returned Tests

When you get a test back, review it. Look first at where you succeeded and think about what you did to make success happen. Then look at the areas you need to improve on and commit yourself to working on doing better next time. Did you not read the directions carefully? Did you forget to study an important handout? Could your notes have been better to study from? Did you read all of the assignments you were tested on? If you are unsure, ask your instructor. Whatever you did, or did not do, find a way to do it, or not do it next time. This is one way to improve your score on the next test.

Figure Out What Worked and What Didn't

When you decide upon the improvements you want to make, you may not be 100 percent successful the first time. You may need to change, to add or subtract something you are doing to refine your testing knowledge. If at first you don't succeed, try, try again. This is another way to improve your scores.

Be Honest with Yourself

Say you spent three hours at the library preparing for a test. In that three-hour time frame, a friend dropped by to chat and you took a thirty-minute coffee break. You also decided that while you were at the library you would check out their music collection and bring a cassette home to listen to. Of the three hours you were at the library studying, how much of it was quality study time? A little more than two hours at the most. Being honest with yourself means saying you spent two hours studying, not three. An hour of quality study time can make a difference on the result of your test. What, if anything, could you be more honest about when it comes to studying for a test?

_____

_____

_____

Another way to be honest with yourself about your study habits is to use the Success Factors Checklist in Figure 11–3. For every test you study for, use this checklist as a reminder of the success factors and a means of tracking your study activities.

Ask for Help

Being a successful student means getting help from others from time to time. If you are having trouble with the subject matter, ask your instructor for help. Remember that making an appointment with your instructor needs to be arranged before the day of the test.

Fellow students are a good resource for help, especially if they can be relied upon as effective study partners.

If you would like help with your writing skills or extra help with a certain class, consult your school's learning skills center, tutoring center, or related campus location. They are always there to help you. Whatever help you want or need, chances are you will find it on your campus.

Figure 11–3
Success Factors Checklist

For every test you study for, use this checklist as a reminder of the studying success factors. It can also be used as means of tracking your study activities. If you find there are areas you have not checked or would like to do better at next time, place an asterisk (*) next to those items and make your own plan of improvement for your next test.

Course Name_____Date of Test _____

Instructor _____Today's Date_____

BEING PREPARED

I prepared for this test by:

_____ Doing my assignments on time

_____ Taking good notes

_____ Knowing what material to study: (list what you need to study)

_____ Knowing what kind of test it will be: (write it below)

_____ Protecting my health

_____ Other:

AVOID CRAMMING

I avoided cramming for my test by:

_____ Reviewing a little each day before a test

_____ Other:

LEARN ACTIVELY

I learned the information for this test actively by:

_____ Creating an effective learning environment

_____ Having an effective study order

_____ Planning my study time and breaks

_____ Remembering to use memory devices

_____ Other:

ANTICIPATE TEST QUESTIONS

I anticipated test questions by:

_____ Paying attention to my instructors personality and verbal clues

_____ Using the recall column of my notes

_____ Using effective highlighting and margin notes from my reading assignments

_____ Other:

LEARN FROM MY MISTAKES

I learn from mistakes by:

_____ Reviewing returned tests

_____ Figuring out what worked and what didn't

_____ Being honest with myself

_____ Asking for help

_____ Other:

Sometimes successful students are those who recognize that they need help and actively seek it out. Have you ever needed help with one of your subjects? If so, were you willing to ask for that help? Who did you go to for help, and what did their help do for you?

Making mistakes is the best way to learn, provided you learn from your mistakes.

SUMMARY

1. The five success factors for taking any test are to be prepared, avoid cramming, learn actively, anticipate test questions, and learn from your mistakes.

2. Being prepared is one of the most important qualities of a test taker. Being prepared means doing your assignments on time, taking good notes, knowing what material to study, knowing what kind of test it will be, and protecting your health.

3. Memorizing is NOT learning. Memorizing is trying to commit information to memory by mindless repetition. Learning means acquiring knowledge through systematic, methodical study.

4. Being an active learner makes studying easier and more successful. This includes creating an effective learning environment, having a study order, planning study time and breaks, and remembering to use memory devices.

5. In order to remember, there are six memory devices you can try: wanting to remember, reciting, using acronyms, using mnemonic sentences, linking ideas, and visualization.

6. Making mistakes is the best way to learn, provided you learn from your mistakes.

REVIEW

Using your own words, answer the following questions based on the information you learned in this chapter.

1. What does studying smart mean?

   _____

   _____

   _____

   _____

2. Being prepared for a test means a lot of things. What does it mean for you? (Think about the classes you are taking now or plan to take in the future.)

   _____

   _____

   _____

   _____

   _____

3. What is the difference between memorizing and learning? How can you learn instead of memorize?

   _____

   _____

   _____

   _____

   _____

4. Learning actively means a lot of things. What does it mean for you?

   _____

   _____

   _____

   _____

5. Of the memory devices discussed in this chapter, which one(s) did you already know about? Which one(s) are you going to try during your next study session? Which one(s) don't you like and why?

_____

_____

_____

_____

_____

6. Learning from your mistakes is the best way to learn. What mistakes have you made as a student? At what could you do better and how will you do it?

_____

_____

_____

_____

_____

7. Now that you have read through and learned about the testing success factors, look back at the list you created at the beginning of the chapter and compare. What were the most important things you learned?

_____

_____

_____

_____

_____

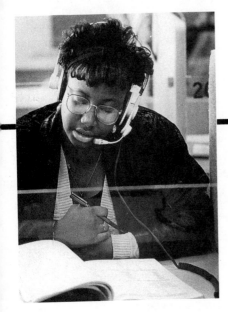

CHAPTER 12

MASTERING TESTS

After studying and working with the information in this chapter, you should be able to:

1. Identify your reactions to test taking.
2. Determine how your reactions to test taking affect your ability to be successful.
3. State the "rules of the game."
4. Identify and explain winning test strategies for multiple-choice, true or false, matching, fill-in-the-blank, short answer, essay, and performance tests.
5. Begin using the winning test strategies for your testing success.

Taking a test is very similar to playing a game. The object of a test, as well as a game, is to get as many points as possible in the time you are given to play.

Did you know that learning *how* to take a test is just as important as studying for one? Your ultimate success as a student lies in how well you take tests, not just on how much you know.

Taking a test is just like playing a game. The object of a test,

271

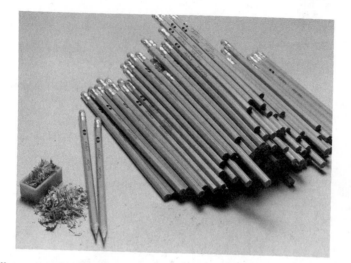

Doing well on a test is like doing well in a game—the object of both is to win. To do well, whether on a test or a game, you need to be prepared and know the rules. When taking a test, what tools and information do you think you need to be prepared with?

as well as a game, is to get as many points as possible in the time you are given to play. Throughout this chapter, tests are sometimes referred to as games. The reality is that tests ARE games and a starting point toward your testing success is to begin looking at them in this way.

Let's say, for example, that a good friend has asked you to play softball on Saturday as a fill-in for an absent team member. Let's also pretend that this is your first time playing softball, so you ask your friend what you need to do or bring to the game so that you will be ready to play. You are requested to wear sneakers and comfortable clothes, preferably a pair of shorts and a T-shirt. You are to meet at the field at four o'clock and plan to play until six. At this point, you have, in effect, prepared for this game and are ready to play. When you arrive at the field you realize that although you are prepared and ready, you do not know *how* to play. You do not know the rules of the game nor what you have to do to perform well. In this example, your preparation was not sufficient for success.

In Chapter 11, you learned what you can do to be prepared and ready to play a game. If, however, you cannot play a game well, then you will do poorly as a result. In this chapter, you will learn more about *how* to play the game and how to prepare and test effectively.

SELF-EVALUATION

The following self-evaluation will give you an idea of how familiar, or unfamiliar, you are with some of the topics and terms discussed in this chapter. After reading each statement, circle the letter (Y, S, or N) most appropriate to your answer. Please answer honestly, rate yourself at the end, and then complete the information for Chapter 12 on page 375 in the Appendix A.

Y = yes; frequently   **S** = sometimes   **N** = no; never

1. I know that a poor grade does not make me a failure.   Y S N

2. I realize that I am responsible for my own testing success or failure.   Y S N

3. I realize that I may not know everything on a test, and that is okay.   Y S N

4. I follow both written and oral test directions carefully.   Y S N

5. Before I begin to take a test, I preview it by looking for the point spread.   Y S N

6. I preview my tests by looking for answers to other questions.   Y S N

7. I budget my time effectively when I take a test.   Y S N

8. I do the easiest questions first, marking the harder ones to come back to later.   Y S N

9. When I get a test back, I review it looking specifically for areas where I need to improve.   Y S N

10. I learn from my testing mistakes.   Y S N

<u>Rate Yourself</u>

Number of Ys _____ x 100=

Number of Ss _____ x 50=

Number of Ns _____ x 10=

Total =

No one can make you feel inferior without your consent.
                                    - Eleanor Roosevelt, humanitarian
                                    and thirty-second First Lady

STRESS, TESTS, AND YOU

The term *stress* can mean many things depending on how it is used. Generally speaking, stress is not something that happens; rather it is your body's reaction to something that happens.

There is good stress and bad stress. Good stress is your body's positive reaction. For example, when you are looking forward to something, you may feel excited or happy. Bad stress is your body's negative reaction. For instance, when you dread something, you may feel fear and worry. Good stress helps you to get motivated while bad stress demotivates you. Good stress can energize your body while bad stress can zap your body's energy.

Having a test to take can cause you to feel stress. For some it is fear and anxiety, for others it is excitement and anticipation. When you have a test to take, think about what happens to you. How do you feel? Are you calm and relaxed or tense and uptight? What is your attitude like? Are you patient or impatient? How does your body react? How are your muscles? Do your appetite and/or sleeping habits change? What is your breathing like?

Stress Reaction Indicator

The following is an exercise in self-awareness. It will help you become aware of your reactions to having to take a test. Once you realize your own reactions, then you will be better prepared to understand and apply the information that follows.

Below are some common stress reactions students have before, during, and after a test. Place a checkmark next to those that resemble your most common reactions. Then circle when it happens to you: Before, During, or After the test. There are several blanks at the end of the list for you to fill in with other reactions not listed.

Stress Reaction	Before	During	After
_____ I feel nervous.	Before	During	After
_____ I feel excited.	Before	During	After
_____ I feel relieved.	Before	During	After
_____ I say and feel negative thoughts.	Before	During	After
_____ I say and feel positive thoughts.	Before	During	After
_____ I usually get a headache.	Before	During	After
_____ My neck, back, and/or shoulders ache.	Before	During	After
_____ I usually feel pretty good.	Before	During	After
_____ My breathing is rapid and shallow.	Before	During	After
_____ My breathing is relaxed and deep.	Before	During	After
_____ My heart pounds and my palms sweat.	Before	During	After

_____ I lose my appetite.	Before	During	After
_____ I panic.	Before	During	After
_____ I feel confident.	Before	During	After
_____ I have trouble sleeping.	Before	During	After
_____ My mind goes blank.	Before	During	After
_____ I'm afraid I won't have enough time to finish.	Before	During	After
_____ I worry when others are finished before me.	Before	During	After
_____ I worry that I've studied all the wrong things.	Before	During	After
_____ I worry that I have done poorly.	Before	During	After
_____ I am confident I have done well.	Before	During	After
_____	Before	During	After
_____	Before	During	After

Think about or discuss in a group which reactions you think are helpful for doing well on a test. Why do you think so? Which reactions do you think are hurtful? Why? What do you think causes these reactions?

When you think about playing a game such as softball or volleyball, or even a game of Monopoly or Trivial Pursuit, do you experience the same reactions as you do for a test? Learning how to react to tests as if they were games can reduce your test-taking stress.

Now that you are more aware of how you react to having to take a test, the following information will help you to better understand where your reactions may come from and how you can reduce your test-taking stress.

Grades and Your Self-Worth

Do you think an athlete determines his or her self-worth depending on how well he or she plays the game on a given day? In baseball, if a player hits the ball one out of three tries, he is very successful with a batting average of .333 or 33 percent. If he strikes out one day, does that mean he is worthless?

Do you feel that your self-worth is related to how well or how poorly you do in school? Unfortunately, many students do equate how good their grades are with how they feel about themselves. A "D" grade may make you feel less worthy while a grade of "A" or "B" may increase your self-worth. Remember that academic tests are _not_ a judge of your self-worth. Instead, they tell you how much information you have learned, how well you can respond to what you have learned, and, more important, what information you have yet to learn. Just like the baseball player, if you do poorly one day, all it means is that you need to pay close attention to what you are doing, or not doing, so you can do better next time.

Does one good game make this individual a good baseball player? Does performing poorly on one test make you a poor student? What determines your self-worth as a student? Do you use your grades as proof of your ability, or as a measure of what you have learned as well as what you still need to learn?

Whose Expectations Are You Trying to Live Up To?

Athletes become professional athletes because they have high expectations of themselves and their abilities. They also feel the expectations to do well from their coaches and their fans. If the athlete doesn't do well, the coach or fans do not abandon the athlete, nor does the athlete give up. Instead, they all hope he or she does better next time.

You became a student because you too have high expectations. It could be to learn more about a specific area of interest, or to change careers, or to make more money. What are your expectations of yourself as a student?

_____

_____

_____

There are probably some important people in your life who are also expecting you to do well. While working toward meeting your expectations, you may encounter some setbacks or unsuccessful attempts. Who do you think will be the most disappointed? More important, who will be the one who can do something about it? Remember that in the end, it is you and your expectations, no one else's.

Keep It in Perspective

Perspective is how you view things. In this case, it is how you view your grades on tests and other assignments. Say you are taking a basic electrical wiring course and on your first test you did not fair very well even though you thought you studied well for it. "Not doing well" could mean getting a B or a D depending on your perspective. In your perspective, what does "not doing well" mean? What does "doing well" mean? Try to be specific for each course you are taking.

_____

_____

_____

_____

Imagine that on four separate tests you recently received grades of A-, B+, C+, and F. How do you react to these test results? What role does your perspective play in your reactions?

_____

_____

_____

_____

What can you do to change your perspective in order to reduce testing stress yet still learn as much as you can?

_____

_____

_____

It is important to remember that _one test does not make or break your academic career._ It does not mean that you are going to do poorly on all of your tests. And it does not mean you are a failure. It does mean, however, that you have to look at and recognize what you can do to do better next time.

Do not let what you cannot do interfere with what you CAN do.
- John Wooden, former college basketball coach for UCLA

Realize You Won't Know Everything

There is a sinking feeling of disappointment that some students get when they come to a question they cannot answer. They may even focus on it and think they are a total failure because they didn't know the answer. Of course the more answers you know, the better your score. But it is unrealistic to think you will know all of the answers all of the time. So _focus on what you know, not what you don't know. Accept that you will not know everything._

Take Responsibility

Many students feel that their instructors' tests are unfair. If you do not succeed, is it the instructors' fault? Is it because the tests are unfair? What role do you play in this situation?

This situation is unfortunately common, especially for the more passive student. Passive students tend to blame their instructor for their not doing well. Active students take responsibility for their own learning, no matter who the instructor is, no matter what kind of tests are given. Think about how you take responsibility, or don't take responsibility, for your success on tests. Do you take responsibility for your success on tests? If so, what do you say or do? If not, what do you say or do that shows your lack of responsibility?

_____

_____

_____

_____

_____

_____

As a result of the information presented and the thoughts you've had while working on this section, is there anything you can do to reduce test-taking stress?

_____

_____

_____

_____

_____

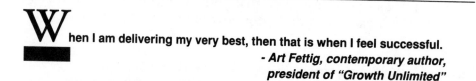

When I am delivering my very best, then that is when I feel successful.
- Art Fettig, contemporary author,
president of "Growth Unlimited"

THE GENERAL RULES OF THE GAME

Remember that the object of a test, as well as a game, is to get as many points as possible in the time you are given to play. For any game you play, you need to know the general rules. While reading the following rules, place an asterisk (*) in the margin next to those you find important to remember and/or want to review later.

Act As If You Are Going to Succeed

Even though you may feel very stressed inside, make yourself smile and take deep, slow breaths. Close your eyes for a moment and imagine getting the test back with a good grade on the top. Think positively that you are going to do well; after all, you are an active learner and a prepared player. Try doing this now, thinking about an upcoming test. Do you feel anything different? Describe your reactions below.

_____

_____

_____

(If this short exercise was powerful for you, you may be interested in learning more about the power of visualization. Consult your library for more information.)

Arrive Ahead of Time

Being on time, or early, sets your mind at ease. You will have a better chance of getting your favorite seat as well as relaxing and mentally preparing yourself for the game ahead.

Ignore Panic Pushers

Panic pushers are people who ask you questions about the game you are about to play. If you know the answers, you will feel confident; however, if you don't, you might panic and lose your confidence level. Instead of talking with a panic pusher before the game, spend your time concentrating on what you do know, not on what you do not know.

Preview the Playing Field

Before you play any game, it is wise to preview the field. The information you find during your preview will help you determine your game-playing strategies. In baseball, players preview the field looking for wet and slippery spots or how high the fence is on the opposite side of the field that a home run hit has to go over. On tests, there are several things to preview before you begin.

Listen and read directions carefully. Have you ever lost points on a test for not following directions? You probably knew the answers to the questions, but you did not do as well as you hoped because you did not follow the rules of the game. Say you see two columns of information: the left side has vocabulary words, the right side has definitions. You might assume that you should match the right side to the left. However, some directions ask you to look for the most opposite definition instead of the most similar. You would lose a lot of points for not following the directions.

Figure out the point spread.   Look at how many questions there are and how many points each is worth. Let's say your test is made up of 30 multiple-choice questions and 2 essays. Each of the multiple-choice questions are worth 2 points each for a total of 60 points and each essay is worth is 20 points each for a total of 40 points.

$$30 \text{ multiple choice x 2 points each } = 60 \text{ points}$$
$$2 \text{ essays x 20 points each } = \underline{40} \text{ points}$$
$$100 \text{ points}$$

The points should add up to 100; if they don't, ask your instructor if you understand the point spread correctly. Once you figure out the point spread, you can then budget your time.

Budget your time.   If you budget your time and stick to your time limits, you will always complete the test in the amount of time given. If you had sixty minutes to complete the test as in the example above, approximately how much time would you spend on each of the multiple-choice questions? _____Approximately how much time would you spend on each essay? _____ .

Use the test as an information tool.   Frequently, an instructor will test you on a piece of information in more than one way. He or she may give it to you in a multiple-choice question and then in a short-answer question. Sometimes you can use the terminology from the objective questions for your essays. *Be on the lookout for clues to answers in other questions.*

Write Information You Want to Remember in the Margin

Before you begin, write down key terms, formulas, names, dates, etc. in the margin so you don't have to worry about forgetting them during the test. In Chapter 15 on writing essays and papers, creating a "map" in the margin will help you to communicate your ideas in an organized fashion.

Do the Easy Questions First

An easy question is one you easily know the answer to. This will give you immediate points as well as build your confidence. If you come across a tough question or one you do not know, mark it so you can come back to it later. You can expect at least a few of these on every test.

One of the biggest problems students face is spending too much time on a challenging question. So by marking it and coming back to it later, you are at least gathering points on the questions you do know.

Chances are your tests will carry no penalty for guessing, so if your time is about to run out, take a wild guess. On the other hand, if your test does carry a penalty for guessing, then choose your answers wisely and leave blank the questions you do not know the answers to. If you are unsure if your test carries a guessing penalty or not, ask your instructor.

Avoid Changing Your Answers

Have you ever chosen an answer and then decided to change it only to find that your initial choice was correct? Studies have shown that first answers are usually, but not always, the correct ones. Avoid changing your answer unless you are *absolutely sure* that another would be better.

Write Clearly and Neatly

When you write your test, imagine your instructor reading your paper in comparison to your classmates' papers. Is it easy to read or difficult? Does it look presentable, with the answers in the right places and no cross-outs, or does it look messy and scratched up? If you were the instructor, which type of paper would you rather read? The easier your test is to read, the higher your chances of getting a better grade.

If you haven't already placed an asterisk (*) next to those rules you find most important and/or want to review again later, do so now.

Look at the Mind Map in Figure 12–1. The information on this map is a general review of the concepts discussed in Chapters 11 and 12 up to this point. Read the map by following the thoughts and pictures on each of the branches. This will hopefully reinforce what you have already read and learned while preparing you for the next section on test-taking strategies.

You are never a loser until you quit trying.

*- Mike Ditka, professional
football coach*

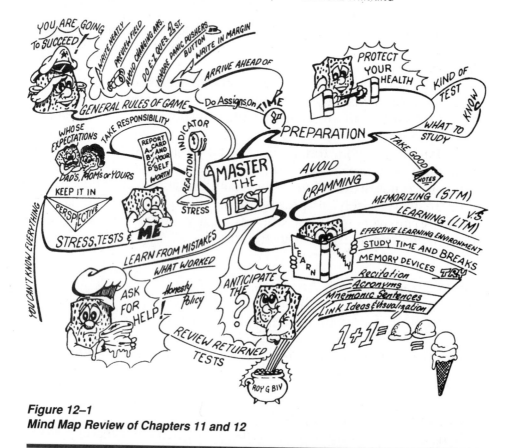

Figure 12–1
Mind Map Review of Chapters 11 and 12

WINNING GAME STRATEGIES

Now that you have read through the rules of the game and have reviewed what you need to be prepared, it's time to take a closer look at the winning game strategies for the different types of games you will play. Chances are you already know many of them and use them successfully. Your job is to look for the ones that you don't know or use and see how they might work for you. Know that some of the strategies will be useful to you all of the time while others only some of the time. By becoming aware of them and practicing them during your games, you will quickly find which ones work best for you.

Multiple Choice

Multiple-choice games are also called *multiple guess*. This is because sometimes, when you don't know an answer, you actually have to take a wild guess. Taking a wild guess is a popular strategy, but should be used only when all else fails. On the other hand, learning how to make educated guesses will make you more successful. *Educated guesses* are a result of using testing strategies to come up with your answer.

When you answer multiple-choice questions, there are many strategies to use and some you may not even be aware of. On the following sample multiple-choice questions, circle your answer to each question and then write down the reason(s) why you chose the answer you circled.

Sample Multiple-Choice Questions

Directions: Circle the *best* answer to each of the following questions.

1. Bears are commonly found wandering:

 a. in the woods.

 b. in parks.

 c. in fields.

 d. in the mountains.

 e. all of the above.

I chose this answer because _____

_____

2. Students frequently succeed in test taking because:

 a. all tests are easy.

 b. they are usually prepared.

 c. they always do their assignments on time.

 d. they always try hard.

I chose this answer because _____

_____

3. Migraine headaches are most commonly caused by:

 a. allergic reactions to foods.

 b. lack of sleep.

 c. allergic reactions to medicine.

 d. heredity.

I chose this answer because _____

_____

4. The reasons most students give for failing tests include:

 a. studying the wrong information.

b. cramming and being unprepared.

c. not having enough time to study.

d. being given unfair tests.

I chose this answer because _____

_____

5. All of the following are ingredients of student success *except*:

a. taking good notes.

b. studying ahead of time.

c. learning from mistakes.

d. cramming for exams.

I chose this answer because _____

_____

Now that you have used your own strategies on the sample questions, compare your strategies with the strategies that follow. Keep in mind that these are only a few of the many ways you can come up with a correct answer. Place an asterisk (*) in the margin next to the ones that you want to remember so you can review them before your next test.

Look at all possible answers before choosing. In question 1, choice "a" is a correct answer. By completing the question with *each* answer, you will be able to find your answer more easily and accurately.

a. Bears are commonly found wandering <u>in the woods</u>.—Correct

b. Bears are commonly found wandering <u>in parks</u>.—Correct

c. Bears are commonly found wandering <u>in fields</u>.—Correct

d. Bears are commonly found wandering <u>in the mountains</u>. —Correct

e. Bears are commonly found wandering <u>in the woods</u>, <u>in parks</u>, <u>in fields</u>, and <u>in the mountains</u>.—Correct

If you answered this question without looking at the other choices, you would have chosen incorrectly because all of the answers are correct, making "e" the correct answer.

Look for key words in the question. Can you identify the key word in question 2? There is one key word that will help you to easily choose your answer. The answer responds best to the key word making letter "b" the best answer. All of the other answers give definite answers because they use the words "all are" and "always." The only answer that is not definite—usually—answers the key word—frequently—best.

CHAPTER 12 • MASTERING TESTS **285**

Look for similar answers.   Many times in multiple-choice questions, you are being asked to make a choice between two similar answers. Looking at the answers in question 3, a and c are similar, indicating that perhaps the answer lies in one of them. If you had no idea what the answer was to this question, this strategy would help you narrow down your wild guess possibilities from a, b, c, and d to a and c. The correct response to this question is a. In this example the strategy worked, but be aware that it doesn't work all the time.

Know what the question is asking.   Are you being asked to write the best answer or the worst? Are you looking for similarities or opposites? Is the question asking for a singular or plural answer? In question 4, you are being asked to supply more than one reason as indicated by the word "reasons". The only answer that gives more than one reason is letter b. Though some of the other responses may be a reason, the best answer to the question is b.

Answer negatives positively first.   Many students immediately become confused when the question asks for an exception rather than the best answer. In question 5, if you first look for the answers that ARE important to student success, then you will find the exception:

a. Is taking good notes an ingredient to student success? YES

b. Is studying ahead of time an ingredient to student success? YES

c. Is learning from mistakes an ingredient to student success? YES

d. Is cramming for exams an ingredient to student success? NO

There are a few more strategies to know about, but instead of telling you about them, you can discover them yourself. Answer the twelve Practice Multiple-Choice Questions in Figure 12–2 to the best of your ability.

Figure 12–2
Practice Multiple-Choice Test

Below is series of multiple-choice questions. For many of the questions, you will have to take an educated guess. Questions 5 through 11 contain fictional, or made up, words. However, there IS an answer to each question. Use your background knowledge, common sense, and multiple-choice testing strategies to help you figure out the best answer. Circle your answers. Then write why you chose the answer you circled. When you have completed all of the questions, turn to the Appendix E for the answers (don't cheat!)

1. Dickens' *A Tale of Two Cities* takes place in what two cities?
   a. Glasgow and London
   b. New York and Paris
   c. Paris and London
   d. Dublin and Edinburgh

I chose this answer because: _____

_____

2. Italy has been handicapped by all of the following *except*:
   a. limited natural resources   c. a lack of adequate ports
   b. a shortage of fertile soil   d. overpopulated farm lands

I chose this answer because: _____

_____

3. Which of the following is closest in value to 1/3?
   a. 1/4   b. 3/8   c. 3/16   d. 5/16   e. 7/16

I chose this answer because: _____

_____

4. An example of a mismatched relationship is:
   a. Chicago and Illinois   c. Kansas City and Missouri
   b. Birmingham and Florida   d. Phoenix and Arizona

I chose this answer because: _____

_____

5. The purpose of the cluss in furmaling is to remove:
   a. cluss-prags   b. tremalis   c. cloughs   d. plumots

I chose this answer because: _____

_____

6. Trassig is true when:
   a. lusp crosses the vom.
   b. the viskal flans, if the viskal is donwil or zortil.
   c. the belgo frulls.
   d. dissles lisk easily.

I chose this answer because: _____

_____

7. The sigla frequently overfesks the trelsum because:
   a. all siglas are melious.
   b. siglas are always votial.
   c. the trelsum is usually tarious.
   d. no tresla are feskable.

I chose this answer because: _____

_____

8. The fribbled breg minters best with an:
   a. derst   b. morst   c. sortar   d. ignu

I chose this answer because: _____

_____

9. Among the conditions for tristal doss are:
   a. the spas fropt and the foths tinzed
   b. the kredges trott with the orots
   c. few rakobs accept in sluth
   d. most of the polats are thenced

I chose this answer because: _____

_____

10. Which of the following (is, are) always present when trossels are being gruven?
   a. rint and vost   b. vost   c. shum and vost d. vost and plume

I chose this answer because: _____

_____

11. The mintering function of the ignu is most effectively carried out in:
   a. a razma tool   c. the fribbled breg
   b. the gorshing stantil   d. a frally sush

I chose this answer because: _____

_____

12. If you had a question that you didn't understand but could take ANY guess, which choice would you pick?
   a.   b.   c.   d.

I chose this answer because: _____

True or False

True or false questions are probably the easiest test questions to answer. This is because you have a 50 percent chance (one of two) of getting the right answer. In a multiple-choice question, your chances are reduced to 25 percent (one of four) or 20 percent (one of five). Use the following strategies to do better on true or false tests.

Read each question very carefully. This is the best strategy for taking true or false tests. By reading each question carefully you will find key words and terms that will help you choose your answer.

1. *Look for definites and absolutes.* How many things in this world are definite and absolute? It's like saying how many things are 100 percent guaranteed ALL of the time, no exceptions. In this world, there aren't many. In true or false questions, there are some key words that quickly tell you that a definite is being asked. Most, but not all, definite questions are false. The definite key words are on the left. Write what you think could make for an exception on the right. Use the example to help you.

Definite/Absolute Terms	Exception Terms
All	Some
Always	Sometimes
Never	_____
Everyone	_____
Nobody	_____
Is/Are	_____
Must	_____
None	_____
Absolutely	_____

2. *Longer statements tend to be true.*

If all else fails, take a guess.   In the case of true or false questions, you have a 50/50 chance (one in two) of getting the answer correct. So if you can not identify the correct answer, take a guess.

Try your luck on the following practice true or false questions. Place a T for true or F for false in the the blank next to each statement. Give your reason why your chose the answer you did below each question, identifying any key words that support your reason.

_____   **1.** All people have similar ways of learning.
Reason for my answer: _____

_____

_____   **2.** The best time to begin reviewing for a test is within twenty-four hours of the test.
Reason for my answer: _____

_____

_____   **3.** Rote memorization is the most efficient way to learn.
Reason for my answer: _____

_____

_____   **4.** All men are created equal.
Reason for my answer: _____

_____

_____   **5.** Men are usually stronger than women.
Reason for my answer: _____

_____

_____   **6.** Some birds do not fly.
Reason for my answer: _____

_____

_____   **7.** College is always harder than high school.
Reason for my answer: _____

_____

_____   **8.** In preparation for a job interview, you must buy new clothes and look presentable.
Reason for my answer: _____

_____

_____   **9.** Eating oat bran reduces cholesterol.
Reason for my answer: _____

_____

_____   **10.** Most students can benefit from learning active study skills.
Reason for my answer: _____

_____

Discuss your answers with your classmates. How effective were your choices? What have you learned about taking true or false tests?_____

_____

_____

Matching

Most of the time, a matching exercise will be a part of a test, not a test in itself. Matching is like a multiple-choice test because you only have to identify the correct response, not state it yourself. Matching tests are a little more challenging because you have to decide from a list of information which best matches the term or idea you are being presented with. There are several things to keep in mind when taking a matching test, some of which you may already know and do.

Understand the format.   A matching test is made up of two columns of information: one on the left and one on the right. Most often, you are asked to match a piece of information in the left column to a piece of matching information in the right. Sometimes the format is reversed and you are asked to match a piece of information in the right with a piece of information in the left.

By reading the directions carefully, you will understand the test format.

Count the possible answers.   Say you are asked to match the information in the left column to the information in the right. The left column has ten vocabulary terms and the right column has twelve definitions. It is obvious that there will be two definitions on the right that do not match the terms on the left. On some tests, you may use the same answer more than once. Given the possible approaches listed below, place a checkmark next to those that you would use to complete the test. Write any other approach you think might help to succeed on matching tests.

_____ I review all possible answers before answering each one.

_____ As I match them, I cross out the answer I matched.

_____ I answer the ones I know first.

_____ I repeat to myself the term on the left and go down each possible answer on the right filling in the possible answer.

_____ _____

_____ _____

Now test your matching ability by completing the Practice Matching Exercise in Figure 12–3.

Figure 12–3
Practice Matching Exercise

Directions: The left column contains a list of terms from this book and on the right is a list of possible information matches. Place the letter of the correct piece of matching information next to its match on the left.

_____ 1. Active Learning	A. A reader's road map
_____ 2. Background Knowledge	B. Notetaking method best used by a random
_____ 3. Cornell Method	learner
_____ 4. Critical Thinking	C. What you already know
_____ 5. Previewing	D. High/fast reading gears
_____ 6. Passive Learning	E. Learning like a sponge
_____ 7. Mind Mapping	F. Notetaking method best used by the
_____ 8. Mind-Wandering	sequential learner
_____ 9. Learning Influences	G. Those things that effect your study
_____10. Skimming and Scanning	concentration.
	H. Learning like a rock
	I. Can only be reduced, not eliminated
	J. Listening for instructor clues
	K. Thinking about thinking
	L. An effective means of time management

Fill-in-the-Blank

Usually, fill-in-the-blank exercises are part of a test, not tests in themselves. Generally, these questions ask you to identify the meaning of new words or words associated specifically with the information you learned for the test. By studying and knowing them well, you should have little trouble on this section.

Fill-in-the-blank questions are more difficult than multiple choice, true or false, or matching because you have to come up with an answer instead of just identifying one. As with the other games, there are several strategies you need to remember when responding to fill-in-the-blank questions.

Do fill-in-the-blank questions LAST.   If your test has other parts to it, do them first. It is very possible to find answers to the fill-in-the-blank questions on other parts of the test.

Make sure your answer makes sense in context.   This means that if the question is asking for more than one thing or the verb is plural, your answer should be plural. If it asks for one thing or the verb is singular, your answer should be singular. If the word "an" appears before the blank, the word in the blank must start with a vowel. Above all, your answer must make sense based on the context in which it is written.

Be aware of the length of the blank. Usually, a short blank means a short answer. A long blank usually means a long or big word answer and two blanks mean a two-word answer.

Try your skill answering the following fill-in-the-blank questions based on the information covered so far in this book. If you have trouble coming up with an answer, look at the chapter identified in the parentheses after each statement.

1. An _____ learner is one who takes responsibility for his or her learning and learns from mistakes. (Chapter 1)

2. The ingredients in the "Recipe for Learning" are _____, _____, and _____. (Preface)

3. A _____ learner is organized and logical, while a _____ learner is more unorganized and creative. (Chapter 2)

4. _____ means putting off doing something unpleasant or burdensome until a future time. (Chapter 4)

5. The best way to build your vocabulary is to use your _____ _____. (Chapter 5)

6. The first two things readers should know BEFORE they start to read is their _____ and _____. (Chapter 6)

7. All readers should know how to read faster because it increases their _____. (Chapter 7)

8. In order to read faster, you can read _____ _____, read _____, and/or use _____. (Chapter 7)

9. In The Cornell Method of Note Taking, the _____ of the notes is for your informal outline and the _____ _____ is for key words and questions to study from. (Chapter 9)

10. The goal of this book is to help you study _____, not _____. (Chapters 1–15)

Short Answer

Short answer questions generally require that you answer the question in a few sentences or fewer. Sometimes you have to define a vocabulary term or identify a person. Other times you have to state the reason for why something happened or provide the date an event took place. Obviously, studying well and being prepared are important to doing well.

To ensure that you answer the question accurately, determine your answer based on the key words in the question. The key words are listed on the left and the answer to provide is on the right.

Key Question Words	Best Answer
Who?	identify the person(s)
When?	provide the date(s)
Where?	name the place
Why?	state the reason(s) or cause(s)
What?	explain it
How?	describe method(s) or reason(s)

There may be times when you are not sure of the answer. If there is no guessing penalty, it would be worthwhile to take a guess. You may be right or get partial credit for being close to the correct answer.

B egin with the end in mind.

- Stephen R. Covey, author of The 7 Habits of Highly Effective People

Essay

Essays are the most challenging types of tests because you really have to know and understand the material well. When a player writes an essay question, he or she should be skilled enough not only to play the game, but also be the referee or umpire. The referee or umpire spends more time learning the game because he or she needs to be the most knowledgeable person on the playing field. This is why studying for essays requires more study time and over a period of time.

There are many strategies to keep in mind as you begin the essay part of a test.

Read the directions carefully. Though reading directions is part of the general rules of the game, it is important to remind you of this on essays. The essay directions will tell you:

1. *How many essays you need to answer.* Sometimes you will be given a choice of questions to answer, such as three out of five. In this case, make sure to only answer three. If you answer four,

chances are that the instructor will count the first three you wrote, not the best three.

2. *How long the essay should be.* Few instructors enjoy reading excessively long essays, especially when they instruct you to write 250 words or one to two pages. Follow the instructions and come as close as you can to the length you are being asked to write.

3. *How to budget your time.* The amount of time you allow for answering essay questions depends on the amount of points the question is worth, the required length of the answers, and how quickly you think you can come up with an answer. This is where previewing the test is very helpful.

4. *The type of answer to give.* Before you answer any essay question, understand first what the question is asking you to do. Always avoid giving your opinion unless you are asked for it. Read and learn Figure 12–4 on understanding essay directions.

Figure 12–4
Understanding Essay Directions

Below are some common words found in essay directions and what they mean. Review and learn them now so you can respond appropriately and accurately.

Direction Word	Its meaning	Example Question
Name List Give	Simply list in 1, 2, 3 order what is asked for; No sentences necessary.	Name the first 5 U.S. presidents. *List* 3 ways to improve listening. Give 2 reasons for taking notes.
Discuss Describe	Write all you can.	*Discuss* active learning. *Describe* life in the 21st century.
Define Identify	Provide a definition; keep answer as brief as possible.	*Define* previewing. *Identify* the parts of a flower.
Explain State	Write all you can; define and give reasons for what is to be explained.	*Explain* why procrastination is a students worst enemy. *State* why jobs are not for life anymore.
Compare	Discuss similarities *and* differences.	Compare computers and typewriters.
Contrast	Discuss differences only.	*Contrast* (or *distinguish* between) computers and typewriters.
Illustrate	Give examples and/or draw a picture labeling its parts.	*Illustrate* how to use Mind Mapping.
Criticize Evaluate	Give evidence on both sides of an issue; draw conclusions and make judgments	*Criticize* (or *evaluate*) the use of force by police.

| Comment | Write your own reaction to the topic; support your opinion with facts or illustrations. | *Comment* on the increase of unemployment in America. |

5. *How many answers you are to write about.* Some essay questions ask you to respond to more than one question. In the following sample essay question, there are actually four responses you would have to give.

Sample essay question: Students benefit from becoming active learners. *Define* active learner and *compare* it to the passive learner. *Discuss* the reasons why it is important to become active in the learning process. *Evaluate* your experiences as an active and passive learner.

Write for the intended audience.   In this case, your intended audience is obviously your instructor. However, *if you write as if the reader knows nothing about the topic, this will force you to communicate simply, clearly, and completely.*

Make your paper easy to read.   Many students forget that someone has to read their paper when they are finished.

❑ Do your best to write in your neatest handwriting and use an erasable pen to avoid messy mistakes

❑ Write on the right-hand side of your test booklet leaving the left side open to write changes or additions

❑ Remember to number and put your name and date on top of every loose page

❑ Summarize your answer in the first paragraph. Restate it in your concluding paragraph

❑ Substitute synonyms for words you use frequently so as not to sound repetitious

❑ Use connecting words to make the essay flow. (See Chapter 15, using connecting words in step #6: writing a rough draft for examples)

Organize your ideas before you start to write.   Too many students begin writing answers to essay questions without thinking about how their ideas will flow. Since one of the grading criterion for papers is organization, it is to your advantage to organize your thoughts *before* you begin writing. In Chapter 15, you will learn about mapping as a prewriting process for essays and papers. *Map-*

ping is a way to create a quick outline of what you want to write about. This outline can be written in the margin to guide you while writing. (Turn to this section now if you want to learn more.)

Proofread your answers. Reread your answers word-for-word, just as if you heard every word in your head. This will help you catch grammatical mistakes. Also review your answers looking for misspellings, flow of ideas, and organization.

Practice answering essay questions in the exercise below. Answer three out of four with approximately 100 words each.

1. *Define* active learner and *compare* it to the passive learner.

_____

_____

_____

_____

_____

_____

_____

_____

_____

_____

2. *Discuss* the reasons it is important to become active in the learning process.

_____

_____

_____

_____

_____

_____

_____

_____

3. *Evaluate* your experiences as an active and passive learner.

_____

_____

_____

_____

_____

_____

_____

_____

_____

4. For a student to be successful, good effective notetaking skills are important. *Describe* two effective notetaking methods.

_____

_____

_____

_____

_____

_____

_____

_____

Performance Tests

Taking your driving test behind the wheel of a real car is an example of a performance test. What other types of performance tests have you taken? What types will you have to take?

_____

_____

_____

_____

Performance tests are sometimes given along with a written test, and sometimes they are not. They are different than written tests because you have to perform or demonstrate what you have learned. Preparing for a performance test means first studying and understanding the information you have to demonstrate. Then it requires a lot of practice to demonstrate something well. For example, say you were taking a computer repair course. A possible performance test may ask you to add a computer chip to the memory. To accomplish this, you need to know how to open the computer, locate where the chip goes, place the chip in its correct slot, and then close the computer safely. How would you go about preparing for this performance test?

_____

_____

_____

_____

Sometimes tests can involve your active performance as well as your ability to articulate information. How would you prepare for a performance test rather than a written test?

If you haven't guessed by now, probably the most effective way to prepare for a performance test is to study, then practice, practice, practice. You may want to work with other classmates to help each other become skilled in the task at hand.

SUMMARY

1. Understanding how you react to tests will provide you with important personal information about how you deal with stress.

2. Your ability to be successful on tests is affected by your reactions to tests. By learning how to reduce your test stress, you may be able to improve your testing success.

3. Taking responsibility for your own learning and learning to keep tests in perspective are two ways to begin reducing test-taking stress.

4. Taking a test is just like playing a game. The object of the game is to get as many points as possible in the time you are given to play.

5. The rules of the game are the important pieces of information you need to know before the game or test begins. The rules include acting as if you are going to succeed, arriving ahead of time, ignoring panic pushers, previewing the playing field, writing information you want to remember in the margin, doing the easy questions first, avoiding changing your answers, and writing clearly and neatly.

6. There are winning test strategies that you can use for every type of test you take. They may not work all of the time, but they do work most of the time.

REVIEW

Using your own words, answer the following questions based on the information you learned in this chapter.

1. What is stress? Give an example of good stress and an example of bad stress.

   _____

   _____

   _____

   _____

   _____

2. How does your reaction to taking a test affect your ability to be successful?

   _____

   _____

   _____

   _____

   _____

3. What can you do to reduce testing stress?

   _____

   _____

   _____

_____

_____

_____

4. In your opinion, what is (are) the most important rule(s) of the game? Which are the most helpful for you and why?

_____

_____

_____

_____

_____

5. What are some winning test strategies for:

a. multiple-choice questions? _____

_____

_____

_____

_____

_____

b. true or false questions? _____

_____

_____

_____

_____

_____

c. matching tests? _____

_____

_____

_____

_____

_____

d. fill-in-the-blank? _____

_____

_____

_____

_____

_____

e. short answer questions?_____

_____

_____

_____

_____

_____

f. essay questions?_____

_____

_____

_____

_____

_____

g. performance tests?_____

_____

_____

_____

_____

_____

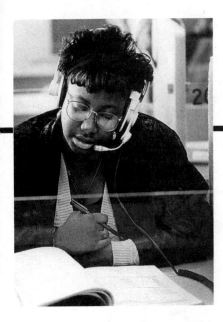

CHAPTER 13

DEVELOPING CRITICAL THINKING SKILLS

After studying and working with the information in this chapter, you should be able to:

1. Explain what critical thinking is.
2. Describe the process of critical thinking.
3. Identify the ways that critical thinking can improve your life.
4. Define the term metacognition and explain its relationship to critical thinking.
5. List the Nine Rules of Critical Thinking.
6. Identify some common mistakes in critical thinking.
7. Begin developing critical thinking skills.

Using the rules of critical thinking can improve your life by making you feel mentally adequate in all kinds of situations.

Have you ever shopped around for the best price on a car or other important purchase? Have you ever discussed a problem with a trusted friend, parent, or teacher? Have you decided that the information in this book is helpful and important? Are you already using some "Tools for Active Learning"?

If your answer to any of these questions is "YES," then you have done some critical thinking. Critical thinking comes naturally and easily to the mind. You do it all the time, quite unconsciously. However, you can improve your critical thinking skills by learning more about them and by consciously practicing the critical thinking techniques presented in this chapter.

Developing good critical thinking skills can help you to do well in your studies and in your work. What critical thinking skills do you already possess that could be helpful in both school and work?

Critical thinking is an important part of learning and living. Many schools today list critical thinking as one of their teaching goals. More and more employers look for people with critical thinking skills because jobs have changed. In the past, most work was done by hand and individuals followed their bosses' instructions. Today the trend is toward work performed in teams using highly technical equipment. This new workplace environment requires independent thinking and problem-solving abilities that are based on habits of critical thinking.

This chapter will acquaint you with some basic critical thinking concepts and provide you with some skills for improving your thinking. Because there's a lot of information about critical thinking, some suggestions for further reading are listed in the recommended bibliography in Appendix F.

SELF-EVALUATION

The following self-evaluation will give you an idea of how familiar, or unfamiliar, you are with some of the topics and terms discussed in this chapter. After reading each statement, circle the letter (Y, S, or N) most appropriate to your answer. Please answer thoughtfully, rate yourself at the end, and then complete the information for Chapter 13 on page 375 in Appendix A.

Y = yes; frequently   **S** = sometimes   **N** = no; never

1. I regularly think about my thinking.	Y S N
2. I know what critical thinking is.	Y S N
3. I make decisions with careful thought and planning.	Y S N
4. I know the definition of the word "metacognition."	Y S N
5. I know when I need more information.	Y S N
6. I know at least five Rules of Critical Thinking.	Y S N
7. I know the difference between "apple polishing" and "name calling."	Y S N
8. I can identify common mistakes in thinking in advertising and political speeches.	Y S N
9. I can identify and describe how critical thinking affects my life.	Y S N
10. I realize that knowledge about thinking can improve thinking.	Y S N

<u>Rate Yourself</u>

Number of Ys _____ x 100=

Number of Ss _____ x 50=

Number of Ns _____ x 10=

Total =

T ake time to think . . . It is the source of power.
- *Anonymous*

WHAT IS CRITICAL THINKING?

C **ritical thinking** is *thinking about thinking in order to decide what to believe and how to behave.* Critical thinking is time consuming. It involves planning and information gathering before decisions get made and actions begin.

Tasks requiring critical thinking fill your life. Using time management techniques, reading labels on food products in order to avoid salt, and deciding how to vote in an election are three familiar activities that involve critical thinking.

List three decisions you've made recently that you believe involved critical thinking:

1. _____

2. _____

3. _____

Select one of the decisions that you listed and describe how you came to the decision you made. Use the following questions to help you with your description.

❑ When did you know you needed to make a decision?

❑ What planning did you do?

❑ What steps did you take? (when begun? when ended?)

❑ Who had to be involved?

❑ What information did you need?

❑ How long did the process take?

❑ Were the results what you wanted?

_____

_____

_____

_____

_____

_____

_____

Critical Thinking Is a Process

As you can see from the previous exercise, critical thinking is a process. It often takes more time than you are used to spending on daily things like cooking, dressing, bathing, etc. You are used to speed in your life. Stopping to think can feel dull and boring. So can memorizing, taking notes, planning schedules, and the other study activities that are described in this book.

Changes in society and technology have added this speed to our lives. Most of us are used to getting results quickly. Slowing down to do such simple, yet time-consuming tasks such as waiting in line, cleaning a room, or mowing the lawn can feel unnatural and unending.

Take a moment and do the following exercise in order to realize how life has sped up in recent years.

How have the following aspects of life sped up in the last 100 years?
Example: Clothing <u>was made at home: now we buy it ready-made at stores</u>.

Bread _____

_____

Transportation _____

_____

Communication _____

_____

Although your daily activities have sped up, *the thinking and learning processes of the brain have not changed*. Education is a process that requires time and practice. It cannot be purchased as a product at a store. You have to do things in order to learn. One of the things you have to do to learn is stop and think things out for yourself.

In Chapter 1 you learned about becoming an active learner, constantly thinking about your reasons for going to school and about some of the strategies you can use to be a successful student. This constant thinking about your learning in order to be a successful student is another example of critical thinking. *Critical thinking is an important part of active learning*.

Improving Life with Critical Thinking

It is true that many ordinary tasks can be done quickly. However, many can be done *better* using critical thinking. For example:

Putting away the groceries: <u>arranging the groceries in categories makes it easier to find things later and to keep track of what's "on hand."</u>

Several other tasks are listed below. In the space provided, describe the thinking that can improve each one.

1. Buying clothes for a new job: _____

_____

_____

2. Deciding on courses for next term: _____

_____

_____

3. Selecting a location for a club party: _____

_____

_____

4. Deciding on charities to support: _____

_____

_____

_____

Deciding what to believe.   Using critical thinking to decide what to believe is important. Careful thinking can save you from being cheated, can keep you pointed toward your goals, can save you time and money, can help you select friends, and so forth.

Often it is difficult to decide what to believe. In the autumn of 1991, millions of American people tried to decide whether to believe Anita Hill or Clarence Thomas. Mr. Thomas was accused of sexually harassing Ms. Hill when she worked for him years earlier. At the time, Mr. Thomas was seeking approval by the United States Senate for an appointment to the highly respected Supreme Court. Mr. Thomas was eventually confirmed, but many people still believe Ms. Hill was telling the truth.

Belief is a big issue in courts of law. The accused are considered innocent until proven guilty. Decisions come from careful consideration by a judge or the vote of a jury. Sometimes justice is unsuccessful and the innocent are found guilty. You have probably read or heard news stories about people being released from prison after years behind bars because of new evidence proving their innocence.

When do you have to decide what to believe in your daily life? You probably are already skeptical about advertisers and politicians. But what about the people you see every day? What claims do they make that you are asked to believe?

Think about recent events in your life and select several situations in which you've wondered whether someone or something was believable.

Examples: Does a friend really like the gift you gave her?
Is a college education really necessary for success in life?

1. _____

2. _____

3. _____

Select one of the examples you listed and think about it or discuss it with your classmates, using the following questions as guides:

❑ How important is it for you to know the truth?

❑ In what ways will you be able to know the truth?

❑ What will you do if you know the truth?

Example: Knowing the truth about my friend and the gift can save me money and make my friend happy. I might learn the truth by noticing if my friend uses my gift. I could also ask her other friends, or I could ask her point blank. If I know the truth, I will know how to make better gift selections in the future.

_____

_____

_____

_____

_____

_____

Many learning activities call for critical thinking about what to believe. Two examples are reading and writing. When you read, you decide whether to believe the author. When you write, you want your readers to decide to believe you.

It is easy to get used to believing what is written in your assignments or told to you by teachers and other sources of information. Have you ever heard of the expression "question authority"? Consider the slick salesman who always has the answers. Remember that a person who knows a lot about a subject can be a better liar than someone who knows nothing.

There is no easy way to be sure that critical thinking will provide correct answers, but it can help you avoid obvious mistakes in thinking. Taking time to think critically can also make you feel better about yourself and the decisions that you make.

The next two sections of this chapter are devoted to helping you develop your critical thinking skills. The first will provide you with some guides called the Rules of Critical Thinking. The second will point out some common mistakes in thinking that are often used to influence your beliefs and your behaviors.

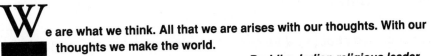

We are what we think. All that we are arises with our thoughts. With our thoughts we make the world.

- Buddha, Indian religious leader

THE RULES OF CRITICAL THINKING

The rules of critical thinking are valuable in several ways. First, they can help you identify situations that can be improved by critical thinking. Second, the rules can also help you feel mentally adequate and enable you to avoid harmful gossip and arguments. Finally, the rules encourage the practice of **metacognition**, or conscious attention to your thinking. Metacognition comes from *meta* which means beyond and *cognition* which means thinking. The regular use of metacognition, or thinking about thinking, will make your thinking better!

The Nine Rules of Critical Thinking, listed in Figure 13–1, are the tools for putting critical thinking to work. A short explanation of each rule follows the list. Use these rules to improve your critical thinking.

Figure 13–1
The Nine Rules of Critical Thinking*

1. Be open-minded about new ideas.
2. Don't argue about things you know nothing about.
3. Know when you need more information.
4. Be aware that different people have different ideas about the meanings of words, gestures, etc.
5. Know the difference between something that must be true and something that might be true.
6. Avoid mistakes in your thinking.
7. Question anything that doesn't make sense.
8. Separate emotional and logical thinking.
9. Develop your vocabulary in order to understand others and to make yourself understood.

* Adapted by L.Loomis [from Anita Harnadeck (1976)].

Explanation of the Rules of Critical Thinking

Read the description for each of the rules for critical thinking carefully. Think about each one and discuss with your classmates any personal examples you can think of. *Using the rules of critical thinking can improve your life by making you feel mentally adequate in all kinds of situations.*

Be open-minded about new ideas. This rule seems easy until a new idea comes along. For you, a new idea could be presented as new information in one of your classes. This idea may seem strange, silly, stupid, boring, artificial, unimportant, etc.

A sign that you are experiencing a new idea is if you feel uncomfortable or feel yourself resisting it. For example, if your instructor decides to change the way you hand in your homework assignments, it is easy to say "I've gotten along fine the other way. Why should I change now?"

Begin to notice when you are feeling uncomfortable or resisting and ask yourself if there is a new idea floating around. Since the world is changing rapidly these days, it is important to become open-minded about new ideas in order to survive.

Think about a time when you experienced open-mindedness. Describe it below.

_____

_____

_____

Don't argue about things you know nothing about. If you feel yourself reacting to a new idea, it is a good idea to hold your tongue until you have enough information on which to base your opinion.

If you hear a rumor, use this rule to avoid gossip that can harm others. A simple "I don't know anything about it" can eliminate hurtful talk.

Think about a time when you tried to argue about something you really didn't know much about. What happened?

_____

_____

_____

_____

Know when you need more information. How do you know when you need more information? Your brain doesn't tell you directly. Instead, it may tell you that you feel stupid, frustrated, incompetent, etc.

The next time you get a "stupid" message, say to yourself "I'M NOT STUPID, I JUST NEED MORE INFORMATION." Then ask a question, make a note to ask someone, or look something up. Remember the reminders in Chapter 1—"I do not understand and will ask my instructor" and "Know when to ask for help and then ask for it." These are two examples of how to use this rule.

Practice saying "I need more information" and learn to get rid of negative self-talk about being dumb or inadequate.

Describe a time when you received a "stupid message." What happened? What can you do in the future to get rid of "stupid messages?"

_____

_____

_____

_____

Be aware that different people have different ideas about the meanings of words, gestures, expressions, etc. This is a rule that could also be called "different strokes for different folks." It is easy to agree with the rule. BUT when someone disagrees with you about something, it is also easy to get angry and refuse to listen to the other point of view.

Getting angry is a signal to use metacognition. Stop and think about the situation. Talk yourself into listening to the other person. The more you practice, the better you get. The old expression "count to ten before answering when you are angry" is a metacognitive strategy for this circumstance. This can help you to avoid saying things you don't mean. Using this rule can also cut down on arguments and fights.

Can you think of a time when someone disagreed with you? What happened? How can this rule help you deal with people better?

_____

_____

_____

_____

Know the difference between something that _must_ be true and something that _might_ be true. This rule will help you separate facts (must be's) and opinions (might be's). It is another useful rule for avoiding rumor and gossip situations.

For example: It is a _fact_ that someone in the class is whispering (must be); it is an _opinion_ that the whispering is about you (might be).

Whenever someone makes a statement that sounds like a fact, ask yourself if the statement is a fact (must be) or an opinion (might be) and look for evidence to support or refute the statement.

Can you think of a time when a fact became confused with an opinion? What happened?

_____

_____

_____

_____

Avoid mistakes in your thinking. There are many kinds of mistakes in thinking. The next section of this chapter describes some of them. A very common mistake is called "hasty generalization." If one taste of a new food leads you to say the food is nasty, then you are guilty of hasty generalization.

Question anything that doesn't make sense. Questioning is a great exercise for developing critical thinking. When you don't understand something someone says, what do you usually do?

_____

_____

_____

It is important to know that when someone wants to trick you, they sometimes try to make you feel stupid in order to keep you from asking questions. They then try to hurry you and give you the feeling you are an idiot when you want to slow down and think critically. They know that you may become suspicious because their answers may not make sense.

If you let a situation go by *without* understanding something someone says, then you have let an active learning opportunity pass you by.

What can you do the next time you don't understand something?

_____

_____

_____

Separate emotional and logical thinking. You have feelings (emotions) and reasons (logical thinking) for everything you experience. Good critical thinking invites you to use both emotions and logic in making decisions. This rule suggests that you do two things. First collect logical information and see where it leads you. Then notice your feelings.

For example: Your logic may tell you that the red dress or tie is a better buy than the blue one. But if you don't like the red item, then purchasing it will be a waste of time and money and a source of regret because you probably will never wear it.

In school you may be unhappy about the results of a test. While you can use your logic to see your mistakes and make plans to improve your work, you also need to express your emotions and recover from your disappointment in the company of supportive friends and family.

This rule is difficult. The ability to use it is considered a sign of maturity.

Develop your vocabulary in order to understand others and make yourself understood.   Chapter 5 is devoted to building vocabulary. Use its tips and guidelines to increase your knowledge of the English language. Enjoy the power provided by a large vocabulary. Your studying will be easier.

The brain loves words. Feed it!

Practicing the Rules of Critical Thinking

Now it's time to practice the rules. Is critical thinking taking place in the following situations? Circle YES or NO and then write a short explanation of your answer citing the rules that are being kept or being broken.

Are you aware of when you are thinking critically? Is the process of critical thinking going on here?

Example: Mary says she is going to drop her psychology course. The professor talks all the time about things she's never heard of and she can't imagine how any of the information could ever be useful.   YES/NO

Mary is not using critical thinking. She is not being open-minded about new ideas.

1. Erin is having problems writing biology lab reports and makes an appointment to get help from her instructor.   YES/NO

_____

_____

_____

2. Ed is upset about failing a test. He tears it up, leaves the room before the professor goes over the questions, and cuts the next two classes. YES/NO

_____

_____

_____

3. Takeisha cannot find her notebook and accuses her roommate of hiding it. YES/NO

_____

_____

_____

4. Whenever Sergei comes across an unfamiliar word he writes it down in a special section of his notebook. After collecting several of these words he stops, looks them up, and records the meaning that fits whatever he is reading. YES/NO

_____

_____

_____

_____

SOME COMMON MISTAKES IN THINKING

This section is devoted to avoiding mistakes in your thinking. There are so many mistakes in thinking that books are written about them and philosophers spend their lives discussing them. Some of the most common mistakes in thinking are described in the following paragraphs. *Your critical thinking will be greatly improved by becoming aware of these mistakes.*

Making decisions is a part of critical thinking. BUT some decisions are not made with the benefit of critical thinking. Going along with the crowd in order to be popular, making fun of someone or something you disagree with, and returning an insult with an insult all involve decisions made without the benefit of critical thinking. These kinds of decisions are considered "mistakes in thinking" and have names: peer pressure, horse laugh, and two wrongs make a right.

Another mistake in thinking was mentioned in the description of this rule. It is called *hasty generalization.* Common examples of this include deciding you don't like someone you've just met, giving up a new sport or hobby after only one or two tries, and refusing to listen to some new music because you didn't understand it the first time you heard it.

Additional common mistakes in thinking are described below:

Name calling.   Name calling substitutes a personal insult for a direct response to another person's statement.

Example: John says, "Being metacognitive about studying is a great help" but Alex responds, "That's a typical nerd statement if I ever heard one!"

Scare tactics, appeals to pity, and apple polishing.   These all focus on emotional thinking and ignore logic. Which one is which in the following examples?

Example A: "Professor Rankin, please let me hand in my paper tomorrow. I had to take care of my sick relative. When I finally started typing I ran out of paper and it was too late to get any. If you accept my paper late, I'll be able to stay off probation."

Mistake : _____

Example B: "We, the membership committee of the Sigma Club, understand that you've been very active with the student newspaper. Did you know that it was *our* club president that was kicked off *your* paper's editorial board last year?"

Mistake : _____

Example C: "Joe, please let me photocopy your notes to study for the exam. Your handwriting is so much neater than mine and you always get more than I do from Professor Thomas's lectures."

Mistake: _____

False dilemma.   People use false dilemma to make you think there are only two choices in a situation: the one they want and an unattractive or terrible alternative.

Example: The statement "Strong men drink liquor—what's the matter with you?" is intended to make you think that you aren't strong if you don't drink. Actually there are many ways to be strong. The peer-pressure tactic mentioned earlier often combines forces with false dilemma.

Slippery slope. Situations involving change often encounter slippery slope thinking. Claims are made that the change will lead to many more changes and that the end result will be awful.

Example: "If we let you have two excused absences from class then you'll want pass/fail exams and before we know it all our academic standards of excellence will have disappeared."

Begging the question. This is also known as circular reasoning. The same statement gets repeated in reverse order. Nothing new is added to the thinking.

Example: "Athletes need a good, healthy diet. Therefore paying attention to what you eat is important if you want to perform well in sports."

Straw man. Have you ever had anyone disagree with you by changing your statement? The changed statement is the "straw man." Notice how your brother changes your "one time clean-up" suggestion to a "daily one" in the following example.

Example: You ask your brother to help you clean the bathroom. He says he can't clean it up every day. It's too much work and a waste of time.

You're another. This last example of common mistakes in thinking is often used by people who spend a lot of time together. It resembles "straw man" because it avoids the subject. Where "straw man" changes the original statement, "you're another" introduces another subject.

Example: If your brother's response to your suggestion about cleaning the bathroom had been, "and when are you going to get me a date for New Year's Eve?" then you would have experienced "you're another." You can respond with: "Let's deal with both of these issues. They are important. Which one shall we discuss first?"

Do you recognize these mistakes in thinking? They are purposefully used in many situations in order to influence your decisions. *Name calling, scare tactics,* and *false dilemma* are favorites of politicians. Advertisers are fond of *apple polishing, peer pressure, slippery slopes,* and *straw men.* Look for these mistakes in thinking when you read or hear political speeches or advertisements.

Practice Identifying Mistakes in Thinking

Practice identifying some of the mistakes in thinking described in this section by doing the following matching exercise.

Can you recognize when you are failing to think critically? What mistake in thinking is this advertisement appealing to?

Wear the shoes that makes the pros great and your teammates more competitive.

Run Faster!

Jump Higher!

Leave your opponents in the dust!

Don't be left behind!

Match mistakes in thinking with their examples by placing the letter of the example next to the number of the mistake. Try not to refer back to the text.

—— **1.** Two wrongs make a right

—— **2.** Hasty generalization

—— **3.** Peer pressure

—— **4.** Scare tactics

—— **5.** Apple polishing

—— **6.** Horse laugh

a. One look at that woman's clothes and I knew we had nothing in common.

b. I'd like to have you on my committee. You're always on time, you have lots of good ideas, and you are great on the telephone.

c. Joe, tell me how to do this assignment. I need to get a good grade and I won't tell your girl friend I saw you out with Sue.

d. Recycling in this town? You've got to be kidding. What a joke.

e. After Anita ruined my dress and made no effort to replace it, I had no problem lending her cashmere sweater to my sister without asking her permission.

f. I don't know if we ought to admit women to this club. The next thing you know

___ **7.** Slippery slope

g. Anna says that regular planning helps her keep on top of her studies. That's too much for me. I can't be bothered jotting things down on my schedule every five minutes.

they'll be running everything their way and all the men will quit.

___ **8.** Begging the question

h. You mean you don't have a tape player? Everyone I know owns one.

___ **9.** Straw man

i. Well, that's just like a freshman to want to know the way to the bookstore.

___ **10.** Name calling

j. Keeping an up-to-date assignment book helps you remember your homework. You won't forget your assignments if you write them all in the same place.

Y**ou see things and you say, "Why?" But I dream things that never were; and I say, "Why not?"**

- George Bernard Shaw, author and playwright

POINT OF VIEW

T he mistakes in thinking that you've been learning in this chapter are frequently used by people who want to persuade you to believe or do something. They have a particular point of view and their messages to you are tilted to favor that point of view. That tilt is called **bias**.

Two common groups of persuaders in our American society are politicians and advertisers. Politicians want you to believe in their ideas and vote for them. Many of their statements are biased in that direction.

What do advertisers want you to believe and do? _____

In order to influence you, a persuader only shows you part of the picture . . . that is, the picture from that person's point of view OR from a point of view that he or she thinks you will like. Presenting part of a picture is often called "card stacking." The persuader only shows you the cards he or she has chosen, instead of giving you the whole deck.

When you recognize bias, several rules of critical thinking are especially useful:

1. Because you realize you are not getting the whole picture *you know you need more information, and you see it's time to separate the facts from the opinions.*

2. If the persuader is playing on your emotions (pity, fear, pride, greed, etc.), then alert yourself to think logically.

3. If the persuader is using unfamiliar terms and trying to make you hurry, *question anything that doesn't make sense and build up your vocabulary.*

4. If the persuader has a different point of view and some new ideas, you might want to learn more about his or her message. Perhaps there is something worthwhile behind the bias. *Keep an open mind, don't argue if you have no information, and know that there can be other points of view than yours.*

Here's an example of an everyday kind of persuasive situation:

An old friend is trying to get you to go to an expensive benefit dinner for a local charity. You recognize a persuasive situation so you do some critical thinking. Identify the rules you use as you go through the following process.

1. "Do I know everything I need to know? What more information do I need?"

_____

_____

2. "Why is my friend pushing so hard for me to attend. It doesn't make sense."

_____

_____

3. "I know that the charity is important but what else might be going on? What might I be getting into?"

_____

_____

4. "I've never been to a benefit dinner for charity. I've always thought it better to give to the charity directly. However, if everything looks O.K., I might give it a try."

_____

_____

_____

Persuasion, bias, and point of view are everywhere. What are some of your points of view? When have you tried to persuade someone to do something? Use the following space to list a few situations in which you've done some persuading.

Example:
Persuasive act: Asking someone to vote for you in an election.
Point of view: You have had experience and will work hard. The incumbent has not kept his campaign promises and doesn't deserve to be reelected. Also, you like to be a winner and you want to be famous. (Notice your emotional bias in the second sentence.)

Now develop your own examples:

1. Persuasive act:

_____

Point of view:

_____

_____

_____

2. Persuasive act:

_____

Point of view:

_____

_____

_____

Looking for points of view is a quality of critical thinking. Determining point of view can help you make decisions. Another person's point of view can be acceptable or unacceptable, depending on your own biases. You'll often choose to believe points of view with which you agree and which you think will help you in your life. HOWEVER, REMEMBER: BE OPEN-MINDED TO NEW IDEAS. Practice using other points of view and accept people who have them. So much new information is being produced these days that new ideas are unavoidable.

Points of view connect with what you believe is important in life. What's important to you carries feelings. Thus, part of your critical thinking is always related to your feelings. (Remember the rule about logic and emotions?) Be a careful critical thinker by continuously noticing your feelings about situations and by examining what you believe is important.

Most sources of information have points of view. This book, for example, is biased in favor of studying and learning. The author feels that education is important and believes that everyone can learn how to learn. The author values learning.

Describe the point of view of a person who would not want to use this book:

_____

_____

_____

Critical thinking asks you to think carefully not only about ordinary events, but also about current environmental and economic topics, such as global warming, the appropriate role of government, and other aspects that can affect your daily life. You probably have some strong feelings about quite a few of these topics. List some of them in the space provided below.

Some current topics that concern me are: _____

_____

_____

Philosophers who study critical thinking and the new knowledge being learned about the brain believe that the human mind has the ability to solve the problems of the world. But to do so will take educating people about critical thinking as well as a commitment to use it. *Study Skills: The Tools for Active Learning* is based on knowledge about the brain. Furthermore, the whole book, not just this chapter, invites you to be a critical thinker . . . to think about yourself, your life, your goals, to believe you can learn, and to act accordingly.

Part of your life as an active learner often includes an essay, a paper, or a speech in which you have to organize and show your thinking. Sometimes you have to do this quickly on a test. In Chapter 15, you will find more information on how to present your point of view.

THE USE OF YOUR MIND

You live in an era about discovery of the power of your mind and your ability to think. New discoveries about the brain are being revealed regularly. Every chapter in this book contains advice and information based on up-to-date information about your brain.

People used to think that mental and physical abilities were set at birth. Now it is known that you can improve both through instruction and practice. In fact, your brain won't age as quickly as your body. Being an active learner and a critical thinker will keep you mentally sharp all your life.

SUMMARY

1. Critical thinking is thinking about thinking in order to decide what to believe and how to behave.

2. Critical thinking is a process. In order to become a critical thinker, you have to learn to stop and think things out for yourself. It helps you to decide what to believe. Critical thinking can also improve your life.

3. Metacognition means thinking about thinking. The regular use of metacognition will make your thinking better.

4. The Nine Rules of Critical Thinking are the tools for putting critical thinking to work. Becoming aware of them is the first step in this learning process.

5. Making decisions is a part of critical thinking. However, it is important to be aware of the common mistakes in thinking that influence your decisions.

6. Becoming an effective critical thinker will give you the intellectual power to succeed in almost any situation.

REVIEW

Using your own words, answer the following questions based on the information you learned in this chapter.

1. In your own words, what is critical thinking?

    _____

    _____

    _____

    _____

2. What is metacognition? What is its relationship to critical thinking?

    _____

    _____

    _____

    _____

3. Describe a situation in which you did some critical thinking.

    _____

    _____

    _____

    _____

4. Explain how critical thinking can improve your life.

    _____

    _____

    _____

    _____

5. Name and explain the importance of three of the Rules of Critical Thinking.

    _____

    _____

    _____

    _____

6. Name and explain three examples of mistakes in thinking.

_____

_____

_____

_____

7. When, where, and how will you use critical thinking in your studies?

_____

_____

_____

_____

PART 5
RESEARCHING AND WRITING PAPERS

CHAPTER 14

USING THE LIBRARY

After studying and working with the information in this chapter, you should be able to:

1. Explain how a librarian can help you.
2. Identify and describe the 3 Rs: Reserves, Reference, and Research.
3. Write a citation.
4. Write a note card.
5. Find books with a catalog.
6. Find periodicals and articles using indexes.
7. Begin using the library for doing school or personal research.

A library is one of the best places to become an active learner.

A **library** is a place where you can find answers to your questions. Libraries come in many varieties and sizes. There are public libraries, school libraries, college libraries, home libraries, and even libraries in companies, called special libraries. Every library has a collection of information that is put together to answer particular questions. Do you remember the first library you ever used? It could have been a shelf in your parent's house, a corner of your first grade classroom, or a big public library.

Using a library effectively can offer great assistance to your learning. Do you know where to go and who to ask for help at your library?

The libraries of then are not the libraries of now. Today's libraries have added computers, compact discs, multimedia, and videotapes to the books, magazines, and newspapers that they have always had. The card catalog is slowly becoming a thing of the past, replaced by computer databases and links to other computer databases.

A library is one of the best places to become an active learner. The books, computers, and magazines that it has on hand can keep you more up-to-date than the textbooks that you use in your classrooms. When there is a new way to treat a disease, a new computer chip to control an electronic device, or a new management technique, the first place to find out about it is in the library.

This chapter is designed to show you how to get started using libraries in your active learning process. The exercises can best be completed during a visit to your school library; however, if time or transportation is a problem, you can use your telephone. What you learn from the exercises will help you tailor your library experience to your own library.

SELF-EVALUATION

The following self-evaluation will give you an idea of how familiar, or unfamiliar, you are with some of the topics and terms discussed in this chapter. After reading each statement, circle the letter (Y, S, or N) most appropriate to your answer. Please answer honestly, rate yourself at the end, and then complete the information for Chapter 14 on page 375 in the Appendix A.

Y = yes; frequently   **S** = sometimes   **N** = no; never

1. I go to the library often.   Y S N
2. I know the librarians and other staff.   Y S N
3. I read current periodicals.   Y S N
4. I use reference books.   Y S N
5. I know what reserve materials are.   Y S N
6. I know how to use the library's computers.   Y S N
7. I use indexes to find articles.   Y S N
8. I make photocopies of articles or reference material. Y S N
9. I know how to create a research plan.   Y S N
10. I know how to write a note card.   Y S N

<u>Rate Yourself</u>

Number of Ys _____ x 100=
Number of Ss _____ x 50=
Number of Ns _____ x 10=
Total =

Great discoveries and achievements invariably involve the cooperation of many minds.

- Alexander Graham Bell, scientist and inventor of the telephone

HOW A LIBRARIAN CAN HELP YOU

Librarians are extremely valuable to your educational process and academic success. Their role is to help you find the materials that will add to what you have learned in class. Librarians know a little about a lot of things, but more important, they also know how to find out almost anything. *Do not be afraid to ask them questions* even if they look busy. Answering your questions is their primary task.

Although librarians have many work responsibilities, their primary role is to help you find what you need. Are you willing to ask for help when you need it, or do you simply hunt around haphazardly for what you want?

There are two things to know about librarians before you go to the library. The first is that not everyone who works in a library is a librarian. There are many employees (some are even students like yourself) who can help you with tasks, such as finding a magazine on the shelf, checking out a book, or using the microfilm machines. They are not librarians. A **librarian** is a person who has advanced training in how to find information. Get to know this individual and he or she can become a strong ally in your active learning process.

The second thing you should know about librarians is that they are not study hall monitors, like they may have been in high school. Quiet is nice in a library because people are trying to read and study. But keeping the peace is not their most important activity. Helping you locate books, periodicals, and other materials in response to your questions is the librarian's most important function.

Let's get to know your library better by learning the answers to the following questions. You might find some answers in your school's student handbook or in a handout that the library may have for every student. Ask a librarian if there is a special library handout. If not, ask for help with the following questions:

Who is in charge of the library (usually this person is called the director)? _____

Who is the main reference librarian? _____

What hours does this person work? _____

Are there other reference librarians? _____ yes _____ no

If the answer is yes, what are their names and their hours?

_____

_____

What are the names and titles of other library staff?

_____

_____

_____

What is the best telephone number to use to reach the reference librarian? _____

What hours is the library open? _____

Are there computers in the library? _____ yes _____ no

    If yes, do they have special names and functions? List them here _____

_____

_____

_____

Where in the library can you find the following sections?

    Reference Area _____

    Reserve Area _____

    Circulation Desk _____

Education is an exercise . . . to learn to want what is worth having.

                                        - Ronald Reagan, former President of the United States 1980–1988

THE THREE Rs

Libraries have many functions helpful to your development as an active learner. These can be summarized by the **Three Rs: R**eserves, **R**eference, and **R**esearch.

    The library has a fourth function that we are mentioning, but will not explain in depth. A library is also a place to **R**elax. Many people come to the quiet and comfort of a library to read the daily newspaper, the latest *Sports Illustrated*, or a new novel. Making the library a part of your daily routine will lead to success in whatever you do.

Reserves

The reserve section of a library is a place where an instructor can store additional reading assignments, such as an article or reference book to be used by students during a term.

Reserve material is put in the library at the request of an instructor. It can be a copy of a particular article, book, or even videocassette or audiotape. These materials usually do not leave the library and must be used there or copied. The cost for copying varies in each library, but it is usually pocket change. If you have the time to spend doing your assignment in the library, then you will save money.

In order to use reserve material, you must know the name of your instructor and the course number. Most libraries keep this material in a special section and have exact requirements for how it is borrowed.

Look at your syllabi (plural of syllabus) from your classes to answer the following questions. If none of your classes have a syllabus, then skip the first three questions and answer the last two.

1. Which of your classes has something on reserve in the library?

_____

2. What is the course number of the class? _____

3. What is on reserve? ____ a book ____ an article ____ other: ____

4. What does your library require to use reserve material?

_____

_____

5. How much does it cost in your library to photocopy a page? ____

Reference

The **reference** section of a library is a place to find a short answer to something you don't know or understand. This can be a definition from a dictionary, an article from an encyclopedia, or a sports statistic.

The books and other items kept in the reference section contain a wealth of information. Almost any question can be given a short answer from this material. The reference section is usually found next to the librarian's or reference desk. Be aware that reference material is not usually allowed to leave the library, so you will have to use it there. Your librarian can help you find the right information for your question. Some helpful materials are the following:

Dictionaries. A **dictionary** is a book that contains words and their meanings listed in alphabetical order. Dictionaries include not only the common *Webster's*, but also dictionaries in specialized fields such as nursing, computers, and law. Close to the general dictionaries you will also find another important tool, the *thesaurus*, which lists more synonyms and antonyms than the dictionary. (See Chapter 5 for more information.)

Directories. A **directory** contains alphabetical information such as names or addresses. The most familiar of these is the local telephone directory. There are many others that list the addresses of anyone from company executives and television personalities to colleges and universities. Directories can be helpful when you are looking for a job.

Handbooks. These are especially important in science and engineering. **Handbooks** contain technical information like the values for information that stay the same, like the speed of light, or an equation like the one to convert Fahrenheit degrees to Celsius.

Almanacs. Facts, facts, and more facts are found in **almanacs**. How many people live in New York? What time is it in Hong Kong when it is five p.m. in Montana? What team won the 1986 World Series? Almanacs are great for becoming a good player of the game "Trivial Pursuit" or "Jeopardy" and for building your background knowledge.

Encyclopedias. An **encyclopedia** is a book, or set of books, containing articles on various subjects from A to Z. Each book, or volume, covers one or more letters with each subject listed in alphabetical order. Each set of volumes has an overall index, usually in the last volume, which is a great help in leading you to the particular information you want.

Among the reference materials available to you in the library, none are more helpful for finding out a lot of information about a subject than an encyclopedia. Can you think of a school assignment that would send you to the library in search of its encyclopedias?

The original encyclopedias were written to include all of the world's knowledge. The ones we know today contain only the most popular information. For example, *Encyclopedia Americana* contains mostly information that an American audience would need. *Encyclopedia Britannica* contains mostly information that a British audience would need. In addition to these, there are also other types of encyclopedias such as the *Encyclopedia of Psychology*, the *Encyclopedia of Sociology*, and the *Encyclopedia of Criminal Law and Justice*. These books will be helpful to you at different times during your education.

What are the names of some of the encyclopedias that your library has?

_____

_____

_____

Encyclopedias will be an especially important tool for doing the third R—**R**esearch. For instance, let's suppose that we are interested in Albert Einstein's theory of relativity. *Go now to any general encyclopedia set in your library. Choose the volume that has **Ein** in it. Locate the subject listing for Albert **Ein**stein.* You will find general information about Einstein as well as some specific information about his theory of relativity. If it is a good encyclopedia, it will lead you to other volumes that have information on this topic by the notation "see also Mathematics."

An easier way to accomplish the same thing is to use the index volume, usually the last one in the set. *Now locate the index for your encyclopedia set. Look up **Einstein, Albert** in the index.* Notice that there are references for not only the main entry in the Ein volume, but several other references as well. It would look something like Figure 14–1. Notice that most of the information about relativity is in the Physics article in the P volume.

Einstein, Albert
    atomic theory
    mathematics
    relativity

Specific related topics

volume "E" for Einstein
page number
E 403
P:372 ← volume "P" for Physics
M:495 ← volume "M" for Mathematics
P:395-400

Figure 14–1
Library Reference for Albert Einstein

Encyclopedias are a great first step in doing research because they can lead you to more material. Take another look at the entry about Einstein in the Ein volume. If we had really been interested in doing a paper on the life of Einstein, we get tremendous help from the section at the end of this listing. This section is usually called a *bibliography*, or *works cited*, or *further reading*. It will give you the titles, authors, and dates of complete books on Albert Einstein. It may look like Figure 14–2.

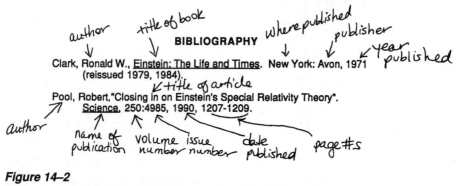

Figure 14–2
Encyclopedia Bibliography References for Albert Einstein

Research

Research is the most important function of the library. You have already done some preliminary research in the previous section of this chapter. You got some information from an encyclopedia, then you found some more in the index. There is even more to find. It's like solving a puzzle.

Doing **research** means locating usable information for a paper or project. It also means finding out about something you want to know more about for personal reasons. Think about the last time you needed to buy something expensive. How do you get the "best buy"? It takes some investigating, or research. Let's take a closer look at a possible method of doing your research.

You first *decide* that you want or need to buy something expensive: a stereo system, a computer, a car. Then you *define* what you want. For example, if you want a new stereo, you decide that it needs to have a compact disc player, a cassette player, and a turntable. Last, you *look for information* about price, quality, and availability. How do you do this? You could use one of the following methods:

1. You can ask friends and family about the models they own.

2. You can look in the newspaper to see what stereo systems were on sale.

3. You can look in consumer rating magazines like *Consumer Reports* for an article on the quality of various brands of stereo equipment.

In the end, you make a choice based on what you learned during your research. You *decide*. You *define*. You *research*. Deciding on a topic and doing research for a paper requires similar research techniques.

WRITING CITATIONS

Citations are a short way of telling your instructor about the books and articles that you read while doing your research. You are usually required to include this with any paper or project you do.

Look again at Figure 14–2 in the encyclopedia section of this chapter. There are two citations there. The first one is a book citation.

Now here is information about several other books. For each one, write a citation using the following format. Use the first listing in Figure 14–2 as an example.

Author's last name first. *Title of book*, (edition used—if given). Place of publication: name of publisher, date of publication.

Book #1: It was written by Abraham Pais, it is called *Subtle is the Lord. . . , the Science and the Life of Albert Einstein*. It was published in New York by Oxford University Press in 1982.

_____

_____

_____

Book #2: It was written by Herman Bondi and called *Relativity and Common Sense: A New Approach to Einstein*. It was published in Mineola, N.Y., by Dover Publishing in 1980.

_____

_____

_____

_____

Book #3: The book is called *Introducing Einstein's Relativity* and was written by R.A. D'Inverno. It was published by Oxford University Press in New York, N.Y., in 1992.

_____

_____

_____

_____

The second citation in the bibliography is for an article. Now here is information about several other articles. For each, write a citation using the following format. Use the second listing in Figure 14–2 as an example.

Author's last name first, "Title of article". *Name of periodical.* Volume number: issue number, date of publication, page numbers.

Article #1: The article was written by Martin C. Gutzwiller called "Einstein" and published in *Scientific American*, volume 266, number 1, on pages 78–85, in 1992.

_____

_____

_____

_____

Article #2: The article was called "Einstein in Love" and written by Dennis Overbye. It was published in *Time* magazine on April 30, 1990, on page 108.

_____

_____

_____

_____

Article #3: The article, called "A Challenge to Einstein" was written by T. Bethell. It was published in *National Review*, November 5, 1990, on pages 69–71.

_____

_____

_____

_____

If you want or need more information on how to construct a bibliography, you can start with the first listing under "Works Cited" in Figure 14–4, *The MLA Style Manual*. Another possible source is the *American Psychological Association Handbook,* which provides the APA style. Check with your instructor for which style he or she prefers you to use.

KEEPING NOTE CARDS

As you know, taking notes is an active form of learning. In this case, the notes you will take are not so much to learn from, but rather to use as tools for writing papers and projects. Writing your own note cards will help you keep track of the important information you have found. It will also help you keep track of where you read the material in each note for use in your bibliography.

You can use index cards of any size (from 3" x 5" to 5" x 8") or notebook paper to write your notes. Look at Figure 14–3. This is a sample of what a note card could look like.

Figure 14–3
Sample Note Cards (5" x 8")

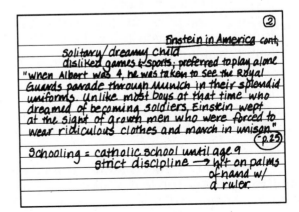

The top of the card or paper is where you write all of the bibliographical information. Make sure to include the title, author, publisher, date published, location of publication, volume numbers, and page numbers. It is frustrating to find later on that you did not get all the information you need to complete your bibliography. You end up wasting time going back to find the missing pieces.

The rest of the card is for your notes about what you read in the book or article you found. You may need to use more than one card for each source you read. In this case, keep track of the cards by numbering them 1, 2, 3, and so forth, and put either the author's last name or book title on each card. Use your effective notetaking techniques to locate and write only the important information. Remember to keep your notes as short as possible using key words and abbreviations.

Plagiarism

If you use direct quotes or any ideas from your reading material, you must tell your reader where you got the ideas you are using in your paper. If you do not, then you are guilty of plagiarism. **Plagiarism** is using other peoples words and thoughts without giving them credit. In most schools plagiarism is serious enough to get you dismissed.

To avoid plagiarism, here are some suggestions about what to write on your note cards:

1. Use quotation marks around words that you are quoting exactly as they appear in the source. Even if you paraphrase and change the wording, you still need to keep track of where you found the information.

2. Keep a list of all the books and articles that you use for your paper; this is known as your **working bibliography**. If you are using note cards, you can write this information there. Write them down in the citation format that you practiced before.

3. Write a citation for *anything* that you did not think of yourself or which you did not read in several sources. You need to acknowledge all of the following: facts not widely known, direct quotations, other people's opinions, statistics, and help which you got from anyone.

At the end of your paper, include an alphabetized list of the sources that you used. It could look something like Figure 14–4. Also see Appendix G for the sources used to write this book.

Figure 14—4
Alphabetical List of Sources Used

WORKS CITED

Achtert, Walter and Joseph Gibaldi. <u>MLA Style Manual</u>. New York: MLA, 1985.
Lunsford, Andrea, et al. <u>St. Martin's Handbook</u>, 2nd ed., New York: St. Martin's Press, 1992.

E ducation is not preparation for life . . . education is life itself.
— *John Dewey, American philosopher and educator*

FINDING BOOKS WITH A CATALOG

The library is full of books. How do you find the ones that will help you with your particular paper?

Let's do a thought exercise first. Think about your own compact disc, record, or tape music collection. How do you find the one tape that you want to listen to? Do you just look through all the ones you have until you find the one you want? If you don't own many, then this may work fine. But what would happen if you owned 30,000 of them? This is the average size of a library's book collection. Would you have them arranged in alphabetical order by singer or band? Would you have them in categories—rock in one section, classical in another, and rap in another? How would each category be arranged? Would you put them in order by singer or would you use the title instead?

What if you had your 30,000-item music collection in the garage because it no longer fit in your house? Would you want to go out there in the dead of winter to look along the shelves to see what you had or would you have an alphabetical list by the musical group, one by title and one by the category?

Is a list the best solution? What would happen if you gave one of your albums away? You would have to rewrite your list. This is why a card for each item would be a better solution. Then, when you discarded an item, you could simply throw the card away.

Libraries have been doing the same thing with their music collection as well as with their books and other materials. They use a card catalog or computerized catalog to keep track of all their materials.

Now, suppose you let your friend Chuck pick from your music collection. Chuck is a nice guy, but he doesn't know anything about music and never remembers that you put things together by musical group, not by album title. He always puts Metallica's . . . *And Justice For All* in the Hip Hop section under A (for . . . *And Justice For All*) instead of M (for Metallica). How could you help Chuck put Metallica where it belongs? Maybe a code would help Chuck. The code could be: **HM** to stand for Heavy Metal, **MT** for Metallica not Megadeth, **A** for . . . *And Justice For All*, not *Metallica*. This code would be written on the cover and also on each card. When you looked in your card file under Metallica, you would find a card like the one in Figure 14–5.

**Figure 14–5
Sample Card for Card
Catalog**

> HEAVY METAL
> HM   Metallica
> MT   . . . And Justice For All
> A

Libraries have been doing this same exercise with books and other materials for centuries. Every book that is brought into the library is given a code, or **call number**. Libraries in the United States usually stick with one of two organizational systems: the *Dewey Decimal System*, which is used in public school and some technical school libraries, and the *Library of Congress System of Organization*, which is used by most college and university libraries. The call numbers are there to get you to the shelf so you can find the book (see Figure 14–6).

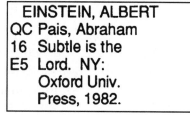

> EINSTEIN, ALBERT
> QC Pais, Abraham
> 16 Subtle is the
> E5 Lord. NY:
>   Oxford Univ.
>   Press, 1982.

> EINSTEIN, ALBERT
> 530   Pais, Abraham
> 0924 Subtle is the
> P149 Lord. NY:
>   Oxford Univ.
>   Press, 1982.

**Figure 14–6
Sample Cards with Call Numbers**

Next, let's think about categories. Most rock fans think of Metallica as a Heavy Metal band. But some call this type of music hard rock. If someone looked in your category section under

HARD ROCK, would they find the works by Metallica? How would you lead them to the HEAVY METAL category?

This problem is solved by something called a **cross-reference**. When you look up Heavy Metal, there would be a note that said "see also" Hard Rock. To make things easier, you might keep all of these notes in one place. In a library, these notes are called **subject headings**. Some libraries have large volumes of them called *Library of Congress Subject Headings.*

Computerized Libraries

In a computerized library there are no card catalog files. Instead, all of the information is contained on the computer in files called *indexes.* But remember that the process of finding the book is still similar. You have three ways to find the book that you want: *author, title,* and *subject.* When you find the listing for the book that you want, you need to note the call number and find the books on the shelf by that number.

Using your library's computerized card catalog, locate the following information. If you can't figure out how to use the computer, ask the librarian to help you. If there is only a card catalog file in your library, use that. You will need to know how to find an item by author, title, and subject.

Find a card for a book about Rock Music in the subject catalog. What are the title of the book and the call numbers? _____

_____

Now find the book on the shelf in your library. Are there other books on the same topic nearby? List the titles. _____

_____

_____

Borrowing Books

Let's go back to your friend Chuck, who always borrows from your music collection. How do you keep track of what Chuck borrows?

Libraries keep track of borrowers with a card. Sometimes this card is separate from your school identification card. Often, especially when the library is highly computerized, the library simply attaches a sticker on the back of your identification card. In a computer system, your book borrowing activities are often tied to your other school records. This may mean that if you have not returned a book by the end of your term, your grades may be withheld until you return it and pay the overdue fine.

The **circulation desk** is the place to go when you want to take out any materials from the library. It is also the place to return the materials.

What do you have to do in order to take materials out from your library? _____

_____

How long can you keep a book? _____ a videotape ?_____
                        a compact disc? _____ an audio tape? _____

How much does your library charge if you keep the material too long? _____

Can you renew the material before it is due?_____

    If so, for how long?_____

FINDING PERIODICALS AND ARTICLES USING INDEXES

Even though a large number of books are published every year, it is nothing compared to the number of periodicals published each month. A **periodical** is a magazine or other publication that is published on a regular basis. Every issue of most magazines has at least twenty to thirty different articles inside. It is the best, most up-to-date source for information.

How do you find articles on the topic you are interested in? As with books, people keep track of each article that is published. Instead of putting a card in a catalog, however, they create lists in what are called **indexes**. An **indexer** is the person who keeps track of the different magazines and makes a list of the articles that are in each issue. The author of the article, the title, and the subject are listed in one alphabetical sequence.

There are many different indexes and each looks at different magazines. One popular index is *The Reader's Guide to Periodical Literature*. It keeps track of general interest magazines such as *Newsweek, Sports Illustrated* and *Mademoiselle*. Specialized indexes keep track of specific subject magazines. For example, the *Applied Science and Technology Index* will list articles from *Electronics Today,* and the *Index Medicus* indexes *RN*, a nursing magazine.

To keep up with the magazines as they are published, the indexes come out every month. At the end of each year, the complete index is republished, creating one that covers the whole year at a time. In searching for an article it is recommended that you start looking at the most recent index volume you can find.

Computer Databases

Computers have made indexes a lot faster to use, but in some ways they are more complicated. Indexes have computerized twins that can be in several different forms. The oldest computerized forms are called **on-line databases**. They work by connecting a microcomputer to a large computer in another location. Because they are expensive, only some libraries can afford these.

The most common form of computerized index is something called **CD-ROM**. CD-ROM looks like a common music compact disc. However, the information stored on it is much more concentrated. One disk can contain three to five years of a single index.

All of these different index formats make it necessary for you to talk to a librarian about your topic before you begin periodical article research. Ask the librarian to show you the paper and computerized indexes in your library.

What paper indexes does your library have? _____

_____

_____

_____

What CD-ROMs does your library have? _____

_____

_____

_____

Ask the librarian to show you which paper index and CD-ROM would work best for our hypothetical project on Einstein. What are their names? _____

_____

_____

_____

Interlibrary Loans

Every library does not have everything you find in an index or a bibliography. Your library tries to have the books that will be the most popular for the teaching being done at your school. However, you may want a book on a subject that is unique to your library. You may also find a reference to an article that your library does not have.

In either case, the librarian can help you find the material in another library. If this library is local or if there is a lot of material that you need located in one place, the librarian may suggest that you go to the library yourself. If you have enough lead time—usually at least six weeks before the paper is due—then the librarian may suggest that you request an **interlibrary loan**. This means that the librarian will make a formal request to another library to have them send a photocopy of an article or to have them lend you the book for a short time.

Always ask a librarian to help you find out where material is. It will save you time in the long run.

A RESEARCH EXERCISE

Now that you know more about how to use a library, let's put that knowledge into practice. Choose a topic based on a course you are currently taking or something you've always wanted to know about.

My topic is: _____

Begin doing research on your topic by starting with the encyclopedia, then books, then articles. Do as much as you can on your own. Ask your librarian for help if you need it. Figure 14–7 will guide you through the beginning stages of any research project. Use it as often as you need throughout your education. Create your working bibliography as you locate your research material:

Citation for your encyclopedia article: _____

_____

_____

_____

Citation for a book:_____

_____

_____

_____

Citation for an article:_____

_____

_____

_____

Figure 14–7
Creating a Quick Reference Guide

This quick reference guide will help you get started on any research project you are assigned. Photocopy this form for use several times during your school years.

Identifying Your Research Task

The first step in doing research is to know what the end result needs to be. Only then can you begin to gather enough information to fulfill its requirements. If you follow the questions and complete the information requested, you will be well on your way to finding the information you need.

Using a syllabus from a class that requires a paper or by consulting with your instructor, begin by answering the following questions:

1. What is your topic? _____

_____

2. How many pages does the instructor want?

___1–3 pages ___ 4–10 pages___ 11–15 pages ___ No limit

3. How many sources does your instructor want? (A source can be a book, a periodical article, or an encyclopedia article.)

___1–5   ___ 6–10   ___ 11–15   ___ No limit

4. Is this paper about a current subject? ___yes ___no
(If the answer is yes, you must concentrate on articles. Only very recent books will have the right material for you.)

Doing Research

Begin doing research for your paper by following the steps below. If you need more citations than the sample provided, use a separate piece of paper to write them.

Step #1: **Find an encyclopedia article about your topic.**
Remember to use specialty encyclopedias where appropriate.
Write your citation here:

_____

_____

_____

Step #2: **Find 2 books about your topic.** Try to find one from the encyclopedia article's bibliography (located at the end of the article) or use the subject part of your library's book catalog. Always choose the most recent material. Check the index of any books that you find to see if it covers the exact topic you are interested in. You may not use the entire book. Maybe a chapter is all you need.

Write your citations below (minimum of two):

1. _____

_____

_____

2. _____

_____

_____

Step #3: Find 3 articles about your topic. Use the information in the "Finding periodicals and articles using indexes" section.

Write your citations below (minimum of three):

1. _____

_____

_____

2. _____

_____

_____

3. _____

_____

_____

SUMMARY

1. Getting to know your library and its librarians is a valuable learning tool. Libraries and librarians can help you find answers to anything you want to know.

2. You will use the library for three basic functions: Reserves, Reference, and Research. You may need to use the library for locating extra reading assignments placed on reserve by your instructor. You may need to find answers to questions in reference material, such as an encyclopedia or handbook. Most important, you may need to use the library for doing research for papers and projects for your classes. The library can also be used for Relaxation.

3. Writing citations and note cards help you to keep track of the information you find. This information is useful and necessary in writing papers.

4. Knowing how to locate the books and articles you need is extremely valuable for doing research.

5. The sooner you get to know and begin using your library, the quicker the doors to this vast world will open.

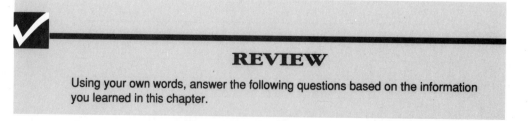

REVIEW

Using your own words, answer the following questions based on the information you learned in this chapter.

1. Can you name four ways that a library can be useful to you?

   _____

   _____

2. How can an encyclopedia help you?

   _____

   _____

3. What is the best way to look up information in an encyclopedia?

   _____

   _____

4. What three ways are there to look up books?

   _____

   _____

5. What do you need from the catalog to locate a book on a shelf?

   _____

   _____

6. What research tools would you use to find an article?

   _____

   _____

7. What is plagiarism? What can you do to avoid it?

   _____

   _____

8. What did you learn from this chapter?

   _____

   _____

CHAPTER 15

WRITING ESSAYS AND PAPERS

After studying and working with the information in this chapter, you should be able to :

1. Identify people who write and be able to explain the ways that writing is used in the real world.
2. Describe the writing process.
3. Select an appropriate topic.
4. Create a thesis statement.
5. Use the 5Ws and H to create an organized outline.
6. Identify the three parts of any essay or paper.
7. Explain what to do to revise your rough draft.
8. Describe what a final draft should include and look like.
9. Begin using the writing process for your writing assignments.

Effectively communicating your thoughts on paper is very important for your success in the real world.

I have known ever since I started writing this book that eventually I would have to write a chapter on writing essays and papers. Even though I have already written most of this book, I do

348

not *think* of myself as a writer. Thinking I am not a writer has made the *thought* of writing this chapter especially difficult.

Before writing this book, I used to *think* of writing essays and papers as overwhelming and impossible. At the time, I did not understand that writing was a process—a series of activities, not a one-time event. With the emphasis of this book on active learning, I have since come to realize that *thinking* about writing scares me more than actually *doing* it. I now understand that *thinking about writing is passive compared to actually doing it.* Once I begin writing, I become *actively* involved. I am too busy to feel overwhelmed or feel as if it is impossible. And once the project is complete, I no longer think, I feel. I feel an incredible sense of relief, pride, and accomplishment.

Writing is not an isolated activity; it's something that you will use every day of your school and work life. How many ways can you think of that you use your writing ability?

In this chapter, I am sharing with you the writing process I have used for every chapter of this textbook. In effect, each chapter was like a research paper. If you too can understand this writing process, then writing will become easier for you.

Learning how to effectively communicate on paper IS an important part of life, not just for school assignments, but for your career and personal growth. Perhaps up until now, you haven't done a lot of writing. Perhaps you think you are not good at it or maybe you just don't know how to get started. This chapter is intended to give you some information and experience to help you understand the writing process. As a result, you will know better how to approach all of your school writing assignments. And in the end, writing may become not only possible, but enjoyable.

This one chapter does not contain all you need to know about writing. Many books have been devoted to the topic and school composition courses are designed to more fully develop your writing skills. But it will certainly give you the tools you need for writing most essays and papers. In the recommended bibliography located in Appendix F of this book, you will find other resources to research for improving your writing. In addition, your school and local library may have several other books in their collection for you to research and reference.

✓ SELF-EVALUATION

The following self-evaluation will give you an idea of how familiar, or unfamiliar, you are with some of the topics and terms discussed in this chapter. After reading each statement, circle the letter (Y, S, or N) most appropriate to your answer. Please answer honestly, rate yourself at the end, and then complete the information for Chapter 15 on page 375 in Appendix A.

Y = yes; frequently   **S** = sometimes   **N** = no; never

1. I know that writing is an important part of any job.   Y S N
2. I understand the writing process.   Y S N
3. I schedule enough time ahead of time for my writing projects.   Y S N
4. I know how to use the library for doing research.   Y S N
5. I know how to go about deciding on a topic.   Y S N
6. I know how to write a good thesis statement.   Y S N
7. I am able to create an organized outline for my paper by using the mapping process.   Y S N
8. I know and can describe the three parts of any written communication.   Y S N
9. I know how to effectively revise my writing.   Y S N
10. I know how to present the final draft of a paper.   Y S N

<u>Rate Yourself</u>

Number of Ys _____ x 100=

Number of Ss _____ x 50=

Number of Ns _____ x 10=

Total =

We do not know who we are until we see what we can do.
> *- Martha Grimes, contemporary*
> *mystery writer*

WRITING IN THE REAL WORLD

Effectively communicating your thoughts on paper is very important to your success in the real world. The *real world* can best be defined as the current world you live and function in, the jobs or careers you choose, and the people with whom you interact. Learning to effectively communicate in your world means that you are not only able to be heard, but also understood. This is especially important in the workplace, in business, and in the pursuit of careers.

When you write essays and papers for a school assignment, you are learning how to effectively talk on paper. Developing this ability enables you to communicate your thoughts and ideas easier, both on paper and for speaking.

In the real world, writing is not limited to essays and papers. These activities are just the training ground for real-life activities. For most professions, there are writing activities essential for doing the job. Here is a partial listing:

❏ memos	❏ meeting minutes	❏ speeches
❏ letters of recommendation	❏ job applications	❏ diaries/journals
❏ letters of complaint	❏ lab reports	❏ policies/procedures
❏ letters of inquiry	❏ technical reports	❏ newsletters
❏ phone messages	❏ directions	❏ resumés
❏ customer service logs	❏ instruction manuals	❏ service reports
❏ advertisements	❏ financial statements	❏ product reviews
❏ magazine articles	❏ research reports	❏ progress reports
❏ annual reports	❏ job descriptions	❏ press releases
❏ cover letters		

Think about and/or talk to the working people you may know in the professions listed in the left column that follows. In the right column, try to come up with some of the writing activities these people need to do. You can use the list above for reference. The first few have been started for you.

Profession	Writing Activities
Nurse	Medical chart updates; patient reports
Business professional	Memos; letters; reports; meeting minutes
Electrician	_____
Secretary	_____
Auto mechanic	_____
Teacher	_____
Job seeker	_____
Computer programmer	_____
Computer technician	_____
Police officer	_____
Lawyer	_____
Building contractor	_____
Entrepreneur	_____
Pharmacist	_____
Doctor	_____
News reporter	_____
Salesperson	_____
Travel agent	_____
Any fields you like: _____	_____

Since writing is such an important part of the real world, then it is important to learn how to do it, and do it well. All it takes is knowing what to do and then doing it.

If God had meant for everything to happen at once, He would not have invented desk calendars.

- Fran Lebowitz, contemporary humorist

WRITING IS A PROCESS

Writing is a **process**. A process is a series of related steps or actions taken to achieve an end. Doctors follow a process when they operate on a patient. Auto mechanics follow a process when they fix a car. Travel agents follow a process when planning vacations for their clients. Event planners follow a process when planning special events and parties. It is not just one action that enables these individuals to do their jobs, but rather a series of steps, activities, or procedures. By understanding that writing too is a process, you will be better equipped to handle any writing task.

This chapter will describe all of the steps necessary for writing research papers. Shorter essays will need only some of them.

Before you do any of the activities in the eight steps of the writing process, it is recommended that you preview the text that follows each one before reading them in detail. This will help you to see the overall flow of each step into the next and understand how you can come up with a quality piece of writing. The eight steps are also listed in Figure 15–1.

Figure 15–1
The Eight Steps in the Writing Process

Step #1: Creating Time to Write
Step #2: Deciding on a Topic
Step #3: Doing Research
Step #4: Creating a Thesis Statement
Step #5: Creating an Outline
Step #6: Writing the Rough Draft
Step #7: Revising the Rough Draft
Step #8: Creating the Final Draft

Step #1: Creating Time to Write   Creating time for writing is the first step in the writing process. This is because any process, especially writing, takes time. The length of time needed depends on the assignment. If you are asked to write an essay on a test in class, then you have to budget your testing time so you can complete it in the time given. This usually means spending about fifteen to thirty minutes, depending the length required, to create an effective essay. If you are asked to write a one- or two-page paper on a topic being discussed in class, you may have several days to do it. And if you are asked to write a five- to ten-page research paper, then you need to arrange for a minimum of six to eight weeks to create it.

Effective writing is done step by step over a period of time, not all at once. Even for essay tests and short compositions, you will need time to create an outline or map of what you will be writing about, time for the actual writing, and time for revising and editing. You will need more time for research papers or those longer in length—time for deciding on a topic, creating a thesis statement, doing research, and creating a final draft.

Working on a research paper does not mean that you are writing for six to eight weeks; it means you schedule time to work on it a little at a time over a six- to eight-week period. Planning for this in advance ensures that you still have enough time for the regular activities in your life like work, school, and personal and family responsibilities.

The following is a suggested time guideline to follow for scheduling a five- to ten-page research paper. This is only a guideline, meaning you can adjust the time frame according to the length of your assignment. It is always wise to plan a little extra time, just in case.

Decide on a topic (may include some research)	1 week
Research time	2 weeks
Creating a thesis statement and outline	1 week
Writing your first draft	2 weeks
Revision	1 week
Final draft	1 week

(See Chapter 4 on Learning Time Management for more information on scheduling time for papers.)

Look at and follow the writing process for research papers in Figure 15–2. Notice that some of the longer, more time-consuming steps are not shown as a one-time activity. Instead, they are repeated several times. By breaking them down into shorter time frames, you are better able to fit them into your life. You are also providing quality time to your writing project, not just quantity.

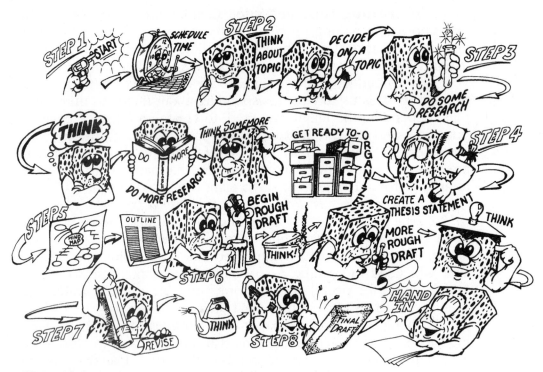

Figure 15–2
The Writing Process for Research Papers

The time you schedule in between each writing process activity gives you time to think. So when you return to do the next activity, you bring a fresh perspective to your process that makes for a better writing result.

Step #2: Deciding on a Topic   Once you have scheduled your time, then you must decide on a topic. The subjects you study are **topics**. Global warming is a topic; gardening is a topic; pollution is a topic; music is a topic. Topics can be very small subjects, such as a dog's diet, or huge ones, such as the universe.

When it comes time to decide on a topic, generally you have three possibilities:

1. You are given the topic to write about, or

2. You are asked to choose a topic in a given subject area, or

3. You can choose any topic you want.

If you are given the topic, then obviously you must write about that topic. If you have your choice, either in a certain subject area or any other one you choose, it is easy to become overwhelmed by your options.

The best topic to choose is one that interests you. If it interests you, then the time and effort you put into it will be more satisfying. You may have a specific topic in mind, one that you have always wanted to know more about, or you may have to do a little research. *Using encyclopedia indexes, tables of contents, and other book indexes are great places to look for possible topic suggestions.* Also, let your instructors help you find an appropriate topic. After all, you *are* writing it for them.

The following is a list of considerations when choosing a topic:

❑ Are you interested in it? If so, then do it; if not, don't.

❑ Depending on the length of the assignment, is there enough information to write about?

❑ Is the subject very new? (If so, you may have trouble finding enough research material.)

❑ Is there *too much* information available? Can you narrow it down and still report on the topic effectively?

Once you find a topic you think you want to write about, check it with your instructor before going on to the next step of doing research. If the instructor prefers you to choose a different topic, then you will not have wasted your time doing unnecessary research.

For the purpose of practicing this writing process, choose a topic. You can use one that has been assigned for a class, one you may have used in the previous chapter, or one you just want to know more about. Use the previous list of considerations before you make your final decision. Then write your topic below:

My topic is: _____

Step #3: Doing Research   Doing research means locating usable information for a paper or project. It also means finding out about something you want to know more about. If you have not already completed Chapter 14, do so now. It provides you with information about how to use the library for doing your research, how to write citations, how to write note cards and how to write a bibliography and a works cited listing. Use the "Doing Research" section of Figure 14–7 in Chapter 14 as a guideline for doing your research.

Step #4: Creating a Thesis Statement   As a result of your research, you have probably found some information that could be easily discussed in a paper. In the research example on Albert Einstein in Chapter 14, you would be overwhelmed with the information available. Creating a thesis statement narrows your topic down so you can focus on one issue surrounding the topic. A thesis is not the same as a topic. A *topic* is what you study while a **thesis** is the conclusion you draw from what you study. A thesis is also the main point of your paper. A **thesis statement** is a summary of your thesis. *Every paper and essay must have a thesis statement because it tells the reader what you are going to prove.*

Creating a thesis statement involves a two-step process. First, it involves identifying the issues that surround your subject. Then it involves stating your position on the issue. An **issue** is an unresolved question about a topic while a **position** is your point of view on an issue.

Identifying an issue.   An issue is best worded using the word "whether." Using some of the topics mentioned earlier, identify several possible issues. The first two topics have been completed as examples. Try to come up with issue statements for the remaining topics, including the one you chose earlier in this chapter.

Topic	Issue
global warming	❑ whether global warming is a threat to people and the environment
	❑ whether global warming should be stopped
	❑ whether global warming is caused by industrial pollution
Albert Einstein	❑ whether Albert Einstein's childhood affected his view of the world
	❑ whether religion played a role in Albert's upbringing
	❑ whether Albert was influenced by Germany at the turn of the century
gardening	❑ whether planting too early in the year affects the plant height
	❑ whether gardening is therapeutic for older people
	❑ whether gardens can help the quality of the earth's air
pollution	❑ _____
	❑ _____
	❑ _____
music	❑ _____
	❑ _____
	❑ _____
abortion	❑ _____
	❑ _____
	❑ _____
AIDS	❑ _____
	❑ _____
	❑ _____
Your topic:	
_____	❑ _____
	❑ _____
	❑ _____

Identifying your position. Now that you have identified several issues, you can begin to identify your position. By identifying your position, you are creating a statement that you will argue in your paper. *Your position, or point of view on an issue, can also be considered a thesis statement.*

Topic	Possible Thesis Statements
Global warming	Global warming is a threat to people and the environment.
Albert Einstein	Albert Einstein's childhood affected his views on the world.
Gardening	Planting a garden can improve the earth's air quality.

Now try to come up with thesis statements based on the issues you listed. Remember to include the topic you chose to work on earlier in this chapter.

Topic	Possible Thesis Statement
Pollution	_____
Music	_____
Abortion	_____
AIDS	_____
Your topic:	
_____	_____

Note that a thesis statement does not give any explanation or reason why you think the way you do. Your explanation is the contents of your paper or essay.

Though you will come up with a thesis statement now, know that you may change it as you develop your ideas. This is okay so long as your paper or essay proves your position.

If you do not know where you are going, you will probably end up somewhere else.

> *-Laurence J. Peter, Canadian*
> *psychologist and educator*

Step #5: Creating an Outline   By the time you get to this step, some of your writing has already been done. If you researched well, you should have a working bibliography and plenty of note cards based on your research. Now it is time to organize your thoughts and information.

An organized paper will always receive a higher grade than an unorganized one. If your paper is unorganized and your written communication is confusing, then your instructor will have a difficult time understanding your thoughts. If, on the other hand, your paper is organized and flows smoothly from one idea to the next, you have succeeded in communicating your thoughts effectively. Organizing your thoughts is easily accomplished by using a pre-writing process called *mapping*.

Mapping and the 5 Ws and H.   In Chapter 9 you were introduced to Mind Mapping® as a notetaking method. If you recall, Mind Mapping is a creative way to take notes that organizes ideas through visual patterns and pictures. In this section, you will learn how to create a similar looking map. **Mapping** is a prewriting thought process that helps you to organize your thoughts and information on paper resulting in an informal outline. This informal outline is the same as the writer's road map—the same one you follow for previewing (see Chapter 6 for more information on previewing).

Begin mapping by drawing a circle in the middle of a blank piece of paper. Then draw about ten lines coming out from it. It will look similar to a spider. Now write your thesis statement in the middle of the circle. On your own piece of paper, do this with your thesis statement. The global warming example is illustrated in Figure 15–3.

Figure 15–3
Beginning the Mapping
Process

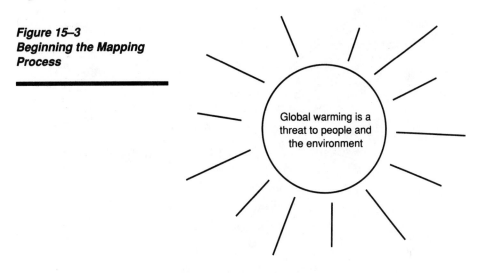

Global warming is a threat to people and the environment

Once you have written down your thesis statement, now it is time to brainstorm. **Brainstorming** is a random, unorganized thought-dumping process that results in new ideas. For writing, this thought-dumping process is guided by using the same 5Ws and H you were introduced to in Chapter 1. To refresh your memory the *5 Ws and H* are:

❏ **W**ho
❏ **W**hat
❏ **W**hen
❏ **W**here
❏ **W**hy
   and
❏ **H**ow

Write these words across the top left of your paper with the thesis statement in the middle.

Using the global warming example, the following questions could be generated from the 5Ws and H and written on the paper as shown on the brainstorm sheet in Figure 15–4. There are no rules to follow for how often or which of the 5Ws and H you use.

Though your paper or essay may not answer all of these questions, you are beginning to think actively and creatively about the paper's contents and organization before you write.

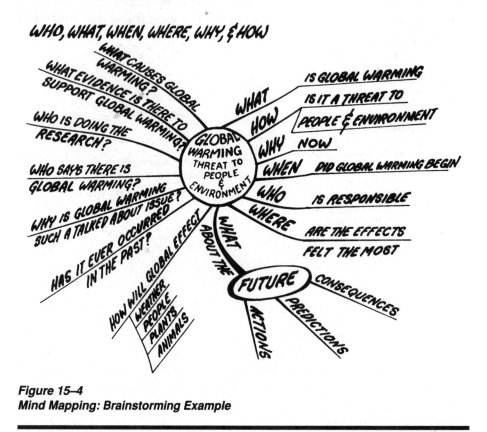

Figure 15–4
Mind Mapping: Brainstorming Example

Now it is your turn to create a brainstorm sheet for your thesis. Start with any of the 5Ws and H and try to come up with any question about your thesis statement. Write your question at the end of one of the legs. You can place a shape of your choice around it such as a circle, square, rectangle, cloud, etc. Continue coming up with as many questions as you possibly can using as many of the question words as appropriate. These questions help you to generate ideas. Try to come up with a minimum of ten questions. Add more legs if you need. The result will be a group of unanswered questions surrounding your thesis.

Organizing an Outline. You now have a lot of good questions about your thesis statement, but they are not organized. To organize them, first review all of your questions. Then decide which question your reader should know about first. On a separate blank piece of summary paper, write your first choice question in the recall column. Place a check mark ✓ next to this question on your brainstorm sheet indicating that the question has been used. Then continue evaluating your questions to decide which question would make the most sense to the reader to read about next, and so on. *Leave at least five blank spaces between each question.* If you see a question that does not relate well to your thesis, cross it off your brainstorm sheet. If you think a question should be reworded or added, then do so.

Figure 15–5 is one suggested way of organizing the questions for the global warming example. Notice that the question "when did global warming begin?" was changed to "when was it first noticed as a problem?" The revised question communicates the message better. The question "has it ever occurred in the past?" can be used as a detail to answer "when was it first noticed?" The question "who says there is global warming?" was not selected.

Figure 15–5
Organizing Questions from
Your Map

Thesis Statement	Global warming is a threat to people and the environment
1. What is global warming? (GW)	
2. Why is GW such a talked about issue?	
3. When was it first noticed as a problem?	
4. What causes GW?	
5. Who is responsible?	
6. What evidence is there to support GW?	
7. Who is doing research?	

Figure 15–5 (continued)
Organizing Questions from
Your Map

8. How is it a threat to people and the environment?	
9. How will global warming effect:	
• weather	
• people	
• plants	
• animals	
10. Where are the effects felt the most?	
Why Now?	
11. What about the future?	
• consequences	
• Predictions	
• Actions	

If this was your paper, you might prefer a different question arrangement. As long as the answers to the questions flow from one to the next, then it will work.

When you have finished either using, changing, or eliminating your questions, read them in order to see if your order makes sense. If you can easily see the organization of your paper in your questions, then you have succeeded in creating the framework of your outline. Does rearranging your questions help? Does adding more questions or taking any out help? Make changes as you see fit.

Mapping with the 5Ws and H is very effective for quickly organizing your thoughts for essay tests. You can create your spider map in the margin or on a separate piece of paper. This does not take long and is well worth the benefit of having your thoughts organized before you begin writing.

Using your note cards to fill in the details. The next step in writing a research paper is to transfer the information on your note cards to full sentences on paper. If you have done some research for your sample topic, then *organize your note cards in the order your questions suggest.* Then, using the body of the summary paper and key words, fill in possible details relating to or answering each question. Be sure to include any statistics, names, quotes, or important dates. If you did not do any research, fill in whatever details you would want to include in your paper.

If you do not have enough information to answer a question and the question is important to your paper, then do a little more research looking for the answer. Figure 15–6 shows some details for each of the questions asked for the global warming example.

Thesis Statement:	Global warming is a threat to people and the environment	8. How is it a threat to people & the environment?	- breathing disorders/asthma - skin cancer from sun exposure - increase in diseases carried by animals - food supply contaminated
1. What is global warming? (GW)	- also known as "Greenhouse Effect" - depletion of ozone layer.	9. How will global warming effect:	
2. Why is GW such a talked about issue?	- effects on people - effects on environment - ozone layer shrinking	-weather	- warmer temp's -↑9 fareinheit from 1992-2025
3. When was it first noticed as a problem?	- ozone layer & sun harmfulness - warmer night temperatures - changing weather patterns - has it ever occurred in the past	- people	- acid rain & water supply - food/air supply
		- plants	- scorched earth theory - drought OR flooding (rising sea level
4. What causes GW?	- chemicals in environment/factor - aerosol cans - cutting down of trees in rainfor. - car emissions	- animals	- food/air supply
5. Who is responsible?	- those involved in the cause - others: _____	10. where are the effects felt most?	
		11. why now?	- time factor - accummulation of causes
6. What evidence is there to support GW?	See #3 - use some examples	12. What about the future?	- temp ↑ - ↑ carbon dioxide causing change in
		-consequences	atmosphere - sun worshippers no more
7. Who is doing research?	- scientists - environmentalists - dept. of public health/gov't - Earth Summit 1992 in Rio de Janiero	- Predictions - Actions	- gas & electric bills ↑ - Florida's weather in New England.

Figure 15–6
Filling in the Details

You may not use all of your note cards or you may need to use a card more than once. If one of your note cards has several ideas on it that are separated on the outline, you can photocopy the card and place a copy in your organized pile where it belongs. Or, if you have time, you can rewrite the piece of information you need on a separate card.

When you have finished filling in your details, you may need to reorganize the order of your details. Do so now. In the end, you will have completed your writer's road map. Make changes to it as you develop your paper. Now you are ready to begin writing your rough draft.

T he great struggle for a writer is to learn to write as he would talk.
- Lincoln Steffens, early twentieth-
century editor and author

Step #6: Writing the Rough Draft The **rough draft** of your paper is just that: rough. It is your first attempt at getting your ideas down on paper. This means you should not expect to have a finished smooth-flowing paper ready to hand in after this step. Truly understanding this means that you need not worry about making mistakes, including spelling and punctuation at this time. This draft is not supposed to be perfect, it is supposed to be rough. You will have an opportunity to revise your rough draft in the next step.

It is recommended that you use a computer with a word processing program for writing your papers. Word processors make writing easier because you can write whatever you want and make changes to it later without having to retype it all. You can also print a typed copy for your instructor, which is easier to read than a hand-written copy. If you do not own a computer with a word processing program, your school may have one you can use. Sometimes your local library will have one. Also, some copy shops rent computer time to the public. If you don't know how to use a word processor, it is to your advantage to learn how, not just for school but for your job or career. It is a marketable skill to have.

When writing your rough draft, either using a word processor, a typewriter, or by hand, make sure to leave a double or triple space between each line you write. This will give you room for making changes and revising later on.

Using a computer to write saves you time and energy, and creates a more attractive final product of your efforts. Are you computer literate? If not, what are you waiting for?

After reading through all of this step, you will be asked to create a rough draft using your sample topic. If you have done some research on your topic, then make your paper at least three pages long. If you did not do research, then make your paper one to two pages long.

Every essay or paper you write must have three parts: *an introduction, a body*, and *a conclusion*. Each of these parts serves a specific purpose.

The Introduction. The **introduction** *tells* the reader what the paper will be about. It includes your thesis statement and begins to generally tell the reader what will be proved or discussed. It is the basis of your discussion. If you are writing an essay in class, then your introduction need only be a paragraph or so in length. If you are writing a ten-page paper, then your introduction needs to be at least several paragraphs long for a total of at least a page or more.

Using stories, analogies, personal examples, or interesting information you found while researching will help in writing your introduction. The introduction should be interesting, creative, and catch the reader's attention.

Using the global warming example for a short essay, a possible introduction to the discussion could be:

> Imagine that every year, the summer will be a little hotter than the summer before. Imagine that it no longer snows in the United States. Imagine that going outside with skin exposed to the sun increases the chances of getting cancer by 25 percent. Imagine having to wear an oxygen mask every day just to survive. Why would anyone want to imagine these situations? Probably because they just might happen. Global warming is the cause and it is a threat to people and the environment.

Now it is your turn to come up with a possible introduction for your discussion. Think about how you can make it interesting for the reader.

_____

_____

_____

_____

_____

_____

_____

The body. The **body** of your paper shows the reader that you know what you are talking about. This is where you discuss your point of view and back up your thesis with facts and specific information. The body of a paper needs to contain background information about your topic, including historical information, important points, and definitions of key words relating to your topic. In addition to your own point of view, the body is where you state other possible points of view. Most of the material you created in your informal outline should be used in the body.

Use the following information to help you create the body of your paper:

1. *Remember to write for your audience.* Your audience is usually your instructor. Even though your instructors probably know a lot about the topic you are writing about, you must *assume that they know nothing.* Write as if you were the instructor telling a student the information. This forces you to include a lot of information and to communicate clearly.

   For example, if you were writing your paper on global warming, you might assume that your instructor is familiar with the term "ozone layer." By pretending he or she is not, you are forced to define it, making your paper easier for the reader to understand.

2. *Write freely and simply.* While writing your rough draft, don't worry about grammar, spelling, or punctuation. It is more important to get your ideas on paper now and revise them later. The following acronym is used by many writers to guide their writing process. It means to avoid long sentences with big words.

   KISS = <u>K</u>eep <u>I</u>t <u>S</u>imple and <u>S</u>hort.

3. *Use connecting words.* Connecting words help to bridge the relationship between sentences. For instance, the word "however" means you are making an exception to something you just said. The words "in addition to" mean you are adding more to what is already said. Below, on the left, is a list of common connecting words. Try to figure out what they mean and how they are used. Use the right side for your suggestions.

Connecting Words	Suggestions for Usage
however	making an exception
in addition to	adding more to what was just said
in other words	restating to explain better
most of all	pointing out the most of something
furthermore	

Connecting Words	Suggestions for Usage
consequently	_____
on the other hand	_____
as a result	_____
besides	_____
therefore	_____
to sum up	_____
for example	_____
first, second, third	_____
for this reason	_____
above all	_____
in conclusion	_____
in short	_____
although	_____
granted that	_____
because	_____
since	_____
previously	_____
ultimately	_____
afterwards	_____
meanwhile	_____
similarly	_____
presently	_____
subsequently	_____
in the end	_____

4. *Document your sources*. When you did your research, you wrote down where you found your information. Now that you will be using the information, you need to document where you found it for your instructor. In recent years, the way to do this has become easier. Instead of creating footnotes for the information you are quoting, you are now required to simply include the author's last name and the pages where you found the specific information you quote. Then, on your works cited list, include the remaining information. According to page 10 of "A Guide to MLA Documentation Style for Research Papers," there are three ways of documenting the following source:

Brooks, John. *Telephone: The First Hundred Years*. New York; Harper, 1976.

a. Cite the author's last name and page number(s) in parentheses. For example:

One historian argues that the telephone created "a new habit of mind—a habit of tense alertness, of demanding and expecting immediate results." (Brooks 117–18)

b. Use the author's last name in your sentence and place only the page number(s) of the source in parentheses. For example:

> Brooks points out that the telephone created "a new habit of mind
> —a habit of tense alertness, of demanding and expecting immedi-
> ate results." (117–18)

c. Give the author's last name in your sentence when you are
citing the entire work rather than a specific section or passage. For example:

> Brooks argues that the history of the telephone is characterized by
> innovations that have changed public attitudes toward technology.

5. *Keep your note cards.* When you have finished using your note
cards for your rough draft, do not throw them away. You may
need them for checking a source or making sure you wrote the
right information. It is suggested that you keep them at least
until your paper has been graded and returned to you.

The conclusion.   The **conclusion** is a summary of your important
points. It lets your reader know you are finished with your argument. The conclusion also allows you to restate your position and
to explain why you believe what you believe. The conclusion for a
five- to ten-page paper is usually more than one paragraph while
shorter papers can be just one.

Now begin writing the rough draft of your paper using the
information in this section.

T here is no such thing as good writing; there's only good rewriting.
> *- Ernest Hemingway, author of The*
> *Old Man and The Sea*

Step #7: Revising the Rough Draft   At this point in your process,
the hardest work is done. You have decided on a topic, done your
research, created a thesis statement and outline, and also written your
rough draft. Now is the time to prepare for the final draft.

Before beginning to revise your rough draft, it is recommended
that you set your writing aside for a day or more before continuing
on. Getting away from it and doing other things for a while fresh-
ens your thought process and allows you to come back to your
paper with a new perspective.

Revising your rough draft means editing it. **Editing** is a process where you correct, add, eliminate, and/or rearrange your
information so that it makes sense to the reader. This also includes
changes in your grammar, spelling, and punctuation.

The questions in Figure 15–7 are meant as a guide for you to follow when revising your paper. Read each question, then go back to your paper and check for the answer. If the answer is "no" (which many will be), then you have to correct, add, eliminate, and/or rearrange your information. If the answer to the question is "yes," then you have completed the revision for that question.

Now use these questions to revise your sample paper.

Figure 15–7
Questions for Revising Any Paper

For the Introduction:
Is your thesis statement included?
Is it interesting and/or catchy?
Is it long enough?
Is it clear?

For the Body:
Does it follow an outline or writer's road map?
Is the first sentence of every paragraph a main idea (topic sentence)?
Does each paragraph support your main idea?
Are your ideas easy to follow?
Are each of your main ideas backed up by research, quotes, or other experiences?
Are your sources quoted properly?
Are your key points clearly stated?
Is the content specific enough?
Are your examples appropriate to your topic?
Did you avoid using the same word over and over again?
Is your grammar correct?
Is your spelling correct?
Is your punctuation correct?

For the Conclusion:
Is your thesis restated in the summary?
Does it summarize your point of view?

Great works are performed not by strength but by perseverance.
- Samuel Johnson, British poet and essayist

Step #8: Creating the Final Draft Creating the final draft is the easy part. This step is where you prepare your paper for your instructor to read. Check with your instructor for any specific guidelines he or she wants you to follow. You can use the ones that follow if there are no guidelines given.

Most instructors prefer that you hand in a typed final copy. If you do this with a typewriter or a word processor, the same guidelines apply:

❑ Leave a one-inch margin on the top, bottom, and sides of your paper. Also double space the entire paper. This leaves room for the instructor to write comments.

❑ Create a cover sheet for your paper by typing a title in the middle of a blank piece of paper. Then, on the bottom right side, include your name, the class number and name, your instructor's name and the date. (See Figure 15–8.)

Figure 15–8
Sample Cover Sheet for a Paper

Global Warming:
A Threat to People and the Environment

Abby Marks-Beale
SCI 101 - Environmental Science
Professor Jack Handey
December 10, 1994

❑ The first page of your paper after the cover sheet should start approximately three inches from the top.

❑ Indent the first line of every paragraph five spaces to the right.

❑ Indent and single space any quotes.

❑ Remember to type up your bibliography and works cited list on separate sheets of paper.

Now that you have typed your paper, this last step is very important: *Read your paper aloud either to yourself or to someone else.*

This is how you will quickly find anything that does not make sense. Listen for grammatical problems and look for typographical errors, including incorrect spelling and punctuation. Make changes as needed.

Neatness DOES count as much as organization. If you think of your paper as a work of art and present it that way, your instructor will see it that way as well. This means the final draft should be clean, with no smudges, coffee stains, or fingerprints. Avoid using white-out unless absolutely necessary. If you do not use a report cover, then staple the pages together in the upper left-hand corner.

Prepare the final draft of your paper now for your sample topic. When you are done, reward yourself for a job well done!

SUMMARY

1. Effectively communicating your thoughts on paper is very important for your success in the real world.

2. Effective writing is a process made up of related steps or activities taken to achieve an end. Creating time for the process is the first step.

3. The second step is deciding on a topic. Sometimes topics are given to you. Others you can choose. Any topic you choose should be of interest to you and narrowed down.

4. The third step is doing research. See Chapter 14 for information on doing research.

5. The fourth step is creating a thesis statement from your topic. This is a two-step process—first identifying an issue and then identifying your position. Your position is your point of view on an issue.

6. The fifth step is creating an outline. Using the 5Ws and H and the prewriting thought process of mapping will help you to create the writer's road map.

7. The sixth step is writing your rough draft. The rough draft needs to include the three parts of any essay or paper: an introduction, the body, and a conclusion.

8. The seventh step is revising your rough draft. This is where you correct, add, eliminate, and/or rearrange your information so it makes sense.

9. The eighth and last step is creating your final draft. This step is where you prepare your paper for presentation to your instructor.

REVIEW

Using your own words, answer the following questions based on the information you learned in this chapter. Use a separate piece of paper if you need more room to write your answers.

1. Pick an occupation—either one in which you currently work or one in which you want to work. Describe the types of writing required to do this job.

   _____

   _____

   _____

2. Without looking back at this chapter, describe the writing process in your own words.

   _____

   _____

   _____

3. What can you do if you have to select a topic for a paper? What are some things to consider?

   _____

   _____

   _____

4. What is a thesis statement? How do you create a thesis statement?

   _____

   _____

   _____

5. What are the 5Ws and H? How can they be used to generate ideas for your essay or paper?

   _____

   _____

   _____

6. Describe "mapping" in your own words.

   _____

   _____

_____

_____

7. What are the three parts of any essay or paper? What purpose does each part serve?

_____

_____

_____

8. What advice would you give another student about how to write the rough draft of a paper?

_____

_____

_____

9. What is involved in revising the rough draft?

_____

_____

_____

10. What do you think a final draft paper should look like?

_____

_____

_____

11. How can learning to communicate on paper be helpful for you?

_____

_____

_____

Appendix A ♦ SELF-EVALUATION PROGRESS CHART AND FINAL SELF-EVALUATION

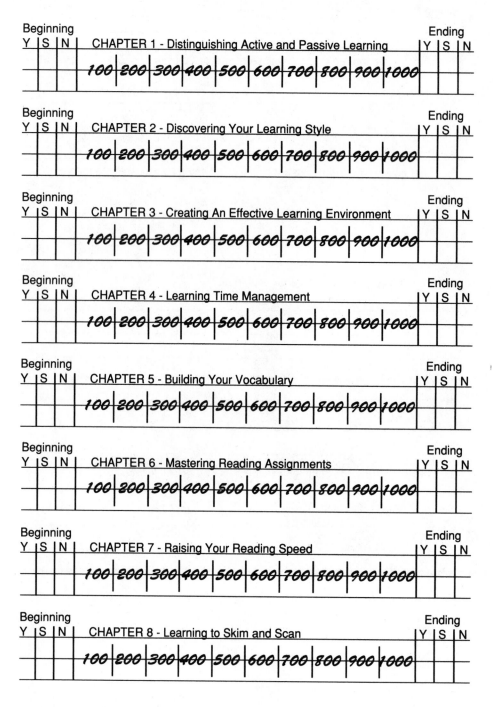

Beginning
Y | S | N   CHAPTER 1 - Distinguishing Active and Passive Learning   Ending
Y | S | N

100 | 200 | 300 | 400 | 500 | 600 | 700 | 800 | 900 | 1000

Beginning
Y | S | N   CHAPTER 2 - Discovering Your Learning Style   Ending
Y | S | N

100 | 200 | 300 | 400 | 500 | 600 | 700 | 800 | 900 | 1000

Beginning
Y | S | N   CHAPTER 3 - Creating An Effective Learning Environment   Ending
Y | S | N

100 | 200 | 300 | 400 | 500 | 600 | 700 | 800 | 900 | 1000

Beginning
Y | S | N   CHAPTER 4 - Learning Time Management   Ending
Y | S | N

100 | 200 | 300 | 400 | 500 | 600 | 700 | 800 | 900 | 1000

Beginning
Y | S | N   CHAPTER 5 - Building Your Vocabulary   Ending
Y | S | N

100 | 200 | 300 | 400 | 500 | 600 | 700 | 800 | 900 | 1000

Beginning
Y | S | N   CHAPTER 6 - Mastering Reading Assignments   Ending
Y | S | N

100 | 200 | 300 | 400 | 500 | 600 | 700 | 800 | 900 | 1000

Beginning
Y | S | N   CHAPTER 7 - Raising Your Reading Speed   Ending
Y | S | N

100 | 200 | 300 | 400 | 500 | 600 | 700 | 800 | 900 | 1000

Beginning
Y | S | N   CHAPTER 8 - Learning to Skim and Scan   Ending
Y | S | N

100 | 200 | 300 | 400 | 500 | 600 | 700 | 800 | 900 | 1000

_____ Beginning Subtotals   Ending Subtotals _____

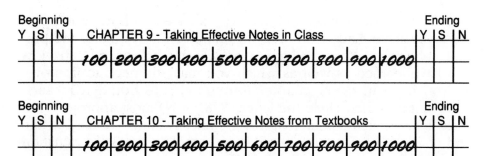

Beginning
Y |S |N | CHAPTER 9 - Taking Effective Notes in Class   Ending Y |S |N
100 |200 |300 |400 |500 |600 |700 |800 |900 |1000

Beginning
Y |S |N | CHAPTER 10 - Taking Effective Notes from Textbooks   Ending Y |S |N
100 |200 |300 |400 |500 |600 |700 |800 |900 |1000

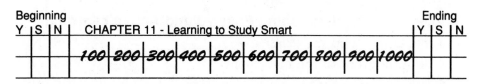

Beginning
Y |S |N | CHAPTER 11 - Learning to Study Smart   Ending Y |S |N
100 |200 |300 |400 |500 |600 |700 |800 |900 |1000

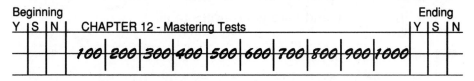

Beginning
Y |S |N | CHAPTER 12 - Mastering Tests   Ending Y |S |N
100 |200 |300 |400 |500 |600 |700 |800 |900 |1000

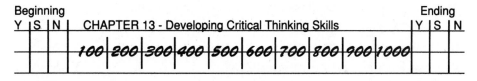

Beginning
Y |S |N | CHAPTER 13 - Developing Critical Thinking Skills   Ending Y |S |N
100 |200 |300 |400 |500 |600 |700 |800 |900 |1000

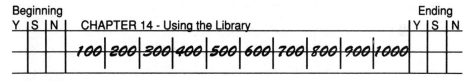

Beginning
Y |S |N | CHAPTER 14 - Using the Library   Ending Y |S |N
100 |200 |300 |400 |500 |600 |700 |800 |900 |1000

Beginning
Y |S |N | CHAPTER 15 - Writing Essays and Papers   Ending Y |S |N
100 |200 |300 |400 |500 |600 |700 |800 |900 |1000

_____ Beginning Subtotals   (this page only)   Ending Subtotals _____
+
_____ Beginning Subtotals   (from previous page)   Ending Subtotals _____
=
_____ Beginning Total   Ending Total _____

This final self-evaluation will give you an idea of how much progress you have made from the beginning of the course to the present. It helps you to see which active learning habits and behaviors you have learned as well as which you may still need to improve. As you have in every chapter throughout the book, read each statement and then circle the letter (Y, S, or N) most appropriate to your answer. Remember to answer honestly, rate yourself at the end of each chapter section and then complete the Self-Evaluation Progress Chart on pages 374 and 375.

Chapter One - Distinguishing Passive and Active Learning

1. I regularly attend my classes.   Y S N

2. I sit in the front of the classroom.   Y S N

3. I actively participate in class discussions.   Y S N

4. I listen carefully and take good notes in all
my classes.   Y S N

5. I choose a proper study environment for learning.   Y S N

6. I take notes or write down questions while reading.   Y S N

7. I am prepared for class and do my assignments on
time.   Y S N

8. I have and follow a study schedule.   Y S N

9. I ask for help when needed.   Y S N

10. I learn from my mistakes as a student.   Y S N

<u>Rate Yourself</u>

Number of Ys _____ x 100=

Number of Ss _____ x 50=

Number of Ns _____ x 10=

Total =

Chapter 2 - Discovering Your Learning Style

1. I know what learning styles are.   Y S N

2. I know *my* learning styles preferences.   Y S N

3. I am familiar with how a sequential learner
prefers to learn.   Y S N

4. I am familiar with how a sequential instructor
prefers to teach.   Y S N

5. I am familiar with how a random learner
prefers to learn.   Y S N

6. I am familiar with how a random instructor
   prefers to teach.   Y S N

7. I can identify the teaching style of my instructors
   by the way they are dressed.   Y S N

8. I can identify the teaching style of my instructors
   by knowing the kinds of questions they ask.   Y S N

9. I can adapt to more than one learning style.   Y S N

10. I know how to adjust my learning style to the
    teaching style of my instructor.   Y S N

<u>Rate Yourself</u>

Number of Ys _____ x 100=

Number of Ss _____ x 50=

Number of Ns _____ x 10=

Total =

Chapter 3 - Creating an Effective Learning Environment

1. I study in a quiet, distraction-free environment.   Y S N

2. I study without a radio or television.   Y S N

3. I avoid taking phone calls while studying.   Y S N

4. I study at a desk or table with good lighting.   Y S N

5. I am aware of, and can change, the room
   temperature.   Y S N

6. I am aware of, and try to take care of, mental
   distractions before I study.   Y S N

7. I am usually relaxed when I have a lot of studying
   to do.   Y S N

8. I know several ways to increase my concentration
   while studying.   Y S N

9. I know I CAN learn anything I WANT to.   Y S N

10. I enjoy learning.   Y S N

<u>Rate Yourself</u>

Number of Ys _____ x 100=

Number of Ss _____ x 50=

Number of Ns _____ x 10=

Total =

Chapter 4 - Learning Time Management

1. I know what is important to me.   Y S N

2. I know where my time is spent.   Y S N

3. I make time to study.   Y S N

4. I study as early in the day as possible.   Y S N

5. I keep and follow a homework assignment planner.   Y S N

6. I keep a term calendar.   Y S N

7. I plan ahead for assignments due in the future
(e.g., tests, writing papers, etc.).   Y S N

8. I set study goals for myself.   Y S N

9. I reward myself when I reach a study goal.   Y S N

10. I know what procrastination is and recognize
how it affects my ability to manage my time.   Y S N

<u>Rate Yourself</u>

Number of Ys _____ x 100=

Number of Ss _____ x 50=

Number of Ns _____ x 10=

Total =

Chapter 5 - Building Your Vocabulary

1. When I come across a word I do not know, I use
context clues to figure out its meaning.   Y S N

2. When I come across a word I do not know, I use
prefixes, roots, and suffixes to figure out its meaning. Y S N

3. When I come across a word I do not know, I use a
dictionary to find its meaning.   Y S N

4. When I come across a word I do not know, I ask
someone what it means.   Y S N

5. I know that there will be new vocabulary to learn
for every class I take.   Y S N

6. When I am reading a textbook chapter, I create my
own vocabulary list for the chapter.   Y S N

7. I keep track of my new vocabulary words either
on 3 x 5 index cards or in a separate notebook.   Y S N

8. I keep a dictionary close to me when I study.   Y S N

9. I think I have a good vocabulary.   Y S N

10. I am interested in learning new words.   Y S N

<u>Rate Yourself</u>

Number of Ys _____ x 100=
Number of Ss _____ x 50=
Number of Ns _____ x 10=
Total =

Chapter 6 - Mastering Reading Assignments

1. I know the difference between nonfiction and fiction material. Y S N

2. I know what previewing is and I can do it effectively. Y S N

3. I know how to preview a nonfiction book or magazine. Y S N

4. I know how to preview a nonfiction chapter or article. Y S N

5. I always know the purpose, or reason why, I am reading. Y S N

6. I know in what way I am responsible for each reading. Y S N

7. If there are questions at the end of a chapter, I look at them before I read. Y S N

8. I know where to find the main ideas in nonfiction reading material. Y S N

9. I always know the organization of my material before I read. Y S N

10. I am confident when approaching my reading assignments. Y S N

<u>Rate Yourself</u>

Number of Ys _____ x 100=
Number of Ss _____ x 50=
Number of Ns _____ x 10=
Total =

Chapter 7 - Raising Your Reading Speed

1. I can handle my reading workload with ease. Y S N

2. I wish there was more reading material in my areas of interest. Y S N

3. I read both for school/work *and* for pleasure.   Y S N

4. I know how to effectively increase my reading
speed when I want to or need to.   Y S N

5. I know how to look for and read key words.   Y S N

6. I know how to look for and read in phrases.   Y S N

7. I know how to use my hands or a white card to
help me increase my reading speed.   Y S N

8. I know how to adjust my reading speed according
to my purpose and background knowledge.   Y S N

9. I realize that learning to read faster takes an active
reading approach.   Y S N

10. I enjoy reading.   Y S N

<u>Rate Yourself</u>

Number of Ys _____ x 100=

Number of Ss _____ x 50=

Number of Ns _____ x 10=

Total =

Chapter 8 - Learning to Skim and Scan

1. I know my reading purpose before I read.   Y S N

2. I change reading gears according to my purpose
and background knowledge.   Y S N

3. I know the difference between skimming and
scanning.   Y S N

4. I know how to move my eyes when skimming.   Y S N

5. I know how to skim effectively.   Y S N

6. I am aware of how quickly my eyes and brain
communicate while scanning.   Y S N

7. I use a pacer to help me scan effectively.   Y S N

8. I can scan accurately.   Y S N

9. I know that reading everything all the time is not
an efficient use of my time.   Y S N

10. I am a flexible reader.   Y S N

<u>Rate Yourself</u>

Number of Ys _____ x 100=

Number of Ss _____ x 50=

Number of Ns _____ x 10=

Total =

Chapter 9 - Taking Effective Notes in Class

1. I use a 3-ring binder, not a spiral notebook, to take notes. Y S N

2. I can pick out the information that is important to write down. Y S N

3. I avoid writing down unimportant information. Y S N

4. I take notes using key words, not full sentences. Y S N

5. I abbreviate a lot when I take notes. Y S N

6. I frequently use my own words when taking notes. Y S N

7. I take notes in every class I take. Y S N

8. My notes are easy to study from. Y S N

9. I know that taking good notes helps me do well as a student. Y S N

10. I know how to take good notes. Y S N

<u>Rate Yourself</u>

Number of Ys _____ x 100=

Number of Ss _____ x 50=

Number of Ns _____ x 10=

Total =

Chapter 10 - Taking Effective Notes From Textbooks

1. I take some form of notes from my textbook reading assignments. Y S N

2. I know how to use a highlighter effectively. Y S N

3. I know how to create margin notes in my texts. Y S N

4. I can find the author's outline in my text and can take effective notes from it. Y S N

5. I take notes from my texts using key words. Y S N

6. I abbreviate words when I take notes from my texts. Y S N

7. I mark areas I don't understand in my text so I can ask my instructor about it. Y S N

8. I know how to study from my texts without a lot of rereading. Y S N

9. When I read my texts I use notetaking as an active way to concentrate and learn. Y S N

10. I learn more when I take effective notes from my texts. Y S N

<u>Rate Yourself</u>

Number of Ys _____ x 100=

Number of Ss _____ x 50=

Number of Ns _____ x 10=

Total =

Chapter 11 - Learning to Study Smart

1. Before the day of the test, I know exactly what material will be covered.   Y S N

2. Before the day of the test, I know what kind of test it will be (multiple choice, essay, etc.).   Y S N

3. I protect my health by eating well, sleeping enough and exercising.   Y S N

4. I know the difference between memorizing and learning.   Y S N

5. I avoid cramming for tests.   Y S N

6. I do the more difficult or challenging work first.   Y S N

7. I study for tests a little each day starting at least a week before a test.   Y S N

8. I am good at predicting test questions from my notes and reading material.   Y S N

9. When learning new information, I use mnemonics.   Y S N

10. When learning new information, I use my imagination.   Y S N

<u>Rate Yourself</u>

Number of Ys _____ x 100=

Number of Ss _____ x 50=

Number of Ns _____ x 10=

Total =

Chapter 12 - Mastering Tests

1. I know that a poor grade does not make me a failure.   Y S N

2. I realize that I am responsible for my own testing success or failure.   Y S N

3. I realize that I may not know everything on a test, and that is okay.   Y S N

4. I follow both written and oral test directions
carefully.   Y S N

5. Before I begin to take a test, I preview it by
looking for the point spread.   Y S N

6. I preview my tests by looking for answers to
other questions.   Y S N

7. I budget my time effectively when I take a test.   Y S N

8. I do the easiest questions first, marking the harder
ones to come back to later.   Y S N

9. When I get a test back, I review it looking
specifically for areas where I need to improve.   Y S N

10. I learn from my testing mistakes.   Y S N

Rate Yourself

Number of Ys _____ x 100=

Number of Ss _____ x 50=

Number of Ns _____ x 10=

Total =

Chapter 13 - Developing Critical Thinking Skills

1. I regularly think about my thinking.   Y S N
2. I know what critical thinking is.   Y S N
3. I make decisions with careful thought and planning. Y S N
4. I know the definition of the word *metacognition*.   Y S N
5. I know when I need more information.   Y S N
6. I know at least five Rules of Critical Thinking.   Y S N
7. I know the difference between "apple polishing"
and "name calling."   Y S N
8. I can identify common mistakes in thinking in
advertising and political speeches.   Y S N
9. I can identify and describe how critical thinking
affects my life.   Y S N
10. I realize that knowledge about thinking can
improve thinking.   Y S N

Rate Yourself

Number of Ys _____ x 100=

Number of Ss _____ x 50=

Number of Ns _____ x 10=

Total =

Chapter 14 - Using the Library

1. I go to the library often.   Y S N

2. I know the librarians and other staff.   Y S N

3. I read current periodicals.   Y S N

4. I use reference books.   Y S N

5. I know what reserve materials are.   Y S N

6. I know how to use the library's computers.   Y S N

7. I use indexes to find articles.   Y S N

8. I make photocopies of articles or reference material. Y S N

9. I know how to create a research plan.   Y S N

10. I know how to write a note card.   Y S N

Rate Yourself

Number of Ys _____ x 100=

Number of Ss _____ x 50=

Number of Ns _____ x 10=

Total =

Chapter 15 - Writing Essays and Papers

1. I know that writing is an important part of any job.   Y S N

2. I understand the writing process.   Y S N

3. I schedule enough time ahead of time for my
writing projects.   Y S N

4. I know how to use the library for doing research.   Y S N

5. I know how to go about deciding on a topic.   Y S N

6. I know how to write a good thesis statement.   Y S N

7. I am able to create an organized outline for my
paper by using the mapping process.   Y S N

8. I know and can describe the three parts of any
written communication.   Y S N

9. I know how to effectively revise my writing.   Y S N

10. I know how to present the final draft of a paper.   Y S N

Rate Yourself

Number of Ys _____ x 100=

Number of Ss _____ x 50=

Number of Ns _____ x 10=

Total =

Common Prefixes
Directions:

1. On each of the following lines, you are given a prefix, its meaning, and an example using the prefix. If you are unsure of the meaning of the example word, use a dictionary to get its exact meaning. Write down the word and its meaning on a separate piece of paper for future use. Notice how the meaning relates to its prefix meaning.

2. Then, in the blank space to the right of the example, give your own example of a word that begins with the prefix which uses the prefix meaning. If you can think of more than one example, make a list of them on a separate piece of paper. Be aware that your example may not carry the meaning of the prefix. Look up your example in a dictionary if you are unsure.

Prefix	Meaning	Example	Your Example
ab	from, away from	abduct	_____
ad	to, forward	admit	_____
ambi	both	ambiguous	_____
an, a	without	anemia	_____
ante	before	antecedent	_____
anti	against, opposite	antipathy	_____
arch	chief, first	archetype	_____
be	over, thoroughly	befuddle	_____
bi	two	bicycle	_____
cata	down	catapult	_____
circum	around	circumspect	_____
com	with, together	communicate	_____
co	with	coeditor	_____
contro (a)	against	controversy	_____
de	down, away	descend	_____
demi	partly, half	demigod	_____
di	two	dichotomy	_____
dia	across	diagonal	_____
dis, dif	not, apart	difference	_____
dys	faulty, bad	dyspepsia	_____
ex, e	out	eject	_____
extra, extro	beyond, outside	extracurricular	_____
hyper	above, excessively	hyperventilate	_____
hypo	beneath, lower	hypoglycemia	_____
in	not	inefficient	_____
im	not	impeccable	_____
inter	between, among	interjection	_____
intra, intro	within	intramural	_____
macro	large, long	macrocosm	_____

mega	great, million	megalomania	_____
meta	involving change	metamorphosis	_____
micro	small	microcosm	_____
mis	bad, improper	misnomer	_____
mono	one	monotheism	_____
multi	many	multitudinous	_____
neo	new	neophyte	_____
non	not	nonentity	_____
ob, of	against	obtrude	_____
pan	all, every	panorama	_____
para	beyond, related	parallel	_____
per	through, completely	pervade	_____
peri	around, near	periphery	_____
poly	many	polyglot	_____
post	after	posterity	_____
pre	before	premonition	_____
prim	first	primordial	_____
pro	forward, in favor of	proponent	_____
proto	first	prototype	_____
pseudo	false	pseudonym	_____
re	again, back	reimburse	_____
retro	backward	retrospect	_____
se	away, aside	seclude	_____
semi	half, partly	semiconscious	_____
sub	under, less	subjugate	_____
sup	under, less	suppress	_____
super	over, above	supervise	_____
sur	over, above	surtax	_____
syn, sym	with, together	synchronize	_____
tele	far	telegraphic	_____
trans	across	transpose	_____
ultra	beyond, excessive	ultramodern	_____
un	not	unwitting	_____
under	below	underling	_____
uni	one	unison	_____
with	away, against	withhold	_____

Common Roots
Directions:

1. On each of the following lines you are given a root, its meaning, and an example using the root. *If you are unsure of the meaning of the example word, use a dictionary to get its exact meaning.* Write down the word and its meaning on a separate piece of paper for future use. Notice how the meaning relates to its root meaning.

2. Then, in the blank space to the right of the example, give your own example of a word that begins with the root which uses the root meaning. If you can think of more than one example, make a list of them on a separate piece of paper. Keep in mind that roots are not only found in the middle of a word, but also in its beginning. Be aware that your example may not carry the meaning of the root. Look up your example in a dictionary if you are unsure.

Root Word	Meaning	Example	Your Example
ac	sharp	acerbity	_____
aev, ev	age, era	medieval	_____
agog	leader	demagogue	_____
agri	field	agriculture	_____
ali	another	alienate	_____
alt	high	altimeter	_____
alter	other	alterego	_____
am	love	amicable	_____
anim	mind, soul	magnanimity	_____
ann, enn	year	perennial	_____
anthrop	man	misanthrope	_____
apt	fit	aptitude	_____
aqua	water	aquatic	_____
arch	ruler, first	archeology	_____
aster	star	asterisk	_____
aud	hear	audible	_____
auto	self	autonomy	_____
belli	war	rebellious	_____
ben	good	benefactor	_____
bon	good	bonus	_____
biblio	book	bibliography	_____
bio	life	biography	_____
breve	short	abbreviate	_____
cap	to take	capture	_____
capit, capt	head	decapitate	_____
carn	flesh	carnage	_____
ced	to yield, to go	antecedent	_____
cess	to yield, to go	process	_____
celer	swift	celerity	_____
cent	one hundred	centipede	_____
chron	time	anachronism	_____
cid, cis	to cut, to kill	homocide	_____
cit	to call, to start	excite	_____
civi	citizen	civilization	_____
clam	to cry out	clamorous	_____
claus, clud	to close	claustrophobia	_____
cognit	to learn	incognito	_____
compl	to fill	complement	_____

cord	heart	cordial	_____
corpor	body	incorporate	_____
cred	to believe	incredulous	_____
cur	to care	curator	_____
curr, curs	to run	excursion	_____
da, dat	to give	data	_____
deb	to owe	indebtedness	_____
dem	people	epidemic	_____
di	day	diary	_____
dic, dict	to say	verdict	_____
doc, doct	to teach	document	_____
domin	to rule	dominant	_____
duc, duct	to lead	viaduct	_____
dynam	power, strength	dynamic	_____
ego	I	egocentric	_____
erg, urg	work	ergonomics	_____
err	to wander	erratic	_____
eu	good, well	eupeptic	_____
fac	to make, do	factory	_____
fic	to make, do	fiction	_____
fec, fect	to make, do	affect	_____
fall, fals	to deceive	fallacious	_____
fer	to bring, to bear	transfer	_____
fid	belief, faith	infidel	_____
fin	end, limit	confine	_____
flect, flex	bend	deflect	_____
fort	luck, chance	fortuitous	_____
fort	strong	fortitude	_____
frag, fract	break	infraction	_____
fug	flee	fugitive	_____
fus	pour	effusive	_____
gam	marriage	polygamy	_____
gen, gener	class, race	generic	_____
grad	go, step	gradual	_____
graph	writing	stenography	_____
gram	writing	telegram	_____
greg	flock, herd	gregarious	_____
gress	go, step	digress	_____
helio	sun	heliograph	_____
it	journey, road	exit	_____
itiner	journey, road	itinerary	_____
jac, jec	to throw	projectile	_____
jur, jurat	to swear	perjure	_____
labor	to work	collaborate	_____
lat	to bring, to bear	translate	_____
leg	to choose, to read	legible	_____
lig	to choose, to read	eligible	_____
leg	law	legitimate	_____
liber, libr	book	libretto	_____

liber	free	liberation	_____
log	word, study	etymology	_____
loqu	to talk	loquacious	_____
luc	light	translucent	_____
magn	great	magnanimity	_____
mal	bad	malevolent	_____
man	hand	manuscript	_____
mar	sea	maritime	_____
mater, matr	mother	matrilineal	_____
mit, miss	to send	dismiss	_____
mob, mov	move	mobilize	_____
mon, monit	to warn	premonition	_____
mori, mort	to die	moribund	_____
morph	shape, form	anthropomorphic	_____
mut	change	immutable	_____
nat	born	innate	_____
nav	ship	circumnavigate	_____
neg	deny	renege	_____
nomen	name	nomenclature	_____
nov	new	renovate	_____
omni	all	omnivorous	_____
oper	to work	cooperation	_____
pac	peace	pacifist	_____
pass	feel	impassioned	_____
pater, patr	father	patriotism	_____
path	disease, feeling	apathetic	_____
ped, pod	foot	impediment	_____
ped	child	pedagogue	_____
pel, puls	to drive	compulsion	_____
pet, petit	to seek	petition	_____
phil	love	philanderer	_____
pon, posit	to place	postpone	_____
port	to carry	export	_____
poten	able, powerful	omnipotent	_____
psych	mind	psychosis	_____
putat	to trim, to calculate	amputate	_____
ques, quir	to ask	inquisitive	_____
reg	rule	regent	_____
rid, ris	laugh	ridiculous	_____
rog, rogat	to ask	interrogate	_____
rupt	to break	interrupt	_____
sacr	holy	sacriligious	_____
sci	to know	omniscient	_____
scop	watch, see	microscope	_____
scrib, script	to write	mistranscribe	_____
sect	cut	bisect	_____
sed	to sit	sedentary	_____
sent, sens	to think, to feel	sensitive	_____
sequi, secut	to follow	consecutive	_____

solv, solut	to loosen	dissolute	_____
somn	sleep	insomnia	_____
soph	wisdom	sophisticated	_____
spec	to look at	spectator	_____
spir	breathe	respiratory	_____
string, strict	bind	stringent	_____
stru, struct	build	constructive	_____
tang, tact	to touch	tangent	_____
tempor	time	extemporaneous	_____
ten, tent	to hold	retentive	_____
term	end	interminable	_____
terr	land	subterranean	_____
therm	heat	thermostat	_____
tors, tort	twist	tortuous	_____
tract	drag, pull	attraction	_____
trud, trus	push, shove	protrusion	_____
urb	city	suburban	_____
vac	empty	vacuum	_____
vad, vas	go	invade	_____
ven	come	intervene	_____
ver	true	verisimilitude	_____
verb	word	verbatim	_____
vers, vert	turn	diversion	_____
via	way	deviation	_____
vid, vis	to see	evidence	_____
vinc, vict, vanq	to conquer	invincible	_____
viv, vit	alive	vivacious	_____
voc, vocat	to call	invocation	_____
vol	wish	voluntary	_____
volv, volut	to roll	convolution	_____

Common Suffixes
Directions:

1. On each of the following lines you are given a suffix, its meaning, and an example using the suffix. *If you are unsure of the meaning of the example word, use a dictionary to get its exact meaning.* Write down the word and its meaning on a separate piece of paper for future use. Notice how the meaning relates to its suffix meaning.

2. Then, in the blank space to the right of the example, give your own example of a word that begins with the suffix which uses the suffix meaning. If you can think of more than one example, make a list of them on a separate piece of paper. Be aware that your example may not carry the meaning of the suffix. Look up your example in a dictionary if you are unsure.

Suffix	Meaning	Example	Your Example
able, ible	capable of	portable	_____
ac, ic	like, pertaining to	dramatic	_____
acious, icious	full of	avaricious	_____
al	pertaining to	logical	_____
ant, ent	full of	eloquent	_____
ary	like, connected with	dictionary	_____
ate	to make	consecrate	_____
ation	the act of	exasperation	_____
cy	state of being	obstinacy	_____
eer, er, or	person who	censor	_____
escent	becoming	pubescent	_____
fic	making, doing	terrific	_____
fy	to make	beautify	_____
iferous	producing, bearing	vociferous	_____
il, ile	capable of	puerile	_____
ism	doctrine, belief	monotheism	_____
ist	dealer, doer	realist	_____
ity	state of being	annuity	_____
ive	like	expensive	_____
ize, ise	make	harmonize	_____
oid	resembling, like	anthropoid	_____
ose	full of	verbose	_____
osis	condition	neurosis	_____
ous	full of	nauseous	_____
tude	state of	certitude	_____

Appendix C ♦ PREVIEWING FICTION (Chapter 6)

Previewing fiction takes more guesswork than nonfiction. (For information about previewing nonfiction, see Chapter 6.) Because fiction writers have the freedom to use any writing style and format they choose, fictional material doesn't have an outline that you can easily follow. Your job then is to use the information available to follow the author and understand what is written. Locate a novel that you can work with while reading this section.

Previewing Fictional Material

Previewing fictional material familiarizes you with some of the important aspects of the writing and helps you to read the material more actively.

The Title.   Though the title of a novel can tell you what the subject is, it can sometimes be misleading. For example, *The Eye of the Needle* by Ken Follet might lead you to believe that it is a book about sewing, but in reality it is a spy novel that uses the "eye of a needle" as a symbol in the plot. A title of a novel can at best give you a clue to the theme of the book, rather than its main idea.

Look at the title of your novel and write it on the blank below. What do you think may be the theme based on the title? If you read the novel, return to this page when you are finished and see how accurate you were.

Title: _____

What it may mean: _____

_____

The Author.   Knowing some information about the author will help you to better understand your story. This information can often be found on either the inside or back cover of the book jacket. For instance, a copy of *The House of the Seven Gables* by Nathaniel Hawthorne might tell you that he was born in Salem, Massachusetts in 1804, that he lived near Boston, and that he died in 1864 after writing several novels. Even this cursory information tells you what era he lived in and what influences he might have had.

Some novels have a *preface* or *introduction* written by the author. By reading this you can get more clues to the writer's personality.

Other questions to think about when learning about an author include: Have they published before? What is their reputation? What is their point of view?

Looking at the information in your novel, what do you know about its author? (Also ask your instructor about what he or she may know.)

_____

_____

_____

_____

The Copyright Date. The copyright date is found within the first few pages of a book. Learning the date the book was written and/or published can give you clues about what to expect.

Example #1: *The House of Seven Gables* by Nathaniel Hawthorne was originally published in 1851, but the current edition reads 1981. This tells you that the book has been very popular and has withstood the test of time. Since it is still read today, then it must be an admired piece of writing as well as popular.

Example #2: *To Kill a Mockingbird* by Harper Lee has a copyright of 1960. This information would tell you that you would NOT read about things that were developed or happened since then, including computers, video games, or McDonald's.

What is the copyright date of your novel? What does it tell you?

_____

_____

_____

_____

The Publisher's Information. A publisher will provide you with several pieces of information that are helpful in the preview process.

A short *plot summary* can sometimes be found on the back cover, inside cover, or book jacket. This will give you an idea of what the story is about as well as what kind of story it is: mystery, romance, thriller, classic novel, etc.

Testimonial quotes, written by famous, well-known, or popular people are sometimes provided on the back cover or within the first few pages of a novel. These quotes attest to the quality of the writing and/or the story. Be wary of these, however. Remember that publishers are out to sell books, so their quotes are like advertising. Have you ever read an unfavorable quote? Use these for general information only.

The *cover design* is also advertising for the book. Some books are more pleasing to the eye than others, but they usually offer little indication as to how good the book really is.

A *table of contents*, though not regularly found in a novel, can be helpful as well for referencing a chapter for study purposes or review.

Look for the publishers information in your book. What does it tell you?

_____

_____

_____

_____

The First Few Pages. By reading the first few pages of a story, you can get a better feel for the writer's style. The *setting*, or where the story takes place, is an important piece of information. If the story takes place on a desert island, it sets your mood to think of an isolated place with lots of sand and ocean. This is quite different than a setting in the middle of New York City.

The *tone*, or the mood of the story, adds information to the setting. The story could take place on a bright, sunny day in a park filled with happy children, or on a dull rainy afternoon in the back room of a dusty office. Each sets a different tone for the part of the story being read.

Notice the *character names*. Are they easy or difficult to remember? It may be helpful to write them down on separate pieces of paper. You can also write some information about who they are related to, in what incidents they were involved, etc., to help you keep track of the characters.

Read the first few pages of your story. What can you tell about the author's style? Do you like it? Why or why not?

_____

_____

_____

At this point, you should feel ready to begin reading your fictional material. Keep the information you obtained from previewing in mind as you read the story.

Appendix D ♦ SKIM AND SCAN
TIMING AND EXERCISES
(Chapter 8)

Several kinds of reading exercises in this book require that you time yourself so that you can measure your progress in speed. Here is the best method for timing yourself when you are not in a classroom and when you do not have a stop watch.

1. Use a watch or clock with a sweep second hand. With a pen and paper handy, wait until the second hand is about ten seconds before the 60 second mark. Then write down the exact time in minutes. This is your *beginning time*. (The hour is unimportant for these short exercises.) When the second hand crosses the 60, begin the reading or reading exercise.

2. As soon as you have finished reading, look at the second hand and write down the exact time in minutes and seconds above your beginning time. This is your *ending time*. Your record will look something like this:

Ending Time:	41 min. 22 sec.
Beginning Time:	39 min. 00 sec.
Total Time:	2 min. 22 sec

3. Subtract your beginning time from your ending time to get your reading time in minutes and seconds. In the above example, the reading time is 2 minutes and 22 seconds.

Figuring Words-Per-Minute

Once you have your reading time, you can figure your words-per-minute.

1. Using the chart below, first translate your seconds into one of the numbers listed under "translated time." This makes it easier to figure words-per-minute. With the example of 2 minutes, 22 seconds, the 22 seconds falls between the 19 and 24 seconds making your translated time into **.3**. Your reading time is now **2.3** minutes.

Seconds	Translated Time
0-6	.0
7-12	.1
13-18	.2
19-24	**.3**
25-30	.4
31-36	.5

37-42	.6
43-48	.7
49-54	.8
55-60	.9

2. Using the simple formula of **WPM = # of words ÷ your translated time**, take the number of words in the reading and divide it by your time. You can use a calculator if you have one. If the number of words was 575 and your time was 2.3 minutes, your words-per-minute would be 250 words-per-minute.

Figuring Percentage of Comprehension

1. Correct your answers to those in this appendix. If you have an incorrect response, write down the correct one and go back to see where you might have had a problem. Learning from your mistakes is a far better education than getting everything right all the time!

2. Now multiply the number of answers you had correct by 10% to get your percent of comprehension. For example, 5 correct answers is 50%, 7 correct is 70%, and 10 correct is 100%.

Skimming Exercise Answers in Chapter 8

Skimming Exercise #1: "Labor Unions"

 # of words: <u>353</u> ÷ your translated time* _____ = _____ WPM
 Answers:
 1. T   2. T   3. F   4. F   5. N   6. T   7. F   8. T   9. F   10. N
 # of correct responses _____ x 10 % = _____ % comprehension

Skimming Exercise #2: "The Changing Workplace"

 # of words: <u>382</u> ÷ your translated time* _____ = _____ WPM
 Answers:
 1. T   2. F   3. F   4. T   5. T   6. N   7. N   8. T   9. F   10. T
 # of correct responses _____ x 10 % = _____ % comprehension

Skimming Exercise #3: "The Attraction of Place"

 # of words: <u>500</u> ÷ your translated time* _____ = _____ WPM
 Answers:
 1. F   2. T   3. F   4. T   5. F   6. N   7. T   8. N   9. T   10. F
 # of correct responses _____ x 10 % = _____ % comprehension

* see "Figuring Words-Per-Minute" in this appendix if you need more information.

Scanning Exercise Answers in Chapter 8

Answers to Course Listing:

1. Health and Physical Assessment in Nursing
2. NUR 216
3. 4 pm on Mondays
4. 7 class sections
5. Manchester Hospital
6. Backus Hospital
7. 3 credits
8. NUR 215
9. From 1/25 to 5/22
10. Central CT ST Univ

Answers to Scanning Exercise #1: Telephone Listing

1. Claude H.
2. Philip J.
3. 3 (Beryl, Howard O. and Childrens Phone)
4. 555–6800 (business is "rl est", or real estate)
5. RE
6. KR
7. 555–6233
8. Belli Blvd. (business is "atty" or attorney)
9. John I.
10. Sydney M.

Answers to Scanning Exercise #2: Cable TV Listing

1. 9 p.m.
2. TBS
3. 7 p.m.
4. UNI
5. 2 1/2 hours

Answers to Scanning Exercise #3: Scanning Text

3A: keep small objects from entering the eye
3B: a typical trade show
3C: 100 (types of cancer)
3D: heart disease
3E: 3/8ths of a page from the top

Appendix E ♦ SUGGESTED ANSWER KEYS

Chapter 7—Adjusting Reading Speed

Things that help me to SPEED UP	Things that cause me to SLOW DOWN
Reading for main ideas (my purpose)	Reading for details (my purpose)
Easy vocabulary	Difficult vocabulary
Some background knowledge	Little background knowledge
For class discussion (responsibility)	For quiz or test (responsibility)
Interest	Lack of interest*
Narrow column width	Wide column width
Quiet	Noisy
Good light	Poor light
Comfortable temperature	Too hot or too cold
Don't have a lot of time	Have plenty of time
Bigger print style	Smaller print style
Author's style	Author's style
Well-rested	Tired*
Early in the day	Late in the day
Previewing	Not previewing
Reading key words	Not reading key words
Reading phrases	Not reading phrases
Using pacers	Not using pacers

* If you are not interested or tired, you tend to read slowly, but with the reading tools and other speed up factors, you can speed up and get your work done quicker.

Chapter 11—Study Order Key and Explanation

Assignments	Study Order
1. Write a one-page essay on The Tools For Active Learning.	1. Study for Test.
2. Read Chapter 12 in Psych Text.	2. Do difficult subject—Math.
3. Study for electrical design test in 3 days.	3. Read chapter.
4. Do 10 math problems on pages 54–57.	4. Write essay.
	5. Review for test.

Explanation. Since time and repetition build long-term memory, then studying for the test first and reviewing for it last ensures plenty of study time and review.

Getting in the habit of doing your most difficult or challenging subject next, or first if you do not have a test to study for, ensures that you spend as much quality brain time on it as possible in order to make it become less difficult. Many students procrastinate and wind up working on their most difficult subject at the end of their study session when they are usually tired and not very eager to tackle it. Frequently, the assignment does not get completed or is not done well, making the course even harder or more challenging.

Given the choice between a reading assignment and a writing assignment, the reading assignment should come first. This is because reading by nature is a more passive process than writing. This is not to say that reading actively is still passive, but compared to writing, it is. By taking notes while reading, you can become even more active.

Writing assignments naturally keep you active. You have to think about what you are going to write and then write it. Writing assignments should be done later in the study session.

Chapter 12—Practice Test Answer Key

Answers to Practice Multiple-Choice Questions

1. C Both Paris and London are mentioned twice in the answers while the other cities are only mentioned once. If you only remembered one of the two cities, you had to make a choice.

2. C Using background knowledge, you would hopefully know that Italy is a peninsula surrounded by water on three sides, thus making "a lack of adequate ports" *not* possible.

3. D First, use the process of elimination. By looking at the five answers, you will see three that are similar (C, D, E). This could indicate that one of the answers lies within as in this case it does. If you didn't know the math for figuring out the answer, at least you could narrow down the possibilities. By knowing the answer is probably in 16ths, then figuring 1/3 into 16ths seem an efficient use of your test-taking time.

4. B The key word is *mismatched*. In order to find the answer, you need to first find the matching ones. This can help eliminate some of your choices. By matching the city correctly to its state, then A, C and D are not the mismatched one. Letter B is.

5. A Because "cluss" is in the answer.

6. B There are two reasons why letter B is the correct one.

    1) It is the longest answer.

    2) It satisfies the condition presented in the question (. . . is true when. . .) by the word *if.*

7. C Letters A, B and D uses definite terms such as *all, always* and *no.* The question uses the word *frequently* making letter C with the word "usually" a better answer.

8. D Letter D best satisfies the grammar rule that a vowel must come after a consonant when using the word *an.* Most instructors don't make it this easy for you but if they do, be aware of it.

9. A Letter A is the only answer that satisfies the plural question of "condition<u>s</u>".

10. B The key word is *always.* Vost is "always" present in all of the answers.

11. C The answer is given in question 8. (Remember that previewing the playing field can help find answers within a test!)

12. C According to studies of instructor created exams (not standardized tests), this is the most common answer given on multiple-choice exams, followed by B, then A, then D. When all else fails, a "C" guess is better than no answer at all!

Answers to Practice Matching Exercise

E.	**1.**	Active Learning	Learning like a sponge
C.	**2.**	Background Knowledge	What you already know
F.	**3.**	Cornell Method	Notetaking method best used by sequential learners
K.	**4.**	Critical Thinking	Thinking about thinking
A.	**5.**	Previewing	A reader's road map
H.	**6.**	Passive Learning	Learning like a rock
B.	**7.**	Mind-Mapping®	Notetaking method best used by a random learner
I.	**8.**	Mind-wandering	Can only be reduced, not eliminated
G.	**9.**	Learning Influences	Those things which effect your study concentration
D.	**10.**	Skimming and Scanning	High/fast reading gears

Answers to Practice Fill-In-The-Blank

1. a<u>n</u> active

2. awareness, knowledge, skills (or tools)

3. sequential; random

4. procrastination

5. background knowledge

6. purpose and responsibility

7. concentration

8. key words, phrases, pacers

9. body, recall column

10. smarter, harder.

Chapter 13—Critical Thinking Exercise Suggestion Keys

Suggested Responses to Practicing the Rules of Critical Thinking.

1. Yes, Erin is using critical thinking. She knows when she needs more information.

2. No, Ed is not using critical thinking. He is not separating emotional and logical thinking.

3. No, Takeisha is not using critical thinking. She does not know the difference between something that must be true and something that might be true.

4. Yes, Carlos is using critical thinking. He is building up his vocabulary.

Answers to the Mistakes in Thinking

How did you do with identifying mistakes in thinking? Here are the answers. Each correct answer is worth 10 points:

1= e, 2= a, 3=h, 4= c, 5= b, 6= d, 7= f, 8= j, 9= g, 10= i

Suggested Responses to Points of View Exercise

1. Know when you need more information.

2. Question anything that doesn't make sense.

3. Know the difference between something that must be true and something that might be true.

4. Be open-minded about new ideas and be aware that different people have different ideas about the meanings of words, gestures, etc.

Sample Note in Informal
Outline Form (Chapter 9)

Text #1
Learning = activity of one who learns
- intentional or random
- may involve new info. or skills
- comes w/Δ in behavior
- goes on thru life

Text #2
Success in class depends on:
1.) effective note-taking
2.) study techniques

Lecture info. formats:
- main ideas w/detail
- vocabulary bldg. w/related examples
- visual aids
    - handouts
    - overheads
    - blackboard

Cornell methods for all formats
- simplifies record of lecture
- provides simple study technique

Text #3
Amer. public schools didn't always exist
Education began in the home
- Mother 1st tchr
Mothers taught
- reading
- writing
- arithmetic
- bible ed.
- discipline
Mothers taught daughters
- sewing
- cooking
- homemaking
Sons learned
- apprenticeship of father

Text #4
People not born w/ bkgd. know.
Bkgd. know. accumulates from birth
    - whatever persons involved in
    - who influences them
    - what learned in school
    - what they read
    - what they see on T.V.
    - who are their friends
    - etc.

Text #4 (con't)
Bkgd. know. valuable tool for rdg.
    - helps to read faster
    - helps to read w/higher concentration
    - " " read w/ " comprehension
3 Ques. good rdrs. ask before rdg:
    1.) what do I need to know?
        - gives purpose
    2.) How well do I already know it?
        - more bkgd. know. means faster rdg. w/greater interest.
    3.) What do I need to know?
        - the readers responsibility
    * The key to bldg. bkgd. know.

Text #5
Listening respectfully to everyone makes people successful.

Listening = set of behavior more than hearing anothers word.
1.) making eye contact w/ spkr.
    - they believe you are hearing them
2.) responsive facial expressions
    - quizical look
    - widening eyes
3.) Nod head, say "uh-huh" or "I see"
4.) Sit or stand in attentive postures
5.) Avoid distractions
    - telephone ringing
6.) Ask questions to clarify your understanding

Appendix F ♦ RECOMMENDED BIBLIOGRAPHY FOR FURTHER READING

GETTING MOTIVATED

Brim, Gilbert. *Ambition: How We Manage Success and Failure Throughout Our Lives*. New York, NY: BasicBooks, 1992.

De Bono, Edward. *Serious Creativity: Using the Power of Lateral Thinking to Create New Ideas*. New York, NY: HarperBusiness, 1992.

Horn, Sam. *Concentration: How to Focus for Success*. Los Altos, CA: Crisp Publications, 1991.

Insights & Ideas. Videocassette. Produced and Directed by John Rees. Career Track Publications, 1992. 1 hour, 36 min.

Marone, Nicky. *Women & Risk: How to Master Your Fears and Do What You Never Thought You Could Do*. New York, NY: St. Martin's Press, 1992.

McWilliams, John-Roger and Peter McWilliams. *Do It! Let's Get Off Our Buts*. Los Angeles, CA: Prelude Press, 1991.

Ottens, Allen J. *Coping with Academic Anxiety*. New York, NY: Rosen Publishing Group, 1984.

Robbins, Anthony. *Personal Power!* Irwindale, CA: Robbins Research International, 1989. Audiocassettes.

Robbins, Anthony. *Awaken the Giant Within: How to Take Immediate Control of Your Mental, Emotional, Physical & Financial Destiny*. New York, NY: Summit Books, 1991.

Siegel, Pete. *Supercharged! The Secrets to Personal Power*. Dallas, TX: Taylor Publications, 1991.

Waitley, Denis. *The Psychology of Human Motivation*. Chicago, IL: Nightingale-Conant, 1991. Cassette recording. Includes a workbook entitled *Psych Up!*

Wexler, Phillip S. *Achieving Personal Excellence*. San Diego, CA: Levitz/Sommer Productions, 1986. 56 min.

BUILDING SELF–ESTEEM

Briley, Richard G. *Are You Positive: The Secret of Positive Thinkers' Success*. Herndon, VA: Acropolis, 1980.

Helmsteter, Shad. *The Self–Talk Solution*. New York, NY: W. Morrow, 1987.

Martarano, Joseph T. and John P. Kildahl. *Beyond Negative Thinking: Breaking the Cycle of Depressing and Anxious Thoughts*. New York, NY: Insight Books, 1989.

McWilliams, John R. and Peter McWilliams. *You Can't Afford the Luxury of a Negative Thought.* Los Angeles, CA: Prelude Press, 1991. Also available on cassette recording.

Robbins, Anthony. *Personal Power!* Irwindale, CA: Robbins Research International, 1989. Audiocassettes.

Robbins, Anthony. *Awaken the Giant Within: How to Take Immediate Control of Your Mental, Emotional, Physical & Financial Destiny.* New York, NY: Summit Books, 1991.

REACHING YOUR GOALS

Covey, Stephen R. *The Seven Habits of Highly Effective People.* New York, NY: Simon & Schuster, 1989. Also on cassette tape from Covey Leadership Center, Provo, UT.

Emmerling, John. *It Only Takes One: How to Create the Right Idea and Then Make It Happen.* New York, NY: Simon & Schuster, 1991.

Fanning, Tony and Bobbie Fanning. *Get It All Done and Still Be Human: A Personal Time–Management Workshop.* Revised Edition. Menlo Park, CA: Kali House, 1990.

Hedrick, Lucy H. *Five Days to an Organized Life.* Dell Trade Paperback, 1990.

Hedrick, Lucy H. *365 Ways to Save Time.* Hearst Books, 1992.

Lakein, Alan. *How to Get Control of Your Time and Your Life.* New York, NY: NAL–Dutton, 1989.

Leonard, George Burr. *Mastery: the Keys to Long-term Success and Fullfillment.* New York, NY: Dutton, 1991.

EXPLORING CAREERS

Basta, Nicholas, *Major Options.* New York, NY: HarperPerennial, 1991.

Bolles, Richard Nelson. *What Color is Your Parachute?: A Practical Guide for Job-Hunters and Career Changers.* Berkeley, CA: Ten Speed Press, 1992.

Encyclopedia of Careers and Vocational Guidance. Chicago, IL: Ferguson Publishing Company 8th Edition, 1990.

Kleiman, Carol. *The 100 Best Jobs for the 1990's and Beyond.* Chicago, IL: Dearborn Financial Publishing, 1992.

Tieger, Paul D. *Do What You Are: Discover the Perfect Career for You through the Secrets of Personality Type.* Boston, MA: Little, Brown, 1992.

IMPROVING YOUR WRITING

(Also, ask your instructors for their personal favorites)

Kerzner, Laurie G. and Stephen R. Mandell. *Holt Handbook,* 2nd Edition, Orlando, FL: HBJ College Publications, 1992.

Leggett, Glen et al. *Prentice Hall Handbook for Writers,* 11th Edition, New York, NY: Prentice-Hall, 1990.

Strunk, William and E.B. White. *The Elements of Style,* 3rd Edition, New York, NY: Macmillan, 1979.

Tyner, Thomas E. *Deep in Thought: A Thematic Approach to Thinking and Writing Well.* Belmont, CA: Wadsworth Publishing Company, 1990.

Appendix G ♦ REFERENCES

Apps, Jerold W. *Study Skills for Today's College Student*. McGraw-Hill Inc.; New York, NY. 1990.

Augarde, Tony. *The Oxford Dictionary of Modern Quotations*. Oxford University Press; New York, NY. 1991.

Baugh, L. Sue. *How to Write Term Papers & Reports*. NTC Publishing Group; Lincolnwood, IL. 1992.

Buzan, Tony. *Use Both Sides of Your Brain*. The Penguin Group; New York, NY. 1991.

Carruth, Gorton and Eugene Ehrlich. *The Harper Book of American Quotations*. Harper and Row; New York, NY. 1988.

Coman, Marcia and Kathy Heavers. *How to Improve Your Study Skills*. VGM Career Horizons, NTC Publishing; Lincolnwood, IL. 1990

Davis, Archie and Elvis Clark. *T-Notes and Other Study Skills*, 2nd Edition, Clark Publishing Company; Metamora, IL. 1986

Dictionary of Contemporary Quotations. Gaylord Professional Publications; Vol. 1–3.

Edson, Lee. *How We Learn*. Human Behavior Series. Time–Life Books; New York, NY. 1975

Effective Study Strategies. Academic Resources Corp.; Acton, MA. 1987. Audiocassettes with workbook.

Flippo, Rona and David Caverly eds. *College Reading & Study Strategy Programs*. International Reading Association; Newark, DE. 1991.

Flippo, Rona and David Caverly eds. *Teaching Reading & Study Strategies at the College Level*. International Reading Association; Newark, DE. 1991.

Fry, Ron. *How to Study Program (Book Series)*. Career Press; Hawthorne, NJ. 1991.

Galica, Gregory S. *The Blue Book: A Student's Guide to Essay Exams*. Harcourt, Brace, Jovanovich; San Diego, CA. 1991.

GED High School Equivalency Exam Review Book. Cambridge Adult Education, Prentice Hall Regents; Englewood, NJ. 1987.

Gibbs, J.J. *Dancing With Your Books: The Zen Way of Studying*. Penguin Group; New York, NY. 1990.

Gross, Ronald. *Peak Learning*. Jeremy P. Tarcher, Inc.; Los Angeles, CA. 1991.

Hanes, Gene R. and Lynne Salop Hanes. *Hanes Guide to Successful Study Skills*. The New American Library; New York, NY. 1981

Harnadeck, Anita. *Critical Thinking Book I.* Midwest Publications Company; Pacific Grove, CA. 1976.

Hermann, Ned. *The Creative Brain.* Brain Books; Lake Lure, NC. 1989.

Herold, Mort. *Memorizing Made Easy.* Contemporary Books; Chicago, IL. 1981.

Jensen, Eric. *Barron's Student Success Secrets,* 3rd Edition. Barron's Educational Series; New York, NY. 1989

Jensen, Eric. "Learning Styles in the 90's: How to Read Them and What to Do About Them". Turning Point; DelMar, CA. 1991. Set of 3 audiocassettes.

Kanar, Carol C. *The Confident Student.* Houghton Mifflin Company; Boston, MA. 1991.

Kesselman-Turkel, Judi and Franklynn Peterson. *Getting It Down: How to Put Your Ideas on Paper.* Contemporary Books; Chicago, IL. 1983.

Kesselman-Turkel, Judi and Franklynn Peterson. *Research Shortcuts.* Contemporary Books; Chicago, IL. 1982.

Kesselman-Turkel, Judi and Franklynn Peterson. *Study Smarts: How to Learn More in Less Time.* Contemporary Books; Chicago, IL. 1981.

Kesselman-Turkel, Judi and Franklynn Peterson. *Test-Taking Strategies.* Contemporary Books; Chicago, IL. 1981.

Killaritsch, Jane. *Reading & Study Organization Method for Higher Learning.* Reading Study Skills Center, Office of Developmental Education, Ohio State University, Columbus, OH.

Knowles, Malcolm S. & Associates. *Andragogy in Action: Applying Modern Principles of Adult Learning.* Jossey-Bass Publishers; San Francisco, CA. 1984.

Lakein, Alan. *How to Get Control of Your Time and Your Life.* Signet Book, The New American Library; New York, NY. 1973.

Merriam-Webster Thesaurus. Pocket Books; New York, NY. 1978.

Moore, Brooke Noel and Richard Parker. *Critical Thinking,* 3rd Edition, Mayfield Publishing Company; Mountain View, CA. 1991.

North, Vanda. *Get Ahead.* BC Books; Bournemouth, England. 1992.

Olney, Claude Dr. "Where There Is A Will, There Is An A". Chesterbrook Educational Publishers, 1988. Audiotape and Videocassette.

Pauk, Walter. *How to Study in College (4th Edition).* Houghton Mifflin Company; Boston, MA. 1989.

Paul, Richard. *Critical Thinking*. Center for Critical Thinking and Moral Critique, Sonoma State University, Rohnert Park, CA. 1990.

Random House Dictionary of the English Language. Random House; New York, NY. 1988.

Ruchlis, Hy & Sandra Oddo. *Clear Thinking*. Prometheus Books; Buffalo, NY. 1990.

Shepherd, James F. *College Study Skills*. Houghton Mifflin Company; Boston, MA. 1990.

Snider, Jean. *How to Study in High School*. Jamestown Publishers; Providence, RI. 1989 (Chapter 11).

Wlodkowski, Raymond J. *Enhancing Adult Motivation to Learn*. Jossey-Bass Publishers; San Francisco, CA. 1990.

Warring, R.H. *Logic Made Easy*. Tab Books, Inc.; Blue Ridge Summit, PA. 1984.

Wyckoff, Joyce. *Mindmapping: Your Personal Guide to Exploring Creativity and Problem Solving*. Berkeley Books; New York, NY. 1991.

Zorn, Robert. *Speed Reading*. Harper Perennial; New York, NY. 1991.

Chapter 14—Works Cited

Bethell, T. "A Challenge to Einstein." *National Review*, 5 Nov. 1990, 69–71.

Bondi, Hermann. *Relativity and Common Sense: A New Approach to Einstein*. Dover; Mineola, NY. 1980.

D'Inverno, R.A. *Introducing Einstein's Relativity*. Oxford University Press; New York, NY. 1992.

Chapter 15 - Works Cited

Gutzweiller, Martin C. "Einstein", *Scientific American*, 266: 1992, 78–85.

Overbye, Dennis. "Einstein in Love", *Time*, 30 April, 1990, 108.

Pais, Abraham. *Subtle is the Lord . . . The Science & Life of Albert Einstein*. Oxford University Press; New York, NY. 1992.

Glossary of Terms

abbreviations a shortened form of a word or phrase

abridged dictionary a shorter version of an unabridged dictionary

abundant in great quantity; plentiful

accountable a responsibility to explain or justify

acronyms words or names formed from the first letters of words or groups of letters in a phrase

active doing something

almanacs books containing facts, facts, and more facts

alphabetically going in order from A to Z

ambidextrous ability to use both hands equally well

analogy make comparison between two things

antonyms those words that are opposite in meaning

appendix contains supplementary information that further explains a subject in the text

auditory learners prefer using their ears to learn

background knowledge what you already know based on your previous experiences and/or learning

bibliography tells you what reading resources the author used in writing the book

boldface words in dark print, usually pointing out a new vocabulary term or heading

brainstorm a random, unorganized thought-dumping process that results in new ideas

call number a code given to every book brought into a library

caption the information below or alongside an illustration that explains it

cause and effect if something happens (the cause), then something happens as a result (the effect)

CD-ROM (<u>C</u>ompact <u>D</u>isk–<u>R</u>ead <u>O</u>nly <u>M</u>emory) a common form of computerized indexes

chronologically going from beginning to end

circulation desk the place to go when you want to take out any materials from a library

citations a short way of telling a reader about the books and articles that were read in a research paper or project

column width how wide or narrow the printed text is on a page

comparing looking at things to emphasize their similarities

comparison looking at two or more things and discovering similarities and differences

conclusion a summary of your important points which lets your reader know you are finished with your argument

context clues the words surrounding the unknown word that provide clues, or hints, to the meaning of the vocabulary word

contrasting looking at things to emphasize their differences

convey to carry or bring

coping attitude neither positive nor negative, but one that helps you cope with the work or situation

copyright date tells you how recent or how old the information in the book is (sometimes referred to as the publishing date)

cramming trying to memorize a lot of information in a very short period of time

critical thinking thinking about thinking in order to decide what to believe and how to behave

daily activity log a simple way for you to see how you spend your time

demotivate remove the inner urge to take action

dictionary a book that contains words and their meanings listed in alphabetical order

directory contains alphabetical information such as names or addresses

distractions that which divides attention or breaks concentration

editing a process where you correct, add, eliminate and/or rearrange your information so that it makes sense to the reader

effective being capable of producing a desired result

efficient accomplishing a job with a minimum amount of time and effort

empowered someone who feels capable of learning anything he or she wants, knows what he or she has to do in order to learn (or asks how), and then proceeds to learn

encyclopedias a book, or set of books, containing articles on various subjects from A to Z

estimation an approximate amount; a guess

etymology word origins indicating where the word comes from

expose to uncover; to make known or disclose

eye span how much information you see at a time when you look down at the page

fiction reading material that is imaginative in nature

flexible reader a reader who can adjust his or her reading techniques according to the reading purpose, difficulty of material and background knowledge

footnotes explanatory comments or reference notes that relate to a specific part of text on a page

full notes taking all of your notes on paper, not in the textbook

5 Ws and H who, what, when, where, why, and how

glossary a specialized dictionary at the back of a book to help you quickly find the specific meaning of a word given in the text

goal something that you want to have, do, or be

handbooks contain technical information

headings provide you with more specific information about the chapter as well as the outline of the information

horizontal something going across from left to right

illustration include any photos, figures, graphs, tables, or charts

incorporate to combine into one

index an alphabetical listing of names, places, and topics along with the numbers of the pages on which they are mentioned or discussed

indexer a person who keeps track of the different magazines and makes a list of the articles that are in each issue

ineffective being unable to produce the desired result

inefficient anything that wastes time and effort

interlibrary loan a librarian may make a formal request to another library to have them send a photocopy of an article or lend you a book that is not available at the requesting library

introduction tells the reader what the paper will be about

issue an unresolved question about a topic

italicized words in slanted print usually indicating something important

jargon vocabulary or terminology specific to a profession or trade

key words the more important words in text

kinesthetic learners prefer using their sense of touch and inner feelings to learn

learning a natural and constant process of gathering and processing information

learning influence something that affects the way you learn

learning environment the combination of learning influences that are present while you are studying

learning style how you prefer to gather information and then what you do with it

librarian someone who has advanced training in how to find information

long-term goal something that takes longer than six months or a year to achieve

mapping a pre-writing thought process that helps you to organize your thoughts and information on paper resulting in an informal outline

margin notes usually indicate an important idea that the author wants you to be aware of

memorizing trying to commit information to memory by rote, or by mindless repetition

mental learning environment what your mind thinks about while you are studying

metacognition conscious attention to your thinking

metaphor using a word or phrase to describe an object or concept. (e.g. the act of reading is like taking a road trip.)

Mind Mapping® a creative way to take notes that organizes ideas through visual patterns and pictures

mind-wandering a momentary lack of concentration or focus

mnemonic sentences an aid to organizing your ideas in which you make up a sentence using your own words (compare to acronyms)

neatniks a slang term for someone who is neat, organized and orderly

nonfiction reading material that is factual in nature

objective tests tests which have a single correct answer such as multiple choice, matching, true or false, or fill-in-the-blank

observers learn by paying careful attention to what they see

obvious easily seen, recognized or understood

omit to leave out

on-line databases   computerized indexes in which a micro-computer is connected to a large computer in another location

osmosis   a passive process by which you learn information or ideas without conscious effort

pacer   can be either your hand or a white card that you can use to help you keep your place while reading and/or to force you to move your eyes down the page faster

participants   learn by getting involved in the learning process

passive   doing nothing

performance test   it measures how well you can execute, or perform a certain task or activity

periodical   a magazine or other publication that is published on a regular basis

peripheral vision   the wide distance you are able to see on your left and right while staring straight ahead

perspective   your point of view

phrase   a group of words that express a thought

physical learning environment   the place you choose to study

physiology   generally how you feel

plagiarism   using other people's words and thoughts without giving them credit

position   your point of view on an issue

possess   to have as one's own; to have knowledge of

preface   tells you why the author wrote the book and/or what you need to know about how the book is organized (usually found after the title page)

prefix   the part of the word that is added to the beginning

previewing   looking over your material before reading it to discover clues to its contents

process   a series of related steps or actions taken to achieve an end

procrastination   to put off doing something unpleasant or burdensome until a future time

publisher   a person or company whose business is to reproduce books, periodicals and the like for sale

purpose   the reason why you are doing your assignment

purpose for reading   the reason why you are reading

random learning style   a less logical, more haphazard approach to taking in information (compare to sequential learning style)

reading actively   includes previewing, reading key words, reading phrases and using pacers

reading responsibility   the way you are accountable for the information you are reading

recall column   the left hand column in The Cornell Method of Note Taking

reinforce   to make effective; stronger

research   locating usable information for a paper or project

responsibility   how you are accountable

reward   something you give yourself in return for your effort

rough draft   your first attempt at getting your ideas down on paper

scanning   looking only for a specific fact or piece of information without reading everything

sequence   the following of one thing after another

sequential learning style   a more logical, step-by-step approach to taking in information (compare to random learning style)

short-term goal   something you want to achieve within the next six months or a year

significant   important

skimming   reading in high gear looking only for the general or main ideas

strategy   a plan or method for obtaining a goal or result

study goal   completing your assignment(s) in a reasonable time frame

study order   the order in which you do your assignments

subheadings   provide you with more specific information about the chapter as well as the outline of the information

subjective tests   tests which evaluate your overall understanding of the material through writing of your opinions or comments, such as short answer or essay (compare to objective tests)

subtitle   gives you more information

suffix   the part of the word added at the end

summary   a brief statement or restatement of main points

syllabus   a schedule of assignments

synonyms   words that are similar in meaning to the vocabulary word

table of contents   the outline of the text

tally   to add up

term calendar   an overview of assignments, papers, projects, etc. that are due on a certain date

testing success factor   something that contributes to a successful test result

thesaurus   a type of dictionary that contains only synonyms and antonyms

thesis   the conclusion you draw from what you study and is also the main point of your paper

thesis statement   a summary of your thesis

title   tells you what the topic or main idea is

topic sentences   they provide you with the main idea of a paragraph and in nonfiction, they are almost always the first sentence of every paragraph

topics   the subjects you study

transform   to change in form, appearance or structure

unabridged dictionary   the most complete type of a dictionary because it includes all words and definitions

vertical   something going up and down, from top to bottom

visual learners   prefer using their eyes to learn

visualization   creating or recalling mental pictures relating to what you are learning

walking dictionary   this is not a book, but rather a person you ask to help you figure out the word you don't understand

weekly activity log   the same as a daily activity log, but it is completed for a full week, or seven days in a row

weekly study schedule   an effective way to keep track of your assignments and plan your study time according to your term calendar

word structures   what words are made out of: prefixes, roots, and suffixes

working bibliography   a list of all the books and articles that are used for a paper

INDEX

416